Yamaha V5[illegible] V75, V80 & V90 Owners Workshop Manual

by Mervyn Bleach

with an additional Chapter on 1979 to 1986 models

by Pete Shoemark

Models covered

V50. 49cc. August 1971 to June 1976
V50 P. 49cc. January 1976 to July 1977
V50 MA. 49cc. January 1977 to April 1983
V50 MDL. 49cc. April 1983 to 1986
V75. 72cc. June 1975 to July 1975
V75 A. 72cc. August 1975 to January 1979
V80. 79cc. May 1979 to April 1983
V80 MDL. 79cc. April 1983 to 1986
V90. 89cc. November 1971 to January 1979

ISBN 1 85010 229 5

ABCDE
FGHIJ
KL

Printed in England *(332-1004)*

Haynes Publishing Group
Sparkford Nr Yeovil
Somerset BA22 7JJ England

Haynes Publications, Inc
861 Lawrence Drive
Newbury Park
California 91320 USA

British Library Cataloguing in Publication Data

Bleach, Mervyn
Yamaha V50, V75, V80 & V90 owners workshop manual.–2nd ed.– (Owners workshop manuals/ Haynes)
1. Yamaha motorcycle
I. Title II. Shoemark, Pete III. Series
629.28'775 TL448.Y3
ISBN 1–85010–229–5

Acknowledgements

Our thanks are due to Mitsui Machinery Sales (UK) Ltd for the technical assistance given whilst this manual was being prepared and for permission to reproduce their drawings.

The model used in the photographic sequences was kindly loaned by Jim Patch of Yeovil Motorcycle Services Ltd.

Brian Horsfall gave the necessary assistance with the overhaul and devised the ingenious methods used for overcoming the lack of service tools, Les Brazier arranged and took the photographs and Mansur Darlington edited the text.

Finally, we would like to acknowledge the help of the Avon Rubber Company for advice about tyre fitting, NGK Spark Plugs (UK) Ltd who furnished advice about spark plug conditions, and Renold Ltd who supplied information on replacement chains.

About this manual

The author of this manual has the conviction that the only way in which a meaningful and easy to follow text can be written is first to do the work himself, under conditions similar to those found in the average household.. As a result, the hands seen in the photographs are those of the author. Unless specially mentioned, and therefore considered essential, Yamaha service tools have not been used. There is invariably some alternative means of loosening a vital component when service tools are not available but risk of damage should always be avoided.

Each of the seven Chapters is divided into numbered Sections. Within these Sections are numbered paragraphs. Cross reference throughout the manual is quite straightforward and logical. When reference is made 'See Section 6.10' it means Section 6, paragraph 10 in the same Chapter. If another Chapter were meant, the reference would read 'See Chapter 2, Section 6.10'. All paragraphs are captioned with a Section/paragraph number to which they refer, and are relevant to the Chapter text adjacent.

Figures (usually line illustrations) appear in a logical and numerical order, within a given Chapter. Fig. 1.1. therefore refers to the first figure in Chapter 1.

Left-hand and right-hand descriptions of the machines and their components refer to the left and right of a given machine when the rider is seated normally.

Motorcycle manufacturers continually make changes to specifications and recommendations, and these, when notified, are incorporated into our manuals at the earliest opportunity.

Whilst every care is taken to ensure that the information in this manual is correct no liability can be accepted by the author or the publishers for loss, damage or injury caused by any errors in or omissions from the information given.

Contents

Left-hand view of 1978 Yamaha V90

Introduction to the Yamaha V50, V75 and V90 models

Following Yamaha's success with the high performance lightweight motorcycles, it was decided to introduce the V50 and V90 models into the U.K. for the commuter motorcyclist. As the models achieved only moderate success in sales, Yamaha concentrated more on the larger motorcycles for a while, until in 1975 they introduced an intermediate lightweight engine size, the V75 model.

With a range of 50 cc, 75 cc and 90 cc models which matched any other manufacturer's range. Yamaha found that sales of the V-models steadily increased.

In August 1975 the V75A model was introduced, being an automatic transmission version of the V75 and destined to replace it. This model automatically changes gear, eliminating the foot operated gearchange lever as well as the clutch lever, to simplify driving procedures.

Due to the legislation in effect in 1975 and 1976, the V50 model was the least popular as it was classified as a small motorcycle and as such was denied moped riders (mainly 16-year-olds), so, in January 1976 the V50 model was offered with pedals in place of the footrests to become the V50P which was classified as a moped.

In August 1977 new legislation came into effect altering the definition of a moped. Yamaha realised that the V50P did not conform to the new specification and introduced a new model that did; the V50MA. This model is a 50 cc engined version of the V75A, having the automatic transmission, but is governed to reduce its top speed.

Model dimensions

Dimensions	V50	V75	V90
Length	1840 mm (72·4 in)	1840 mm (72·4 in)	1845 mm (72·6 in)
Width	645 mm (25·4 in)	645 mm (25·4 in)	645 mm (25·4 in)
Height	1005 mm (39·6 in)	1005 mm (39·6 in)	1010 mm (39·8 in)
Wheelbase	1170 mm (46·1 in)	1170 mm (46·1 in)	1170 mm (46·1 in)
Seat height	740 mm (29·2 in)	730 mm (28·8 in)	735 mm (29·0 in)
Weight	70 kg (154 lbs)	75 kg (165 lbs)	80 kg (176 lbs)

Ordering spare parts

When replacement parts are required for your Yamaha, it is advisable to deal direct with a recognised Yamaha agent or with the area distributor. They are better placed to supply the parts ex-stock and should have the technical experience that may not be available with other suppliers. When ordering parts, always quote the engine and frame numbers in full, since these will identify the model and its date of manufacture. It will sometimes help if the old part is presented when the replacement is ordered, to aid correct identification.

Always fit replacement parts of Yamaha manufacture and do not be tempted to use pattern parts. Although the pattern parts may appear similar they often give inferior service and may prove more expensive in the long run.

The engine number is stamped on the left-hand crankcase immediately above the flywheel generator. The frame number is stamped on the right-hand side of the steering head. There is also a nameplate on the left-hand side just below the petrol tank, which also gives the model and serial number.

Some of the more expendable parts such as spark plugs, bulbs, tyres, oils and greases etc., can be obtained from accessory shops and motor factors, who have convenient opening hours, and can often be found not far from home. It is also possible to obtain parts on a Mail Order basis from a number of specialists who advertise regularly in the motor cycle magazines.

Engine number location

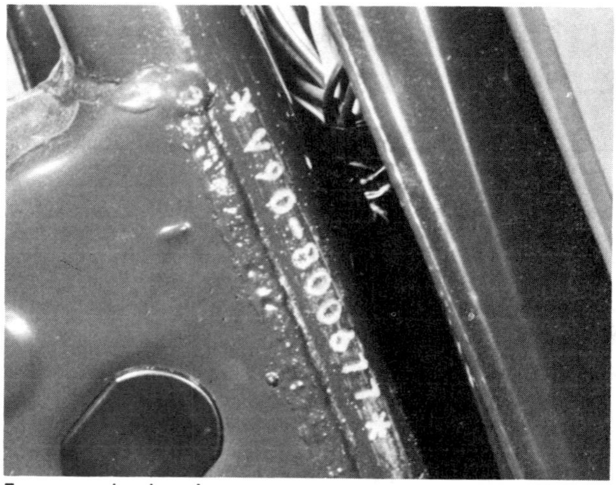

Frame number location

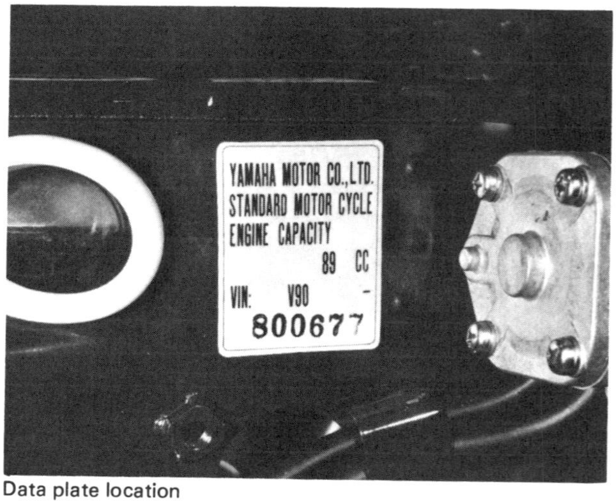

Data plate location

Safety first!

Professional motor mechanics are trained in safe working procedures. However enthusiastic you may be about getting on with the job in hand, do take the time to ensure that your safety is not put at risk. A moment's lack of attention can result in an accident, as can failure to observe certain elementary precautions.

There will always be new ways of having accidents, and the following points do not pretend to be a comprehensive list of all dangers; they are intended rather to make you aware of the risks and to encourage a safety-conscious approach to all work you carry out on your vehicle.

Essential DOs and DON'Ts

DON'T start the engine without first ascertaining that the transmission is in neutral.
DON'T suddenly remove the filler cap from a hot cooling system – cover it with a cloth and release the pressure gradually first, or you may get scalded by escaping coolant.
DON'T attempt to drain oil until you are sure it has cooled sufficiently to avoid scalding you.
DON'T grasp any part of the engine, exhaust or silencer without first ascertaining that it is sufficiently cool to avoid burning you.
DON'T allow brake fluid or antifreeze to contact the machine's paintwork or plastic components.
DON'T syphon toxic liquids such as fuel, brake fluid or antifreeze by mouth, or allow them to remain on your skin.
DON'T inhale dust – it may be injurious to health (see *Asbestos* heading).
DON'T allow any spilt oil or grease to remain on the floor – wipe it up straight away, before someone slips on it.
DON'T use ill-fitting spanners or other tools which may slip and cause injury.
DON'T attempt to lift a heavy component which may be beyond your capability – get assistance.
DON'T rush to finish a job, or take unverified short cuts.
DON'T allow children or animals in or around an unattended vehicle.
DON'T inflate a tyre to a pressure above the recommended maximum. Apart from overstressing the carcase and wheel rim, in extreme cases the tyre may blow off forcibly.
DO ensure that the machine is supported securely at all times. This is especially important when the machine is blocked up to aid wheel or fork removal.
DO take care when attempting to slacken a stubborn nut or bolt. It is generally better to pull on a spanner, rather than push, so that if slippage occurs you fall away from the machine rather than on to it.
DO wear eye protection when using power tools such as drill, sander, bench grinder etc.
DO use a barrier cream on your hands prior to undertaking dirty jobs – it will protect your skin from infection as well as making the dirt easier to remove afterwards; but make sure your hands aren't left slippery. Note that long-term contact with used engine oil can be a health hazard.
DO keep loose clothing (cuffs, tie etc) and long hair well out of the way of moving mechanical parts.
DO remove rings, wristwatch etc, before working on the vehicle – especially the electrical system.
DO keep your work area tidy – it is only too easy to fall over articles left lying around.
DO exercise caution when compressing springs for removal or installation. Ensure that the tension is applied and released in a controlled manner, using suitable tools which preclude the possibility of the spring escaping violently.
DO ensure that any lifting tackle used has a safe working load rating adequate for the job.
DO get someone to check periodically that all is well, when working alone on the vehicle.
DO carry out work in a logical sequence and check that everything is correctly assembled and tightened afterwards.
DO remember that your vehicle's safety affects that of yourself and others. If in doubt on any point, get specialist advice.
IF, in spite of following these precautions, you are unfortunate enough to injure yourself, seek medical attention as soon as possible.

Asbestos

Certain friction, insulating, sealing, and other products – such as brake linings, clutch linings, gaskets, etc – contain asbestos. *Extreme care must be taken to avoid inhalation of dust from such products since it is hazardous to health.* If in doubt, assume that they *do* contain asbestos.

Fire

Remember at all times that petrol (gasoline) is highly flammable. Never smoke, or have any kind of naked flame around, when working on the vehicle. But the risk does not end there – a spark caused by an electrical short-circuit, by two metal surfaces contacting each other, by careless use of tools, or even by static electricity built up in your body under certain conditions, can ignite petrol vapour, which in a confined space is highly explosive.

Always disconnect the battery earth (ground) terminal before working on any part of the fuel or electrical system, and never risk spilling fuel on to a hot engine or exhaust.

It is recommended that a fire extinguisher of a type suitable for fuel and electrical fires is kept handy in the garage or workplace at all times. Never try to extinguish a fuel or electrical fire with water.

Note: *Any reference to a 'torch' appearing in this manual should always be taken to mean a hand-held battery-operated electric lamp or flashlight. It does* **not** *mean a welding/gas torch or blowlamp.*

Fumes

Certain fumes are highly toxic and can quickly cause unconsciousness and even death if inhaled to any extent. Petrol (gasoline) vapour comes into this category, as do the vapours from certain solvents such as trichloroethylene. Any draining or pouring of such volatile fluids should be done in a well ventilated area.

When using cleaning fluids and solvents, read the instructions carefully. Never use materials from unmarked containers – they may give off poisonous vapours.

Never run the engine of a motor vehicle in an enclosed space such as a garage. Exhaust fumes contain carbon monoxide which is extremely poisonous; if you need to run the engine, always do so in the open air or at least have the rear of the vehicle outside the workplace.

The battery

Never cause a spark, or allow a naked light, near the vehicle's battery. It will normally be giving off a certain amount of hydrogen gas, which is highly explosive.

Always disconnect the battery earth (ground) terminal before working on the fuel or electrical systems.

If possible, loosen the filler plugs or cover when charging the battery from an external source. Do not charge at an excessive rate or the battery may burst.

Take care when topping up and when carrying the battery. The acid electrolyte, even when diluted, is very corrosive and should not be allowed to contact the eyes or skin.

If you ever need to prepare electrolyte yourself, always add the acid slowly to the water, and never the other way round. Protect against splashes by wearing rubber gloves and goggles.

Mains electricity

When using an electric power tool, inspection light etc which works from the mains, always ensure that the appliance is correctly connected to its plug and that, where necessary, it is properly earthed (grounded). Do not use such appliances in damp conditions and, again, beware of creating a spark or applying excessive heat in the vicinity of fuel or fuel vapour.

Ignition HT voltage

A severe electric shock can result from touching certain parts of the ignition system, such as the HT leads, when the engine is running or being cranked, particularly if components are damp or the insulation is defective. Where an electronic ignition system is fitted, the HT voltage is much higher and could prove fatal.

Routine maintenance

Periodic routine maintenance is a continuous process that commences immediately the machine is used. It must be carried out at specified mileage recordings or on a calendar basis if the machine is not used frequently, whichever is sooner. Maintenance should be regarded as an insurance policy, to help keep the machine in the peak of condition and to ensure long, troublefree service. It has the additional benefit of giving early warning of any faults that may develop and will act as a safety check, to the obvious advantage of both rider and machine alike.

The various maintenance tasks are described below, under their respective mileage and calendar headings. Accompanying diagrams are provided, where necessary. It should be remembered that the interval between the various maintenance tasks serves only as a guide. As the machine gets older or is used under particularly adverse conditions, it would be advisable to reduce the period between each check.

No special tools are required for the normal routine maintenance tasks. The tools contained in the toolkit supplied with every new machine are limited, but will suffice if the owner wishes to carry out only minor maintenance tasks.

When buying tools, it is worth spending a little more than the minimum to ensure that good quality tools are obtained. Some of the cheaper tools are too soft or flimsy to do an adequate job. It is infuriating to have to stop part way through a job because a spanner has splayed open or broken, and a replacement must be found.

A deep rooted knowledge of engineering principle is by no means necessary before the owner undertakes his or her own maintenance tasks but familiarity with a few of the more commonly used terms and a basic knowledge of how to use tools will help.

The following list of tools will suffice to undertake the routine maintenance tasks described in the Section, but where reference is made to another Chapter for the dismantling procedure, additional tools may be required.

A tyre pressure gauge
A tyre pump
A pair of pliers.
Two cross head screwdrivers, size 2 and 3.
A small electrical screwdriver
A set of feeler gauges.
A 14 mm spark plug spanner.
A set of metric open-ended spanners
Box spanners to include 12 mm, 21 mm and 23 mm sizes.
An adjustable spanner (this tool to be used only as a last resort).

Weekly or every 300 miles (500 km)

1 Check the tyre pressures

The tyre pressure should be 20 psi for the front tyre and 28 psi for the rear tyre measured when the tyres are cold.

Remove the dust cap, flick the valve centre to blow out any dirt or water and push on the pressure gauge. If the pressure is too low, pump up the tyre with the pump or a garage air line to the correct pressure. If the pressure is too high, push the valve centre to release the air until the correct pressure is reached. Replace the dust cap because it is a second seal.

2 Checking the oil tank level.

The oil tank capacity is 1·4 litres (2·4 pints) and a self-mixing two-stroke oil should be used.

The level can be checked either by looking through the window on the frame or by lifting the seat, pushing the oil tank lighting switch, and reading the level gauge. Refill the tank, if required.

On no account run the engine when the oil tank is empty as engine seizure will result.

3 Oil and adjust the brake cable and rod

The standard brake cables should be lubricated with a light machine oil, but if a nylon lined cable has been fitted on no account use oil on it.

Similarly, the cable nipples and pivot points should be oiled including those of the brake rod. Normally, rain and the washing of the machine will provide sufficient lubrication for the nylon and plastic parts. Before the winter sets in each year, it is advisable to remove the cables completely and thoroughly lubricate them as shown in the accompanying sketch, to ensure troublefree riding during the more arduous conditions to be found in winter.

The brakes need adjusting when there is too much movement on the lever or the pedal ie; when the brake lever comes close to the handlebar when the brake is applied or if there is too much movement of the brake pedal. To adjust either brake turn the adjusting nut until the brake just starts to rub when the wheel is spun. Slacken back the adjusting nut until the brake just stops rubbing. Ensure that the adjusting nut cut-outs are seating correctly on the brake operating arm on the rear brake and that the locknut is fully tightened on the front brake.

4 Check, adjust and lubricate the final drive chain

Place the machine on its centre stand on level ground. Check the up and down movement of the chain, midway between the two sprockets. Rotate the back wheel until the up and down movement is at the minimum. This is the 'tight spot' on the chain and the up and down movement here should be between 10 mm (0·40 inch) and 20 mm (0·79 inch).

If the play is greater than 20 mm (0·79 inch) the chain should be adjusted as follows:

Slacken the wheel spindle nuts so that they are finger tight. Make sure that each adjusting nut is turned the same amount, to keep the wheels in line, until the play is reduced to within the limits. Tighten the wheel spindle nuts and recheck the amount of play on the chain.

When the wheels are properly aligned both the adjusters should match the swinging arm markings.

An SAE 90 oil or a chain lubricant should be spread on the chain for lubrication. The latter is applied from an aerosol pack, to make application easier.

Check the oil level through the window

Use a self-mixing 2-stroke oil in the oil tank

Adjust the back brake with the special nut

Check the chain through the inspection hole

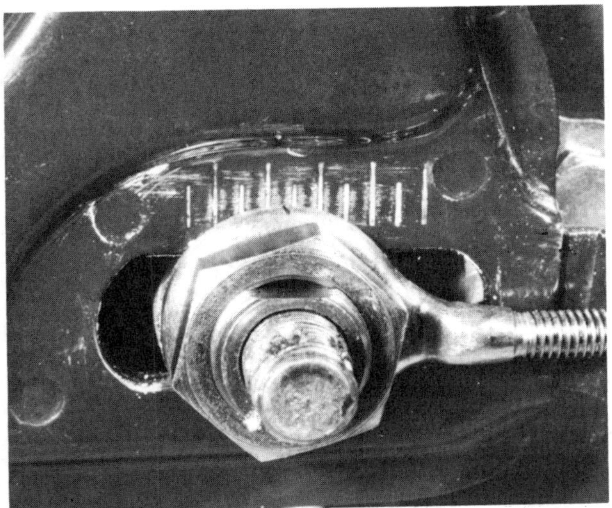
The adjusters should match the frame markings on each side

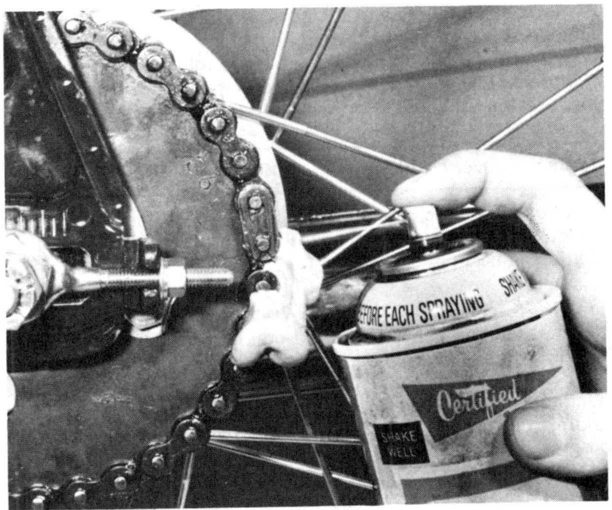

Lubrication is easier from an aerosol can

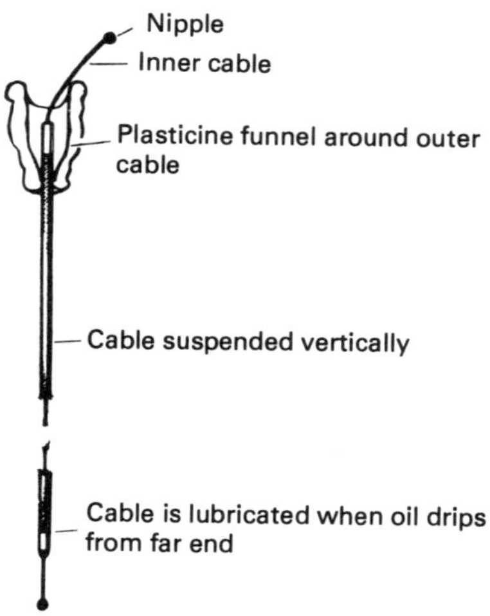

Oiling a control cable

5 *Check the lights and horn*

Check that all the lights are working properly. Renew any defective bulbs and if any lights are dim, clean the connections and earthing points, to restore the lights to their original brightness.

Check that the horn works, again checking the connection if the performance is poor.

6 *Visual inspection*

Give the whole machine a close visual inspection, checking for loose nuts and fittings, frayed control cables or missing parts which may have fallen off.

7 *Check the battery*

Remove the side panel, release the battery and slide it out. Remove the top cover, if fitted, and unscrew the vent plugs on top of the plates. On translucent batteries, the level of the liquid is marked on the outside of the battery. If the liquid level is low, the separate cells in the battery should be topped up to the correct level with distilled water. Tap water should not be used as the impurities in the water will have an adverse effect on the battery life.

Replace the plugs and the cover and refit the battery to the machine, finally replacing the side panel.

If any liquid is spilt out of the battery this should be washed off immediately with plenty of water as it will corrode any metal parts and burn the skin if left unattended.

Monthly or every 1000 miles (1600 km)

Check the tyres, brakes, lights and horn as described in the weekly/300 miles service and then carry out the following additional tasks:

1 *Check the gearhox oil level*

The gearbox capacity is 650 cc (1·14 pints), and an SAE 20W/50 oil is recommended.

Place the machine on its centre stand on level ground. If the machine has just been run, allow the oil to settle for 5 minutes before checking the level. Remove the plastic filler cap with its integral dipstick. Wipe the oil off the dipstick. Replace the dipstick without screwing it in, remove it and check that the oil level is between the upper and lower limit marks on the dipstick. Add oil if necessary, to bring the oil to the correct level, and replace the filler cap dipstick after ensuring that the sealing O ring is in good condition.

Check the oil level, using the dipstick provided

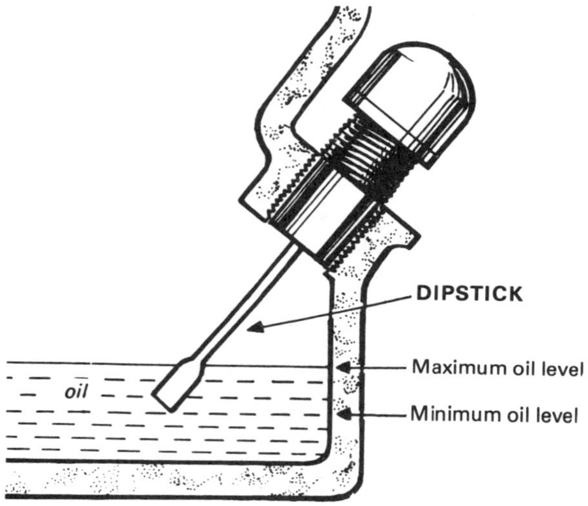

Crankcase dipstick

2 *Check the spark plug*

An NGK type B–7HS is fitted as standard equipment to the Yamaha V50, 75 and 90 models. The recommended gap of the plug is 0·5 mm – 0·6 mm (0·020in – 0·024 in).

Pull off the spark plug gap and unscrew the plug. Clean the electrodes to remove any oil or carbon. Check that gap between the electrodes with a set of feeler gauges. If the gap needs resetting, bend the outer electrode to bring it closer to the central electrode. Do not try to move the centre electrode as the insulation will break and ruin the plug.

Refit the spark plug and push on the plug cap. Do not overtighten the spark plug as this can cause the thread to strip in the cylinder head. A normal plug spanner has the correct length tommy bar or handle to make overtightening impossible.

A new spark plug should be fitted every 5000 miles (8000 km), or if it is damaged or excessively worn.

3 *Check and adjust the throttle cable*

The throttle should have about 1 mm – 2 mm (0·04 in – 0·08 in) free play movement.

To adjust the amount of free play, slide the rubber sleeve up the cable to reveal the adjusting nut. The adjusting nut is turned to provide the correct play and locked in position with the locknut. Slide the rubber sleeve back down the cable to exclude the dirt.

4 Check and adjust the carburettor slow running adjustment

Any checks or adjustments that are made on the carburettor should be undertaken only when the engine has reached its normal working temperature and not when the engine is cold.

The engine should continue to run slowly when the throttle is closed. If the engine stops every time the throttle is closed, adjustment is necessary. As the machine has an automatic clutch, if the engine runs too fast, the machine will tend to creep forward when it is in gear unless the brakes are applied to stop it .

Slacken the throttle cable to ensure that there is plenty of slack so that cable tension does not give false adjustment on the carburettor.

On the side of the carburettor are two screws, the upper one is the throttle stop screw, the lower the air mixture screw.

To adjust the slow running of the engine, turn the throttle stop screw until the engine is running at approximately 1300 rpm. Turn the air mixture screw until the highest engine speed is obtained. If the engine speed is then too fast, unscrew the throttle stop screw to reduce it, then turn the air mixture screw to find the highest engine speed again. This process is repeated until the engine runs slowly and evenly. Readjust the throttle cable slack to the limit as set out under the previous heading.

5 Check the tyre condition

By law a motorcycle must have a minimum depth of tread of 1 mm (0·04 inch) for at least 75% of the tyre width all the way round the circumference of the tyre. In the interest of safety it is better to renew the tyre long before the legal minimum is reached.

When checking the tyre condition, remove any stones in the tread, check for any bulges, splits or bald spots and renew the tyre if any doubt exists by following the procedure given in Chapter 6, Section 17.

6 Check the Autolube pump adjustment

When the throttle cable has its correct free play of 1 mm – 2 mm (0·04 in – 0·08 in) turn the twistgrip to take up the slack and the oil pump guide pin should line up with the mark on the oil pump pulley. The cable adjuster and locknut are situated just above the oil pump but the legshields need removing if adjustment is necessary.

Six monthly or every 3000 miles (5000 km)

Complete all the checks under the weekly and monthly headings taking into account the additional work required by the following items.

Hole in legshield allows easy carburettor adjustment

1 Change the gearbox oil

As stated previously the gearbox capacity is 650 cc (1·14 pints) of SAE 20W/50 oil.

Place the machine on its centre stand on level ground. Run the engine for a few minutes to warm up the oil so that it will run out easier. Place a container under the engine and remove the drain plug, which is situated on the underside of the engine. When all the oil has drained, replace and tighten the drain plug, ensuring that the sealing washer is in good condition.

Refill the engine with oil of the correct viscosity, checking the level as described in the weekly check.

2 Clean the air filter

The air filter is located under the main frame tube, immediately behind the steering head, clearly visible when the legshields have been removed.

To clean the air filter, remove the legshields to gain access to the air filter box. Remove the centre nut and bolt from the air box and pull off the end plates. The filter element can then be pulled clear of the rubber intake hose and slid out of the air box. Accumulated dust can be removed from the element either by tapping it lightly and brushing with a soft brush or by using a vacuum cleaner on the outside taking care not to damage the element as it is only made of paper. If it is torn, disintegrating or oiled up, fit a replacement.

Oil or water will reduce the efficiency of the filter element and may upset the carburation.

It is advisable to replace the element at less than the recommended 6000 miles if the machine is used in very dusty conditions. The usual signs of a filter element in need of replacement are reduced performance, misfiring and a tendency for the carburation to run rich.

On no account should the machine be run without the filter element in place because this will have an adverse effect on carburation. Reassembly of the air filter is the reverse of the dismantling procedure.

3 Clean the carburettor

Over a period of time sediment and water will collect in the carburettor. A drain screw on the carburettor enables the float chamber to be flushed out with petrol to remove nearly all of the dirt but Chapter 3 Sections 8 to 10 will describe how the carburettor itself is removed, stripped, cleaned and reassembled, if any trouble still persists.

4 Clean the fuel tap filter

The fuel tap filter should stop any dirt, rust or water from getting into the carburettor from the petrol tank.

Unscrew the small bowl on the bottom of the tap and lift out the gauze filter. Clean the filter and the sediment bowl and refit to the tap ensuring that the sealing ring is in good condition.

Adjust oil pump so that screw and mark align

5 Remove, clean and lubricate the final drive chain

Although the final drive chain is fully enclosed, the oil and grease lubricant on the chain will tend to pick up dust and grit, so every six months it is advisable to remove the chain from the machine for thorough cleaning.

To remove the chain, place the machine on its centre stand on level ground, remove the four bolts and the two chaincase halves.

It may be necessary to release the bottom of the rear suspension unit to enable the top half of the chaincase to be removed without being scratched.

Rotate the rear wheel until the spring link is in a convenient position, preferably on the rear wheel sprocket. Use a pair of pliers to remove the spring clip and then remove the side plate and the linkplate, thus disconnecting the chain. Connect to one end of the chain a second chain, either an old worn out one or a brand new one which is kept in readiness for fitting to the machine. Pull the first chain off the machine, feeding the second chain on, until the first chain can be disconnected from the second chain. If the second chain is usable, reconnect it, ensuring that the closed end of the spring clip is facing the direction of travel of the chain. Adjust the chain as described in the weekly maintenance section and refit the chaincase.

The chain which has just been removed should be washed thoroughly in petrol or paraffin to remove all the dirt and grease.

To check whether the chain is due for renewal, lay it lengthwise in a straight line and compress it so that all play is taken up. Anchor one end and then pull on the other end to take up the play in the opposite direction. If the chain extends by more than the distance between two adjacent links, it should be renewed in conjunction with the sprockets.

The chain should be lubricated by immersing it in a molten lubricant such as Linklyfe or Chainguard and then hanging it up to drain. This will ensure good penetration of lubricant between the pins and rollers, which is less likely to be thrown off when the chain is in motion.

To refit the chain to the machine, connect it to the second chain, pull the second chain and feed the first chain back onto the machine. Reconnect the chain, ensuring the spring clip is correctly fitted as stated before. It is easier to reconnect the chain if the ends are fitted onto the rear wheel sprocket whilst the connecting link is inserted. Adjust the chain, following the weekly maintenance procedure, and refit the chaincase.

6 Check and adjust the ignition timing

The ignition timing is determined by when the contact breaker points open. The flywheel operates the contact breaker and the heel of the contact arm will wear, altering the ignition timing. The flywheel inspection cover should be removed so that the contact breaker can be viewed through one of the apertures in the flywheel. When the line marked on the flywheel lines up with the timing plate the contact breaker should just start to open. If adjustment is necessary, the fixed contact can be moved by slackening the clamping screw and using a screwdriver in the slot provided. Retighten the clamping screw and check the adjustment again, to ensure that it has not altered.

When the ignition timing is correct, rotate the flywheel to determine the position at which the contact breaker points are fully open. When fully open the contact breaker gap should be between 0·3 mm and 0·4 mm (0·012 and 0·016 in).

If the gap is too small, the contact breaker points need renewing, as described in Chapter 4, Section 6.

Refit the flywheel cover and the spark plug and plug cover, if these have been removed.

After checking the timing, rotate the engine and check again before replacing the covers. The accuracy of the ignition timing is critical in terms of both engine performance and petrol consumption. Even a small error in setting can have a noticeable effect on both.

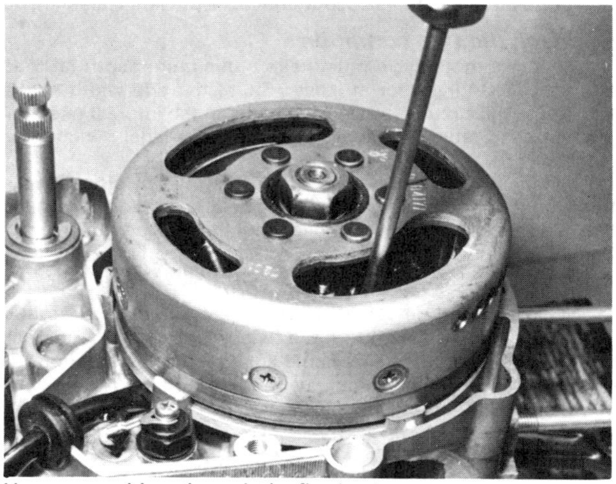

Use a screwdriver through the flywheel aperture ...

... to adjust the contact breaker

Check the contact breaker gap

7 Decoke the engine and exhaust system.

This task although not too difficult is very messy. Chapters 1 and 3 fully describe the necessary procedures required to remove and replace the cylinder head and cylinder barrel and the exhaust system.

8 Grease the leading link forks

Apply a grease gun to the nipples on the leading links and the fork blades. Pump grease into the bearings until clean grease emerges from the joints. Wipe away any excess grease as this will collect dirt and make the machine look unsightly.

9 Grease the throttle twist grip and oil the throttle cable

Remove the two screws and the indicator switch from the handlebar. This releases the twisting sleeve which slides off the handlebar with an anti-clockwise twist. The sliding block can now be lifted out of the handlebar and the inner cable unhooked. The outer cable stop can then be removed from the handlebar and unhooked from the cable.

10 Check the centre and prop stand springs

Check the condition of the centre and prop stand springs and renew them if they are worn or heavily corroded. If the stand drops when the machine is moving, it may catch in some obstacle in the road and unseat the rider. Grease the springs and the stand pivot points.

11 Grease the speedometer cable

Once the headlamp lens has been removed, the speedometer cable can be unscrewed from the speedometer head and pulled clear. The inner cable can then be pulled out. Clean off the old grease by washing in petrol or paraffin. Spread new grease along the length of the cable except for the top 15 cm (6 inch) and feed the cable back into the outer casing. Reconnect the cable to the speedometer head.

If the top of the cable is greased, the grease will work its way into the speedometer head and stop it functioning, thus necessitating a replacement as the speedometer head cannot be stripped for cleaning.

Yearly or every 5000 miles(8000 km)

Complete all the checks listed under the weekly, monthly and six monthly headings, then complete the following additional tasks:

1 Lubricate the felt wick of the contact breaker cam

When the ignition timing is checked, the felt wick of the contact breaker cam can be seen. A few drops of light machine oil, should be put on the wick to reduce wear on the heel of the contact arm. Do not over oil. If oil finds its way on to the contact breaker points it will act as an insulator and prevent electrical contact from being made.

Lubricate the felt wick for the contact cam

2 Check the condition of the sprockets

When the final drive chain is cleaned and checked, ensure that the sprockets are not badly worn, before replacing the chain. If the sprocket teeth are badly worn, they will probably have a hooked appearance and should be renewed as described in Chapter 1, Sections 9 and 6 and Chapter 6, Section 12.

3 Adjust and lubricate the steering head bearings

Dismantling and reassembly of the steering head is a task that should be undertaken only if the problems involved are understood. Chapter 5, Sections 2 and 4, fully describe the necessary procedures.

4 Examine and lubricate the wheel bearings

Dismantling and reassembly of the wheel bearings is also a task to be undertaken only if an understanding of the problems involved is realised. Chapter 6 fully describes the necessary procedure.

5 Examine both front and rear brake assemblies

The brake assemblies should be cleaned to remove any dust and checked to ensure that the brake linings are not wearing too thin. This task is fully described in Chapter 6.

Grease the leading link fork pivots

Greasing the speedometer cable

Quick glance maintenance adjustment and capacities

Engine oil tank capacity	1·4 litre (2·4 pints)
Gearbox oil capacity	650 cc (1·14 pints)
Contact breaker gap	0·3 – 0·4 mm (0·012 – 0·016 inch)
Spark plug gap	0·5 – 0·6 mm (0·020 – 0·024 inch)
Tyre pressures:	
Front	20 psi
Rear	28 psi

Recommended lubricants

Component	Type of lubricant
Engine	Self-mixing two stroke oil
Gearbox	SAE30 motor oil or 20W/50 engine oil
Final drive chain	Multi-grade engine oil or graphited grease
All greasing points	Multi-purpose high melting point lithium based grease
Cables etc. (not nylon-lined)	Light machine oil

Working conditions and tools

When a major overhaul is contemplated, it is important that a clean, well-lit working space is available, equipped with a workbench and vice, and with space for laying out or storing the dismantled assemblies in an orderly manner where they are unlikely to be disturbed. The use of a good workshop will give the satisfaction of work done in comfort and without haste, where there is little chance of the machine being dismantled and reassembled in anything other than clean surroundings. Unfortunately, these ideal working conditions are not always practicable and under these latter circumstances when improvisation is called for, extra care and time will be needed.

The other essential requirement is a comprehensive set of good quality tools. Quality is of prime importance since cheap tools will prove expensive in the long run if they slip or break and damage the components to which they are applied. A good quality tool will last a long time, and more than justify the cost. The basis of any tool kit is a set of open-ended spanners, which can be used on almost any part of the machine to which there is reasonable access. A set of ring spanners makes a useful addition, since they can be used on nuts that are very tight or where access is restricted. Where the cost has to be kept within reasonable bounds, a compromise can be effected with a set of combination spanners – open-ended at one end and having a ring of the same size on the other end. Socket spanners may also be considered a good investment, a basic $\frac{3}{8}$ in or $\frac{1}{2}$ in drive kit comprising a ratchet handle and a small number of socket heads, if money is limited. Additional sockets can be purchased, as and when they are required. Provided they are slim in profile, sockets will reach nuts or bolts that are deeply recessed. When purchasing spanners of any kind, make sure the correct size standard is purchased. Almost all machines manufactured outside the UK and the USA have metric nuts and bolts, whilst those produced in Britain have BSF or BSW sizes. The standard used in the USA is AF, which is also found on some of the later British machines. Other tools that should be included in the kit are a range of crosshead screwdrivers, a pair of pliers and a hammer.

When considering the purchase of tools, it should be remembered that by carrying out the work oneself, a large proportion of the normal repair cost, made up by labour charges, will be saved. The economy made on even a minor overhaul will go a long way towards the improvement of a tool kit.

In addition to the basic tool kit, certain additional tools can prove invaluable when they are close to hand, to help speed up a multitude of repetitive jobs. For example, an impact screwdriver will ease the removal of screws that have been tightened by a similar tool during assembly, without a risk of damaging the screw heads. And, of course, it can be used again to retighten the screws, to ensure an oil or airtight seal results. Circlip pliers have their uses too, since gear pinions, shafts and similar components are frequently retained by circlips that are not too easily displaced by a screwdriver. There are two types of circlip pliers, one for internal and one for external circlips. They may also have straight or right-angled jaws.

One of the most useful of all tools is the torque wrench, a form of spanner that can be adjusted to slip when a measured amount of force is applied to any bolt or nut. Torque wrench settings are given in almost every modern workshop or service manual, where the extent is given to which a complex component, such as a cylinder head, can be tightened without fear of distortion or leakage. The tightening of bearing caps is yet another example. Overtightening will stretch or even break bolts, necessitating extra work to extract the broken portions.

As may be expected, the more sophisticated the machine, the greater is the number of tools likely to be required if it is to be kept in first class condition by the home mechanic. Unfortunately there are certain jobs which cannot be accomplished successfully without the correct equipment and although there is invariably a specialist who will undertake the work for a fee, the home mechanic will have to dig more deeply in his pocket for the purchase of similar equipment if he does not wish to employ the services of others. Here a word of caution is necessary, since some of these jobs are best left to the expert. Although an electrical multimeter of the AVO type will prove helpful in tracing electrical faults, in inexperienced hands it may irrevocably damage some of the electrical components if a test current is passed through them in the wrong direction. This can apply to the synchronisation of twin or multiple carburettors too, where a certain amount of expertise is needed when setting them up with vacuum gauges. These are, however, exceptions. Some instruments, such as a strobe lamp, are virtually essential when checking the timing of a machine powered by a CDI ignition system. In short, do not purchase any of these special items unless you have the experience to use them correctly.

Although this manual shows how components can be removed and replaced without the use of special service tools (unless absolutely essential), it is worthwhile giving consideration to the purchase of the more commonly used tools if the machine is regarded as a long term purchase. Whilst the alternative methods suggested will remove and replace parts without risk of damage, the use of the special tools recommended and sold by the manufacturer will invariably save time.

Chapter 1 Engine and gearbox

For modifications, and information relating to later models, see Chapter 8

Contents

Specifications

Engine

Type	Air cooled two-stroke with reed valve inlet and loop scavenging
Cylinder arrangement	Single cylinder, horizontally disposed
Bore and stroke:	
V50 models	40·0 x 39·7 mm (1·575 x 1·563 in)
V75 models	47·0 x 42·0 mm (1·850 x 1·654 in)
V90 models	50·0 x 45·6 mm (1·969 x 1·795 in)
Capacity:	
V50 models	49 cc
V75 models	72 cc
V90 models	89 cc
Compression ratio:	
V50 models	6·6 : 1
V75 models	6·8 : 1
V90 models	6·8 : 1
bhp:	
V50 models	4·5 @ 6000 rpm
V75 models	6·2 @ 6500 rpm
V90 models	7·5 @ 6500 rpm

Cylinder barrel

Type	Cast iron
Maximum ovality	0·05 mm (0·002 in)

Piston

Type	Flat top, cut away skirt
Oversizes available	+ 0·25 mm (+ 0·01 in), + 0·5 mm (+ 0·02 in), + 0·75 mm (+ 0·03 in) and + 1·0 mm (+ 0·04 in)

Piston rings

Number	Two
End gap	0·15 – 0·35 mm (0·006 – 0·014 in)

Crankshaft

Type	Pressed-up with caged roller big and small end bearings

Gearbox (manual)

Ratios	
Top	1·200 : 1
Second	1·833 : 1 (1·812 : 1, V90 models)
First	3·250 : 1
Primary reduction ratio	3·578 : 1 (68/19T)

Gearbox (automatic)

Ratios	
High	2·333 : 1
Low	3·250 : 1
Primary reduction ratios	
High	2·107 : 1 (59/28T)
Low	3·833 : 1 (69/18T)
Final drive ratio*	
V50 models	3·000 : 1
V75 models	2·571 : 1
V90 models	2·333 : 1
Engine sprocket size	
V50 models	13 teeth
V75 models	13 or 14 teeth
V90 models	14 or 15 teeth

* This ratio may vary depending on engine sprocket used

Torque wrench settings

Stud size	kg m	ft lb
6	1·0	7·5
7	1·6	11·25
8	2·1	15·0
10	3·5 – 4·0	25·0 – 29·0
12	4·0 – 4·5	29·0 – 33·0
14	4·5 – 5·1	33·0 – 37·5
17	5·6 – 7·0	41·5 – 50·0

1 General description

The engine fitted to the Yamaha V50, 75 and 90 models is of the two stroke type, with a reed inlet valve, working on the 'loop scavenging' principle. A flat top piston is used, fitted with pegs to retain the piston rings in a set location so that they cannot rotate and permit the ends to become trapped and broken in the ports. Cutaways in the base of the piston skirt facilitate the opening and closing of the transfer ports.

Engine lubrication is by Yamaha's Autolube system which uses an oil pump to introduce oil into the engine from a separate oil tank. The oil, after lubricating the engine, is burnt in the combustion chamber, hence the system is known as 'total loss lubrication', because no oil is returned to the oil tank.

The primary drive and gearbox depend upon separate lubrication and run in oil in a separate compartment of the crankcase assembly.

All models are fitted with an automatic clutch and the V50 MA and V75A models are fitted with the automatic two speed gearbox, whilst the remaining models are fitted with the manually operated three speed gearbox.

The engine and gearbox are of unit construction hence when the crankcases are separated the crankshaft and gearbox internals are exposed.

It should be noted that the V50 MA is restricted in performance to classify it as a moped and it is illegal to increase the performance without reclassification.

2 Operations with engine in frame

It is not necessary to remove the engine unit from the frame unless the crankshaft assembly and/or gearbox internals require attention. Most operations can be accomplished with the engine in place, such as removal and replacement of:

1 Cylinder head
2 Cylinder barrel and piston
3 Flywheel generator
4 Clutch assembly
5 Contact breaker assembly

When several operations need to be undertaken it will probably be advantageous to remove the complete engine unit from the frame, an operation that should take approximately fifty minutes. This will give the advantage of better access and more working space.

3 Operations with engine removed

1 Removal and replacement of the main bearings.
2 Removal and replacement of the crankshaft assembly.
3 Removal and replacement of the gear cluster, selectors and gearbox main bearings.

4 Method of engine/gearbox removal

As described previously, the engine and gearbox are built in unit and it is necessary to remove the unit complete in order to gain access to either assembly. Separation is accomplished after the engine unit has been removed and refitting cannot take place until the crankcases have been reassembled. When the crankcases are separated the gearbox internals will also be exposed.

5 Removing the engine/gearbox unit from the frame

1 Place the machine on the centre stand and make sure it is standing firmly on level ground.
2 Remove the rear plastic side panel to obtain the tool kit.
3 Remove the screws that retain the legshields and lift the legshields clear of the machine, thus allowing easy access to the engine.
4 Remove the crankcase drain plug and drain the oil into a suitable container.
5 Remove the two bolts holding the exhaust pipe to the cylinder barrel and unscrew the silencer support nut. On the later models the swinging arm pivot nut needs to be removed as there is an additional support bracket. The exhaust system will pull clear once the rear brake return spring has been unhooked. Remove the exhaust gasket.
6 Using a punch, mark the kickstart arm and shaft before removing the kickstart arm so that on reassembly the correct position for the arm can be readily found.
7 Remove the metal side and cover plates from both sides of the frame.
8 Slide the battery out and disconnect the wires. Pull out the wiring harness to disconnect the plastic four way socket. Push the engine half of the socket back into the frame so that it will not catch on anything when the engine is removed.
9 Remove the two long headed bolts to release the oil pump cover. Gently ease the cover off and disconnect the control cable from the pump pulley. Slide the spring clip up the oil feed pipe, prise the pipe off the pump and either plug the end or allow the oil to drain into a suitable container.
10 Remove the spring clip and pull the intake hose off the carburettor. Slacken off the pinch bolt and gently ease the carburettor off the inlet stub and tie it up out of the way. Ensure that the petrol tap is not in the 'prime' position because petrol will leak if the carburettor is tipped.
11 Ensure that the machine is in neutral and remove the gearchange lever bolt which allows the lever to slide off its shaft (manual models only).
12 On the V50P model only, remove the cotter pin from the left-hand pedal crank. The cotter pin may be very tight so care should be taken not to damage the thread. Remove the three screws in the pedal chain cover and let it drop down the pedal crank. Displace the circlip retaining the pedal drive sprocket and slide the sprocket and crank off together, followed by the spring and drive dog. Pull the other crank, with the spindle, from the right-hand side of the machine.
13 Remove the screws and the left-hand side cover, including the screw and retaining plate on the manual models, to reveal the generator and final drive sprocket.
14 Rotate the rear wheel until the chain spring link is accessible. Disconnect the chain at the spring link and pull the chain clear of the engine sprocket. If the chain is reconnected, it will ease finding both ends of the chain when reassembling. It may be necessary to remove two bolts and the top half of the chainguard to obtain greater access to the chain.
15 Remove the engine bottom mounting bolt and the two shorter bolts so that the footrest assembly can be removed (not V50P). Note that the right-hand side short bolt has its head inside the frame. Replace the engine bolt so that it can act as a pivot for the engine.
16 Remove the spark plug cap.
17 On V50P models remove the rear brake light switch from its mounting bracket.
18 Remove the two engine top mounting bolts and allow the engine to pivot on the bottom bolt so that it rests on the ground.
19 Remove the engine bottom bolt and pull the engine clear of the machine.

5.5a Remove the two bolts holding the exhaust pipe

5.5b Remove the silencer support nut

5.5c Unhook the brake return spring

5.6 Centre-punch the kickstart lever to aid assembly

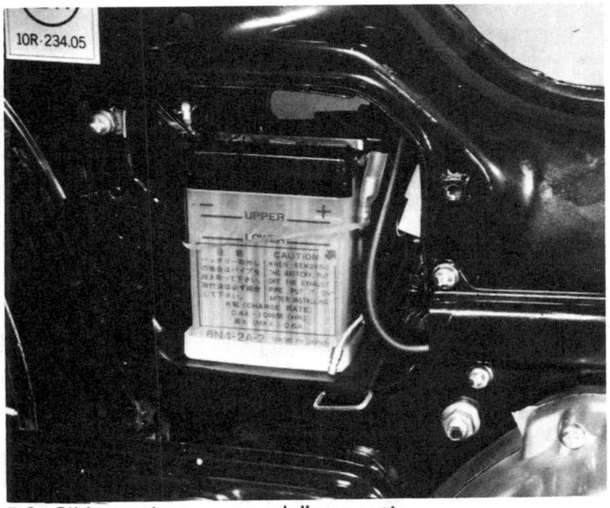

5.8a Slide out the battery and disconnect

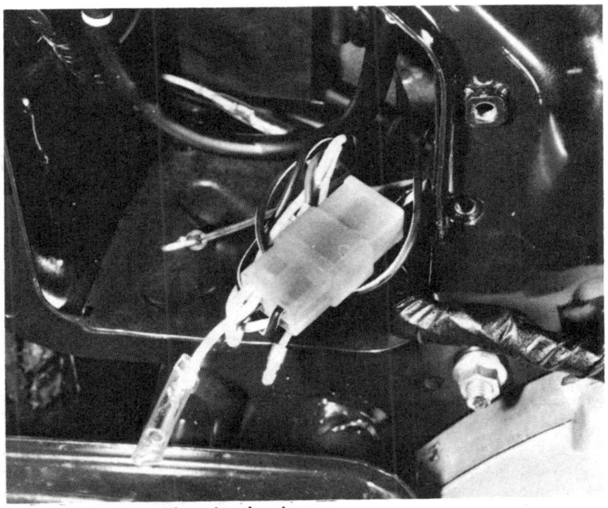
5.8b Disconnect the plastic plug

5.9 Disconnect the cable from the pump pulley

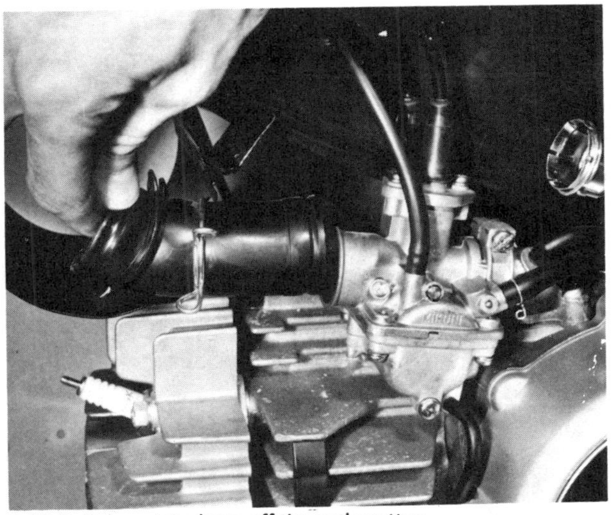
5.10 Pull the intake hose off the carburettor

5.13 Remove the side cover to reveal the generator

5.14 Disconnect the chain at the spring clip

5.15 Remove the bolts to release the footrest assembly

5.18a Remove the two engine top bolts ...

5.18b ... and allow the engine to pivot down

6 Dismantling the engine, clutch and gearbox: general

1 Before commencing work on the engine unit, the external surfaces should be cleaned thoroughly. A motorcycle engine has very little protection from road grit and other foreign matter, which will find its way into the dismantled engine if this simple precaution is not observed. One of the proprietary cleaning compounds such as Gunk can be used to good effect, particularly if the compound is allowed to work into the film of oil and grease before it is washed away. When washing down, make sure the water cannot enter the inlet or exhaust ports or the electrical system, particularly if these parts have been exposed.

2 Never use undue force to remove any stubborn part, unless mention is made of this requirement. There is invariably good reason why a part is difficult to remove, often because the dismantling operation has been tackled in the wrong sequence. Dismantling will be made easier if a simple engine stand is constructed that will correspond with the engine mounting points. This arrangement will permit the complete unit to be clamped rigidly to the workbench, leaving both hands free.

7 Flywheel generator: removal

With the engine in the frame

1 As stated in Section 2 of this Chapter, removal of the generator is possible whilst the engine is still in the frame. Removal of the generator should be preceded by carrying out the dismantling procedure detailed in Section 5 paragraphs 1 – 3 and 11 – 13. In addition the battery cover should be detached. Having accomplished this continue as if the engine were removed as described in the remainder of this Section.

Engine removed from the frame

2 If the whole of Section 5 has been completed, continue with the following dismantling procedure.
3 Hold the generator securely and remove the central nut and washer.
4 Use a Yamaha extractor tool to remove the rotor as it is a keyed taper fit. If the extractor is not available a two legged sprocket puller can be used in the slots of the rotor but extreme care should be taken to avoid damaging the rotor, or the coils affixed to the baseplate.
5 Disconnect the wire to the neutral warning light switch. If the stator plate is to be removed completely the wires in the plastic four way plug need to be removed as there is insufficient room to get the plug past the engine when it is still in the frame.
6 Remove the two screws and the stator plate and if further dismantling is required prise out the Woodruff key from the crankshaft.

8 Cylinder head, barrel and piston : removal

With the engine in the frame

1 As stated in Section 2 of this Chapter, it is possible to remove the cylinder head, barrel and piston, whilst the engine is still in the frame.Only paragraphs 1 to 3, 5, 10 and 16 of Section 5 need to be completed before proceeding with the following dismantling procedure.

With the engine removed from the frame

2 If the whole of Section 5 has been completed continue with the following dismantling procedure:
3 Unscrew the four nuts which retain the cylinder head in position and remove them together with their washers. The cylinder head can now be lifted off the holding down studs.

7.5 Disconnect the wire to the neutral switch

4 Slide the cylinder barrel up the holding down studs, taking care to support the piston when it falls clear of the cylinder bore. If only a limited amount of dismantling is being undertaken, it is advisable to pad the crankcase mouth with clean rag as soon as the cylinder barrel is raised, otherwise particles of broken piston ring may fall into the crankcase and necessitate further dismantling to retrieve them.
5 Remove the two circlips from the piston, using a pair of long nosed pliers. The gudgeon pin can now be pushed out of position, allowing the piston complete with rings to be removed from the connecting rod.
6 If the gudgeon pin is a tight fit, warm the piston by placing a rag soaked in hot water on the crown. Never drift the gudgeon pin out of position without supporting the piston, otherwise there is risk of bending the connecting rod. Throw away the circlips, they should **never** be re-used.
7 Note that the piston crown is marked with an arrow and when reassembling the piston this arrow should point down (toward the exhaust port).
8 The small end is a caged roller assembly and will slide easily out of the connecting rod.

7.4 Prise out the Woodruff key

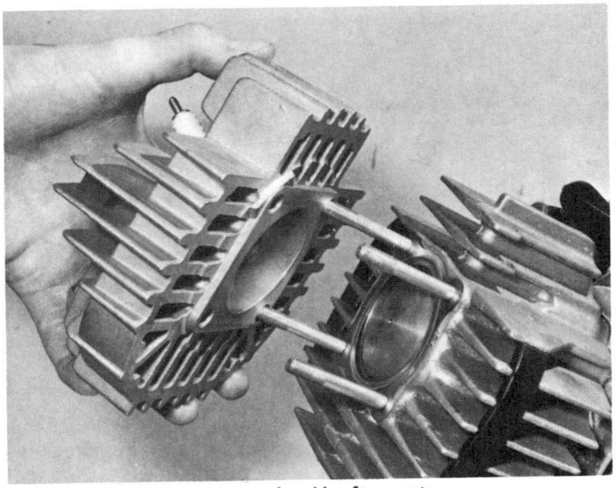

8.1 The cylinder head is retained by four nuts

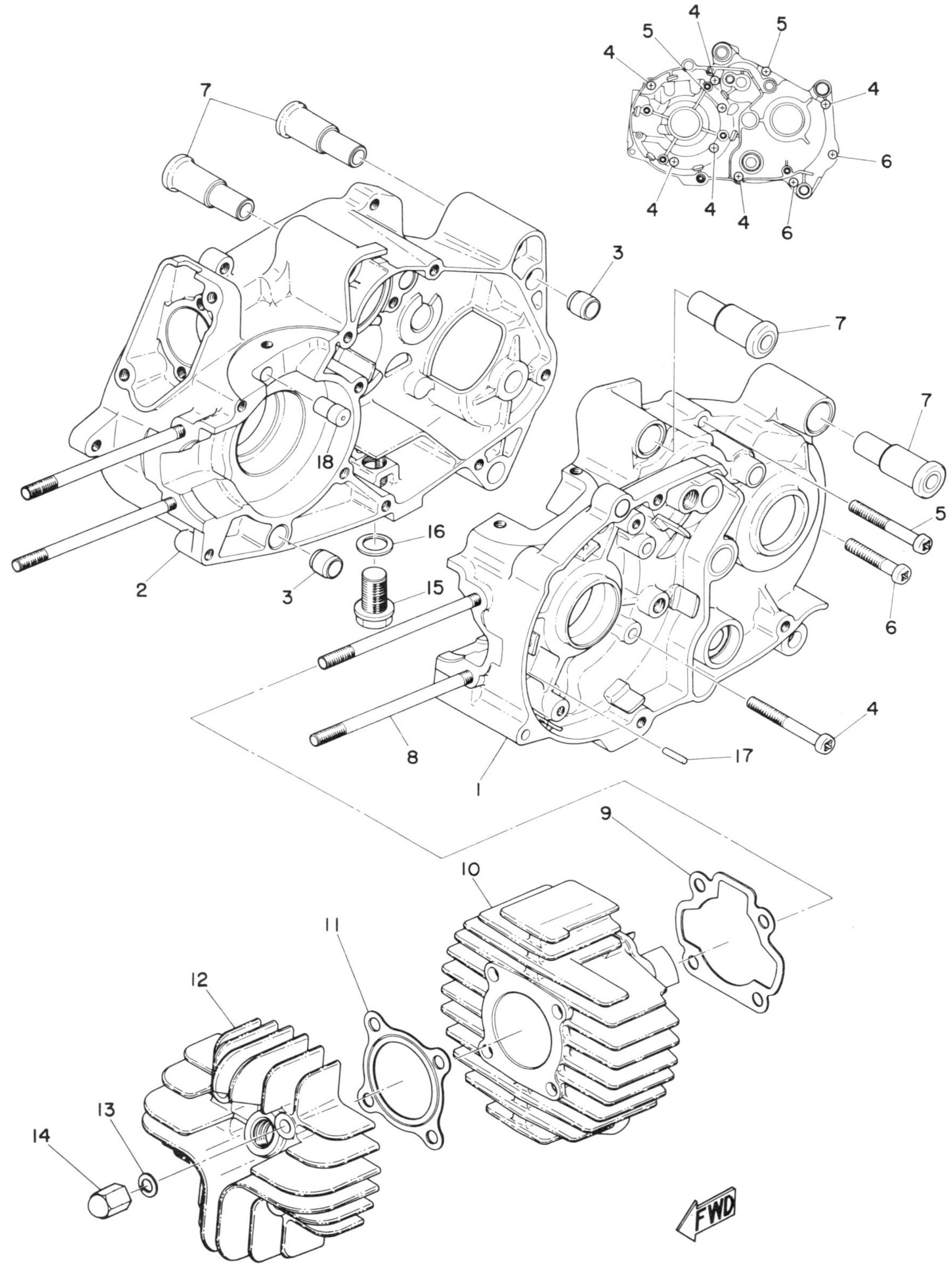

Fig. 1.1 Cylinder head, barrel and crankcase halves

1 LH crankcase half
2 RH crankcase half
3 Hollow dowel – 2 off
4 Screw – 6 off
5 Screw – 2 or 3 off
6 Screw – 1 or 2 off
7 Rubber bush – 4 or 6 off
8 Stud – 4 off
9 Cylinder base gasket
10 Cylinder barrel
11 Cylinder head gasket
12 Cylinder head
13 Washer – 4 off
14 Nut – 4 off
15 Drain plug
16 Sealing washer
17 Dowel pin
18 Nozzle assembly (early models)

8.2 Slide the barrel up the holding down studs

9 Final drive sprocket: removal

1 If the left-hand side cover and the final drive chain have been removed as described in Section 5 paragraphs 1 to 3 and 11 to 14, proceed as follows.
2 On the early and automatic models, prise down the tab washer and remove the nut, washer and sprocket. If further dismantling is required, pull out the spacer that runs in the oil seals.
3 On the later models, remove the circlip and slide the sprocket off its splines.
4 On the V50P models, remove the circlip, slide off the spacer, remove the second circlip and slide the sprocket off its splines.

9.3 A circlip retains the final drive sprocket

10 Clutch and primary drive: removal

With the engine in the frame
1 As stated in Section 2 of this Chapter it is possible to remove the clutch and primary drive, whilst the engine is still in the frame. Only paragraphs 1 to 4 and 6 need to be completed before proceeding with the following dismantling procedure:

8.6 The small end roller assembly is a push fit

With the engine removed from the frame
2 If the whole of Section 5 has been completed continue with the following dismantling procedure:

Early models
3 Remove the seven screws holding the right-hand cover, noting that the longest one fits in the front lower position, through the dowel.
4 Remove the cover with the engine over a small tray to catch any oil that is left in the engine.
5 Securely hold the crankshaft and remove the central nut and washer.
6 The clutch drum and plates assembly will slide off the splines as a unit. The primary drive gear assembly can now be slid off the spline followed by the bush.
7 If further work on the clutch is required Chapter 2 will provide all the information that is necessary.
8 Remove the circlip from the gearbox mainshaft and catch the two half collets that it holds in place. Slide the primary gear pinion off its splines.
9 If further dismantling is required the oil pump gear can be pulled off the crankshaft and the drive pin removed followed by the O-ring.
10 The spacer for the oil seal can now be removed although this is easier once the crankcase halves have been separated.
11 Remove the seven screws holding the right hand cover, noting that the long one fits in the front lower position, through the dowel.
12 Remove the cover with the engine over a small tray to catch any oil that is left in the engine.
13 Securely hold the clutch and remove the central nut and washer.
14 The clutch will lift off as a unit, followed by the bush and thrust washer.
15 If further work on the clutch is required, Chapter 2 will provide all the information that is necessary.
16 Securely hold the crankshaft and remove the end nut and washer. The primary drive pinion will slide off the shaft, and the parallel key can be prised out of the crankshaft.
17 If further dismantling is required, the oil pump gear will pull off the crankshaft and the drive pinion and O-ring can be removed.
18 The spacer for the oil seal can now be removed although this is easier once the crankcase halves have been separated.

Automatic models
19 Remove the seven screws holding the right hand cover, noting that the long one fits in the front lower position, through the dowel.

20 Remove the cover with the engine over a small tray to catch any oil that is left in the engine.
21 Remove the circlip from the gearbox mainshaft, and catch the two half collets that it holds in place. Slide the top gear pinion off its spline.
22 Securely hold the crankshaft and remove the central nut, a washer and a thrust washer.
23 The clutch will lift off as a unit followed by the bush and another thrust washer.
24 If further work on the clutch is required Chapter 2 will provide all the information that is necessary.
25 The bottom gear pinion complete with the pawl carrier will now slide off the mainshaft. Note that there is a thrust washer between the pinion and the carrier which is easily misplaced, especially if the carrier and pinion are separated to examine the pawls and pawl spring.
26 If further dismantling is required, the oil pump gear will pull off the crankshaft and the drive pin can be removed, followed by the O-ring.
27 The spacer for the oil seal can now be removed, although this is easier once the crankcase assembly has been separated.

10.12a Remove the clutch as a unit ...

11 Oil pump: removal

1 Unless the oil pump is suspect, it should not be removed as the engine can be stripped with the oil pump left in place. On the later models, the oil feed pipe from the pump to the inlet stub needs to be disconnected if the engine is being stripped.
2 To remove the oil pump, paragraphs 1 to 3 and 9 of Section 5 must be completed as an absolute minimum although usually a complete engine rebuild is required if the oil pump malfunctions.
3 Remove the two large screws and gently ease the oil pump out of the crankcase half. There is either one or two O-rings round the body of the pump for sealing purposes and these may tend to stick so care should be used to avoid damage to the pump or the housing.
4 Chapter 3 describes the operation of the oil pump and any further dismantling that can be undertaken.

10.12b ... followed by the bush and thrust washer

12 Kickstart mechanism: removal

1 The kickstart mechanism can be removed once the right-hand side cover has been removed. Reference to the previous Section will show how this is done.
2 Unhook the kickstart return spring and slide the assembly out, making a note of the position of the centre punch mark to aid reassembly.

11.3 Gently ease the oil pump out of the case

12.2 Lift the kickstart assembly out

13 Gearchange mechanism and index arm: removal – manual change models only

1 When the clutch and the primary drive gears have been removed, the circlip and washer on the gearchange shaft on the other side of the engine have to be removed, which, after the pawl arm has been lifted clear of the gearchange cam, will allow the shaft assembly to be withdrawn. The pawl spring and the gearchange return spring should be checked and renewed, if necessary.
2 Remove the shouldered bolt holding the index arm and unhook the spring, which allows the arm to be removed.

14 Assorted retaining plates: removal

1 Remove the screw and the retaining plate that keeps the crankshaft oil seal in position.
2 Remove the two screws and the bearing retaining plate from the gearbox mainshaft. This is only necessary if the bearing is suspect or needs replacing.
3 On the manual change models, remove the two screws and the retaining plate that limits the end float on the selector drum.

15 Reed valve and inlet stub: removal

1 Remove the four screws and prise off the inlet stub and reed valve assembly.
2 If the reed valve assembly is undamaged, it is pointless to remove it from the inlet stub unless the gasket between the two has been leaking.

16 Separating the crankcase halves

1 Slacken evenly and remove the screws securing the crankcase halves. There are three different lengths of screw so a note should be made of which screw fits in which hole.
2 Before trying to separate the crankcase halves, ensure that the oil pump gear drive pin and the rotor Woodruff key have been removed.
3 The right-hand crankcase should lift off but light tapping with a rawhide mallet may be necessary.
4 Never use the point of a screwdriver to aid the separation of the crankcase. A leaktight crankcase is an essential requirement of any two-stroke engine. If the crankcase joint is damaged in any way, air will be admitted, which will dilute the incoming mixture. This will cause poor starting and indifferent running, mainly due to the weakened mixture that results.
5 Note that there are two locating dowels fitted in the crankcases.
6 The spacer for the oil seal can now be removed easily from the crankshaft or the oil seal, if it was left in place as suggested in Section 10.
7 Check the ends of the shafts and the crankcase half to see if any washers or shims have been fitted and after noting their position, remove them to avoid loss.

17 Gearbox components: removal

1 The gearbox shafts should now slide out of the crankcase half as a cluster. Where fitted, the selector arms and shaft should be removed at the same time as the gear assemblies.
2 Light tapping on the end of the output shaft may be required to remove it from its bearing.
3 The final drive spacer will probably be left in the oil seal in the crankcase half and can be easily pulled out.

13.1a Remove the circlip and washer ...

13.1b ... and slide out the gearchange shaft

13.2 Remove the shouldered bolt to release the index arm

14.1 A single screw holds the oil seal retaining plate

14.2 Two screws hold the bearing retaining plate

14.3 Two screws hold the drum retaining plate

15.1 Lift off the inlet stub and the reed valve together

16.3 The right-hand crankcase lifts off

17.1 The gearbox components lift out as a cluster

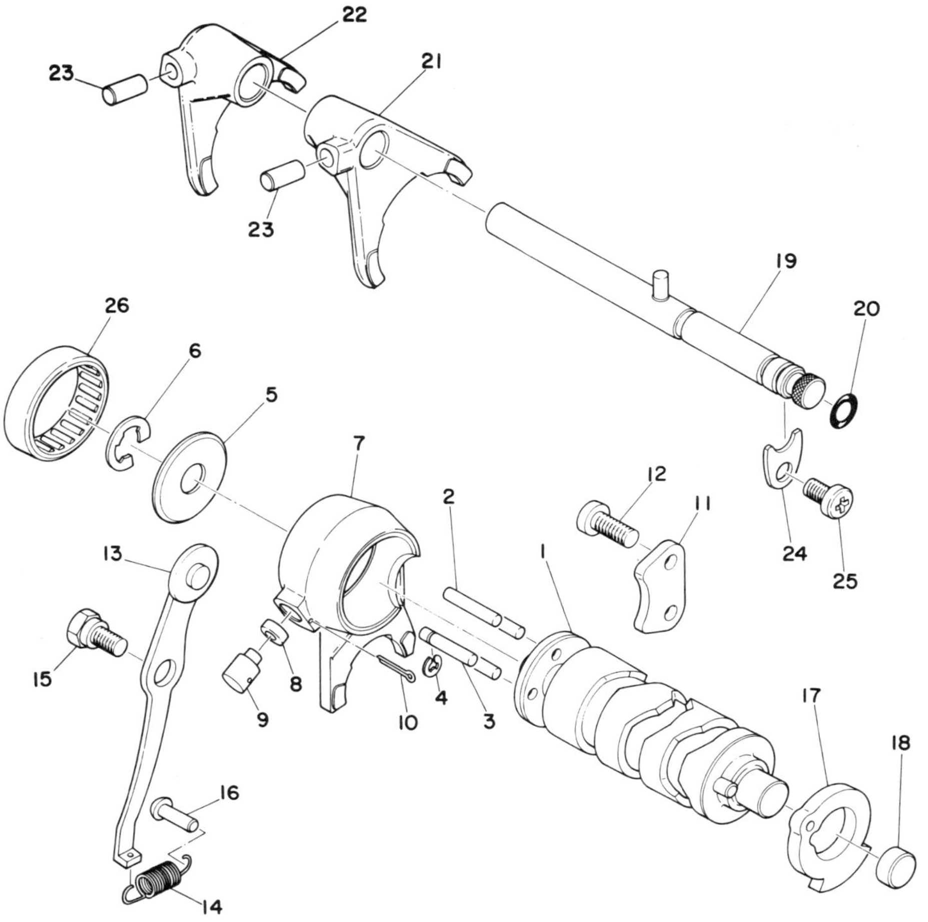

Fig. 1.2 Gear selector mechanism (non-automatic models)

1 Barrel cam
2 Pin – 3 off
3 Locating pin
4 Circlip
5 Plate
6 Circlip
7 Selector fork
8 Cam follower roller (early models only)
9 Cam follower pin
10 Split pin
11 Retaining plate
12 Screw – 2 off
13 Positive stop arm
14 Spring
15 Pivot bolt
16 Spring anchor
17 Plate
18 Plug
19 Selector fork shaft
20 O ring
21 Selector fork
22 Selector fork
23 Cam follower pin – 2 off
24 Retaining plate
25 Screw
26 Bearing

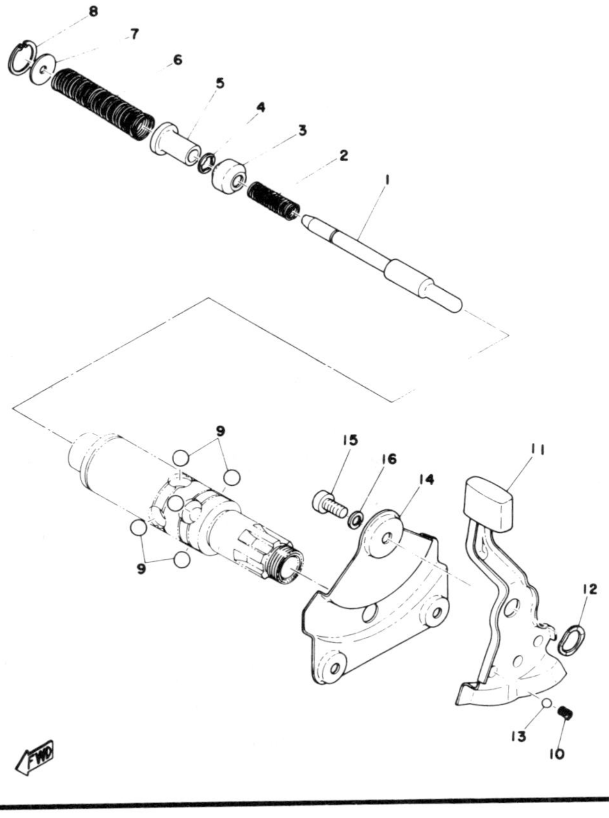

Fig. 1.3 Gear selector and change mechanism (automatic models)

1 Selector rod
2 Spring
3 Selector head
4 Circlip
5 Retainer
6 Spring
7 Washer
8 Circlip
9 Steel ball – 8 off
10 Spring
11 Gearchange lever
12 Wave washer
13 Steel ball
14 Dust seal
15 Screw – 3 off
16 Spring washer – 3 off

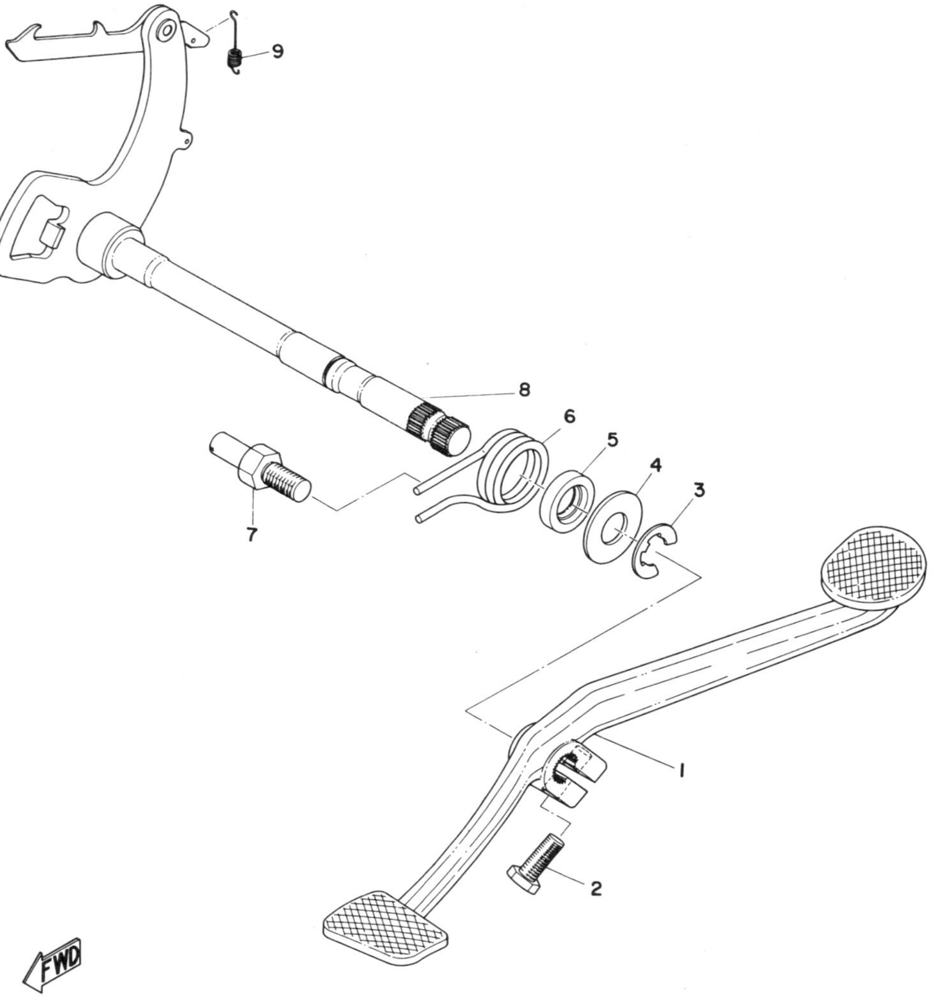

1 Gear lever
2 Bolt
3 Circlip
4 Washer
5 Oil seal
6 Return spring
7 Spring anchor
8 Gear change shaft
9 Spring

Fig. 1.4 Gear change mechanism (non-automatic models)

18 Crankshaft assembly: removal

1 Support the crankcase half and tap the end of the mainshaft with a rawhide mallet until the crankshaft assembly is free. A rawhide mallet is used to avoid damaging the thread on the end of the crankshaft. If one is not available, a small piece of wood can be used to protect the thread.

19 Neutral indicator switch: removal

1 Removal of the neutral indicator switch is not strictly necessary unless it is faulty and renewal is required. The switch, however, does project from the crankcase half, and it is recommended that it be removed to prevent damage during subsequent dismantling.
2 The plastic body of the switch should be unscrewed carefully from the casing and removed, together with the sealing washer.

18.1 Drift out crankshaft from casing half

19.1 Remove the switch to avoid damage

20.1 The different bearings can clearly be seen

20 Crankshaft and gearbox bearings: removal

1 The crankshaft assembly runs in two journal ball bearings, the gearbox mainshaft runs in a journal ball bearing and a needle roller bearing, the output shaft runs in a journal ball bearing and a plain bush and the gear selector drum on the manual change models runs in a needle roller bearing and directly in the crankcase half.
2 Before removing any of the bearings, prise out the oil seals and ensure that the bearing retaining plates have been removed as described in Section 14.
3 Because the bearings are a tight fit, it is advisable to heat the crankcase halves, before driving the bearings out, as it makes the task easier. Always use a mandrel of a suitable size, and drive the bearings out squarely, because the soft aluminium crankcase halves can otherwise be damaged irreparably.
4 The casing in question may be heated by immersion in boiling water or by being placed in an oven at approximately 100°C (212°F). The use of a blowlamp is not recommended because of the danger of uneven heating and subsequent warping of the case.

21 Oil seals: examination and replacement

1 Two-stroke engines are particularly vulnerable to wear or damage which may occur to the oil seals. This is even more so on the Yamaha engine. Apart from the oil leakage that will result, worn crankshaft seals will admit air to the crankcase and dilute the incoming mixture.
2 Early warning of failing crankshaft oil seals is given by difficulty in starting and a general reluctance of the engine to run smoothly.
3 The oil seals can be prised out of the crankcase but if removed, new ones must be fitted.
4 The oil seals must be fitted with the manufacturer's marks and letters facing outward.
5 When fitting new oil seals, extreme care should be taken when they are inserted over a shaft. To prevent damage to the feather edge of the seal, grease both the shaft and the centre of the oil seal itself.

22 Crankshaft assembly: examination and renovation

1 Wash the complete crankshaft assembly with a petrol/paraffin mix to remove all surplus oil.
2 Replace the small end caged roller bearing and the gudgeon pin. Check for play between the gudgeon pin and the crankshaft. The play should not exceed 2 mm (0.080 in).
3 If there is more play than is allowable, the whole of the crankshaft assembly should be renewed as it is the connecting rod which has worn. To separate the flywheels is a highly specialised task, beyond the normal home garage facilities.

22.1 Clean the crankshaft assembly thoroughly

23 Cylinder barrel: examination and renovation

1 There will probably be a lip at the uppermost end of the cylinder barrel which marks the limit of travel of the top piston ring. The depth of the lip will give some indication of the amount of bore wear that has taken place, even though the amount of wear is not evenly distributed.
2 Remove the rings from the piston, taking great care because they are brittle and very easily broken. There is more tendency for the rings to gum in their grooves in a two-stroke engine. Insert the piston in the bore so that it is positioned about 13 mm ($\frac{1}{2}$ inch) below the top of the bore. If it is possible to insert a 0.10 mm (0.004 in) feeler gauge between the piston and the bore, a rebore and the fitting of an oversize piston is necessary.

3 Give the cylinder barrel a close visual inspection. If the surface of the bore is scored or grooved, indicative of an earlier seizure or a displaced circlip and gudgeon pin, a rebore is essential. Compression loss will have a very marked effect on performance.
4 Check that the outside of the cylinder barrel is clean and free from road dirt. Use a wire brush on the cooling fins if they are obstructed in any way. The engine will overheat badly if the cooling area is obstructed in any way.
5 Clean all carbon deposits from the exhaust ports and try and obtain a smooth finish in the ports without in any way enlarging them or altering their shape. The size and position of the ports predetermines the characteristics of the engine and unwarranted tampering can produce very adverse effects. An enlarged or re-profiled port does not necessarily guarantee an increase in performance.

24 Piston and piston rings: examination and renovation

1 Attention to the piston and piston rings can be overlooked if a rebore is necessary because new replacements will be fitted.
2 If a rebore is not considered necessary, the piston should be examined closely. Reject the piston if it is badly scored or if it is badly discoloured as the result of the exhaust gases by-passing the rings.
3 Remove all carbon from the piston crown and use metal polish to finish off. Carbon will not adhere so readily to a polished surface.
4 Check that the gudgeon pin bosses are not worn or the circlip grooves damaged. Check also the piston ring pegs, to make sure that none has worked loose.
5 The grooves in which the piston rings locate can also become enlarged in use. The clearance between the piston and the ring in the groove should not exceed 0.05 mm (0.002 inch).
6 Piston ring wear can be checked by inserting the rings in the cylinder bore from the top and pushing them down about 40 mm (1½ inches) with the crown of the piston so that they rest square in the cylinder. If the end gap exceeds 0.35 mm (0.014 inch) the rings should be replaced.
7 Examine the working surface of the rings. If discoloured areas are evident, the rings should be replaced since the patches indicate the blow-by of gas. Check also that there is not a build-up of carbon behind the tapered ends of the rings, where they locate with the piston ring pegs.
8 It cannot be over-emphasised that the condition of the piston and rings in a two-stroke engine is of prime importance, especially since they control the opening and closing of the ports in the cylinder barrel by providing an effective seal. A two-stroke engine has only three working parts, one of which is the piston. It follows that the efficiency of the engine is very dependent on the condition of this component and the parts with which it is closely associated.

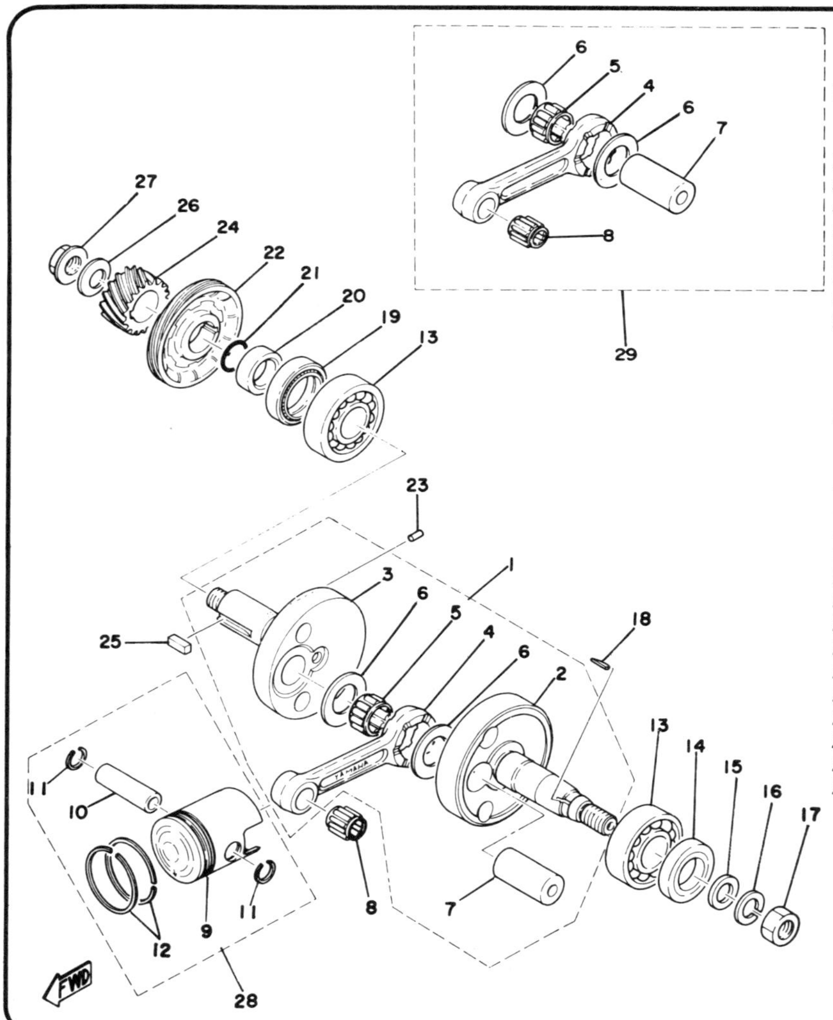

Fig. 1.5 Crankshaft assembly

1 *Crankshaft assembly*
2 *Left-hand crank*
3 *Right-hand crank*
4 *Connecting rod*
5 *Big end roller bearing*
6 *Thrust washer – 2 off (late models only)*
7 *Crank pin*
8 *Small end roller bearing*
9 *Piston*
10 *Gudgeon pin*
11 *Circlip – 2 off*
12 *Piston ring set*
13 *Main bearing – 2 off*
14 *Oil seal*
15 *Washer*
16 *Spring washer*
17 *Nut*
18 *Woodruff key*
19 *Oil seal*
20 *Spacer*
21 *O ring*
22 *Oil pump drive gear*
23 *Dowel pin*
24 *Gear*
25 *Straight key*
26 *Washer*
27 *Nut*
28 *Piston assembly*
29 *Connecting rod assembly*

24.4 Check the piston ring pegs

25 Small end: examination and renovation

The small end is a caged roller bearing and should be checked at the same time as the crankshaft assembly.

26 Cylinder head: examination and renovation

1 It is unlikely that the cylinder head will require any special attention apart from removing the carbon deposit from the combustion chamber. Finish off with metal polish; a polished surface will reduce the tendency for carbon to adhere and will also help improve the gas flow.

2 Check that the cooling fins are not obstructed, so that they receive the full air flow. A wire brush provides the best means of cleaning.

3 Check the condition of the thread where the spark plug is inserted. The thread in an aluminium alloy cylinder head is damaged very easily if the spark plug is overtightened. If necessary, the thread can be reclaimed by fitting what is known as a Helicoil insert. Most agents have facilities for this type of repair, which is not expensive.

4 If the cylinder head joint has shown signs of oil seepage when the machine was in use, check whether the cylinder head is distorted by laying it on a sheet of plate glass. Severe distortion will necessitate a replacement head but if the distortion is only slight, it is permissible to wrap some emery cloth (fine grade) around the sheet of glass and rub down the joint using a rotary motion, until it is once again flat. The usual cause of distortion is uneven tightening of the cylinder head nuts.

27 Crankcase: examination and renovation

1 Inspect the crankcases for cracks or any other signs of damage. If a crack is found, specialist treatment will be required to effect a satisfactory repair.

2 Clean off the jointing faces using a rag soaked in methylated spirit to remove old gasket cement. Do not use a scraper because the jointing surfaces are damaged very easily. A leak-tight crankcase is an essential requirement of any two-stroke engine. Check also the bearing housings, to make sure they are not damaged. The entry to the housings should be free from burrs or lips.

28 Reed valve: examination and renovation

1 A reed valve is fitted to the engine to control the inlet part of the two-stroke cycle. As the piston rises, the crankcase pressure falls, and the valve is opened by the incoming charge. When the piston falls, the crankcase pressure rises, and shuts the valve. This system has the advantage, that the inlet port timing varies according to the engine speed, rather than being fixed as in the case of a piston or disc valve control.

2 The reed is made from 0.2 mm (0.008 in) stainless steel and hence is rather delicate, so avoid touching it. Visually check the reed to ensure that it is not cracked or broken and check that it is seating on the rubber gasket. If any faults are found it is advisable to renew the whole reed valve assembly.

3 Ensure that the valve assembly is thoroughly clean because dirt and grit will impair its efficiency.

29 Gearbox components: examination and renovation

Manual change models

1 This group of components was removed from the crankcase as a unit, with care being taken to avoid losing any shims or washers from the ends of the shafts. The parts fall naturally into three sub-assemblies; the selector drum, the mainshaft and the output shaft.

2 Check that the selector forks are not bent or excessively worn. On the early models the selector drum sub-assembly should be examined to ensure that the selector forks will slide easily on the drum, without too much play. To renew the selector fork, remove the spring clip and the cam track follower and slide the selector fork clear. When reassembling, ensure that the selector fork is fitted the right way round.

3 The mainshaft and output shaft sub-assemblies should be examined closely for any signs of wear or damage, such as broken or chipped teeth, worn dogs and damaged or worn splines. Renew any parts found unserviceable as they cannot be reclaimed. To renew any parts, removal of the circlips, washers and gears until the defective part is reached is straightforward and if the parts are laid out in sequence, reassembly should be present no problems.

Automatic models

4 This group of components is removed from the crankcase as a unit, with care being taken to avoid losing any shims or washers from the ends of the shafts. The parts fall naturally into two sub-assemblies; the mainshaft and the output shaft.

5 Examine the sub-assemblies closely for any signs of wear or damage such as broken or chipped teeth, worn dogs or splines. Renew any parts found unserviceable as they cannot be reclaimed. To renew any parts, removal of the circlips, washers and gears until the defective part is reached is straightforward and if the parts are laid out in sequence, reassembly should present no problems. The output shaft has a shim immediately under the circlip on the end. If any parts are renewed, ensure that the correct thickness of shims is used to control the end-float of the gears, whilst still allowing them to rotate freely.

6 Inside the output shaft is the selector mechanism. Remove the circlip in the end with care, as the return spring is under the retaining washer. The whole mechanism will now slide out so that the wear on the selector head and the condition of the springs can be checked.

7 Renew any damaged or suspect parts as they cannot be reclaimed. Reassembly is straightforward because the eight $\frac{9}{32}$ inch balls that select the gears cannot get into the centre but the gears may need turning to allow the selector head to seat properly.

28.3 Ensure that the reed valve is clean and undamaged

29.2a A large circlip retains the end plate on the selector drum to hold the pins in place

29.2b The pip operates the neutral indicator switch

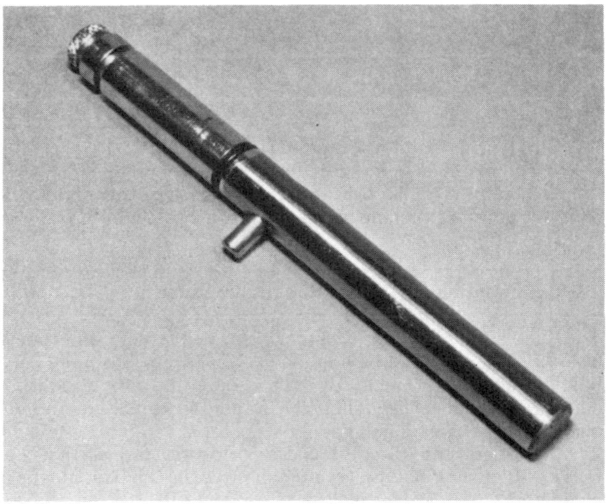
29.2c Ensure that the selector shaft is not bent

29.3a The mainshaft if damaged must be replaced as a complete assembly

29.3b The second gear pinion slides off the output shaft

29.3c Remove the circlip ...

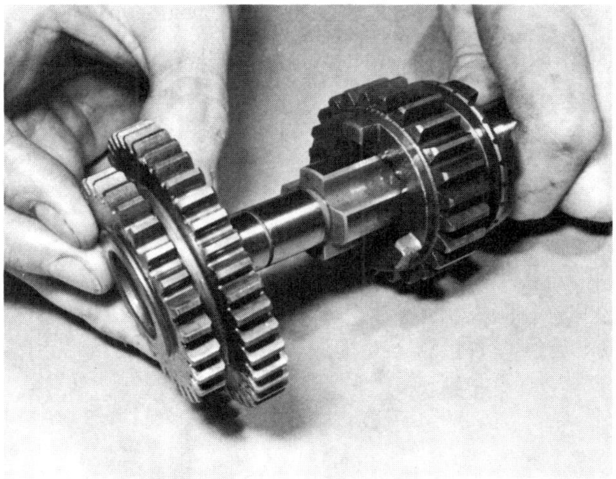

29.3d ... to release the first gear pinion ...

29.3e ... and slide off the top gear pinion

30 Gearchange mechanism and index arm: examination – manual change models only

1 Examine the gearchange mechanism and the index arm for any signs of damage, renewing any of the springs which may have become weak or broken.
2 Check for wear on the gearchange lever pawls as this can cause missed gearchanges.

31 Gear selector lever: examination – automatic models only

1 The gear selector lever is bolted onto the left-hand cover by three bolts. Visually check for wear and check the condition of the spring located under the index ball.

32 Kickstart assembly: examination

1 Give the kickstart assembly a close visual inspection for signs of wear or damage such as broken or chipped teeth, removing the necessary circlips if dismantling for the renewal of any parts.
2 Examine the kickstart return spring for weakness or damage. This component is often overlooked, even though it is tensioned every time the kickstart is depressed. It is best to renew as a precaution during a major overhaul, to prevent a further stripdown later.

33 Primary drive: examination

1 The primary drive gears should be examined closely to ensure that there is no damage to the teeth. The depth of mesh is predetermined by the bearing locations and cannot be adjusted.
2 On the automatic models carefully remove the pawl carrier assembly to examine the condition of the pawls, the spring and the ratchet teeth. Renew any damaged or worn parts as they cannot be reclaimed. When reassembling, ensure that the thrust washer between the gear and the pawl carrier does not get misplaced.

34 Engine reassembly: general

1 Before reassembly is commenced, the various engine and gearbox components should be thoroughly clean and placed close to the working area.
2 Make sure all traces of the old gaskets have been removed and the mating surfaces are clean and undamaged. One of the best ways to remove old gasket cement is to apply a rag soaked in methylated spirit. This acts as a solvent and will ensure the cement is removed without resort to scraping and the consequent risk of damage.
3 Gather together all the necessary tools and have available an oil can filled with clean engine oil. Make sure all the new gaskets and oil seals are to hand; nothing is more frustrating than having to stop in the middle of a reassembly sequence because a vital gasket or replacement has been overlooked.
4 Make sure the reassembly area is clean and that there is adequate working space. Refer to the torque and clearance settings wherever they are given. Many of the smaller bolts are easily sheared if they are over-tightened. Always use the correct size screwdriver bit for the crosshead screws and never an ordinary screwdriver or punch.

32.1 Check for worn or broken teeth

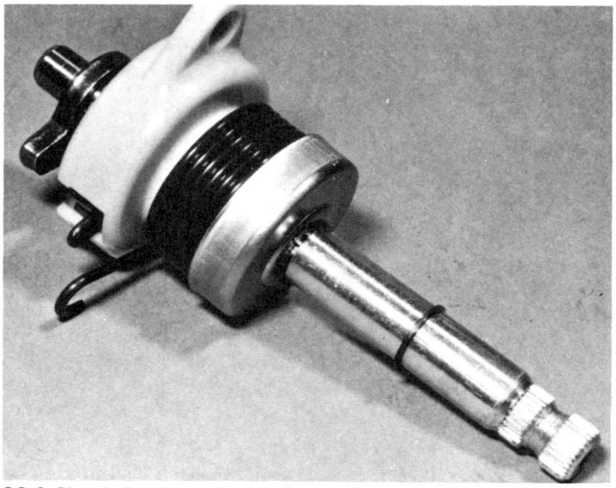

32.2 Check the return spring for weakness or damage

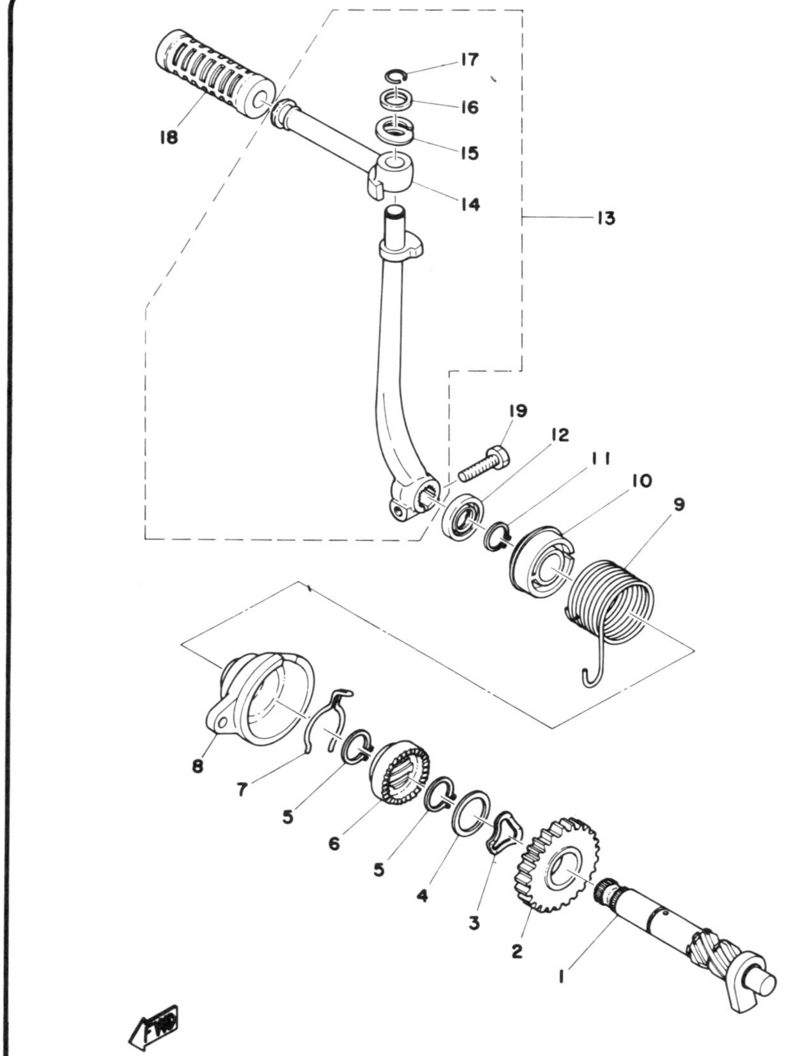

1 Kickstart shaft
2 Gear pinion
3 Wave washer
4 Shim
5 Circlip – 2 off
6 Ratchet wheel
7 Friction spring
8 Return spring guide
9 Return spring
10 Spring cover
11 Circlip
12 Oil seal
13 Kickstart lever assembly
14 Kickstart pedal
15 Double spring washer
16 Washer
17 Circlip
18 Pedal rubber
19 Bolt

Fig. 1.6 Kickstart assembly

35 Fitting the bearings and oil seals to the crankcases and clutch cover

1 Before fitting the crankcase bearings, make sure that the bearing surfaces are scrupulously clean and that there are no burrs or lips on the entry to the housings. Press or drive the bearings into the cases, using a mandrel and hammer, after first making sure that they are lined up squarely. Warming the crankcases will help when a bearing is a particularly tight fit.
2 When the bearings have been driven home, lightly oil them and make sure they revolve freely. This is particularly important in the case of the main bearings.
3 Using a soft mandrel, drive the oil seals into their respective locations. Do not use more force than is necessary because the seals will damage very easily. Good crankcase seals are essential to the efficient running of any two-stroke engine and if there is any doubt about the condition of the old seals they should be replaced without hesitation. Poor starting and indifferent running can often be attributed to worn or damaged oil seals, which allow air to enter the crankcase and dilute the incoming mixture.
4 Replace the bearing retaining plate on the gearbox main bearing, and the oil seal retaining plate for the crankshaft oil seal.
5 Lightly oil all the other moving parts as a prelude to reassembly. This will ensure all working parts are lubricated adequately during the initial start-up of the rebuilt engine.

36 Crankshaft assembly: refitting

1 Feed the crankshaft assembly into the left-hand crankcase. Fit suitable spacers and the rotor nut and draw the crankshaft assembly into the crankcase. Several spacers will be required as the thread length for the rotor nut is relatively short, so several 'bites of the cherry' will be required.
2 On no account drive the crankshaft in by hitting on the primary drive end because this will alter the setting up of the crankshaft assembly and render it unserviceable.

37 Gearbox components: refitting

1 Place the left-hand crankcase on wooden blocks or an engine stand so that the inner side faces upwards.
2 On the automatic models the mainshaft and output shaft, when meshed, should simply slide into the crankcase but light tapping may be required to fit the output shaft into the journal bearing.
3 On the manual change models, put the mainshaft and output shaft in mesh in one hand and rest the selector drum on top, pyramid fashion. On early models, the selector should be positioned locating with the mainshaft. Feed the two selector forks into position on the shafts and locate them in the selector drum. Hold everything in place with the other hand and feed the cluster into the crankcase half. Again, light tapping to fully seat the output shaft may be necessary.
4 Do not use excessive force during reassembly. If the components do not fit, remove the cluster and check that everything is in its correct position. Check that the shafts rotate when they have been refitted.

38 Rejoining the crankcase halves

1 Smear the joint face with Golden Hermatite or other jointing compound and stick the gasket to the crankcase joint.
2 Ensure that the crankcase dowels are in position and that any shims and washers are on their shafts.
3 Lower the other crankcase half into position. Gentle tapping may be required to fit the two halves together as the bearings and dowels are a tight fit.
4 Rotate all the shafts to ensure that they will turn and that no binding occurs.
5 Excessive force should not be used as this shows something has been wrongly assembled or is out of alignment.
6 Replace the screws which hold the crankcase halves together.
7 The crankshaft spacer and the output shaft spacer, where fitted, can be pushed into their respective oil seals. Use great care so that the seal is not damaged.
8 Replace the oil drain plug after checking that the sealing washer is in good condition.

39 Neutral indicator switch: refitting

Screw the neutral indicator switch back into the crankcase after checking that the sealing washer is in good condition.

40 Selector drum retaining plate: refitting

Refit the selector drum retaining plate and secure it with its two screws.

35.1 Ensure that the housings are clean before driving the bearings into place

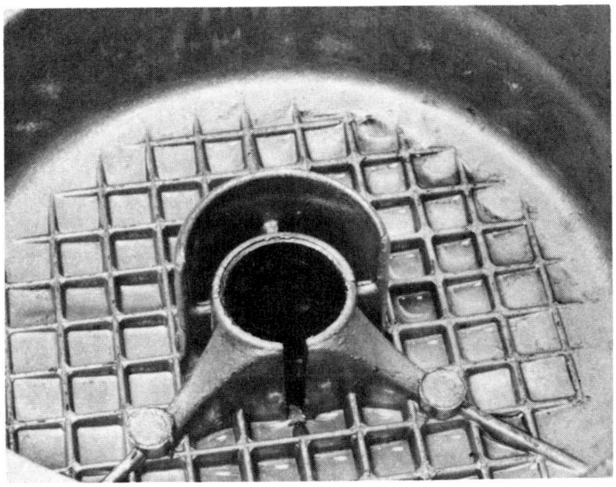

35.3 Check the oil seal in the clutch cover

Fig. 1.7 Gearbox components (early models)

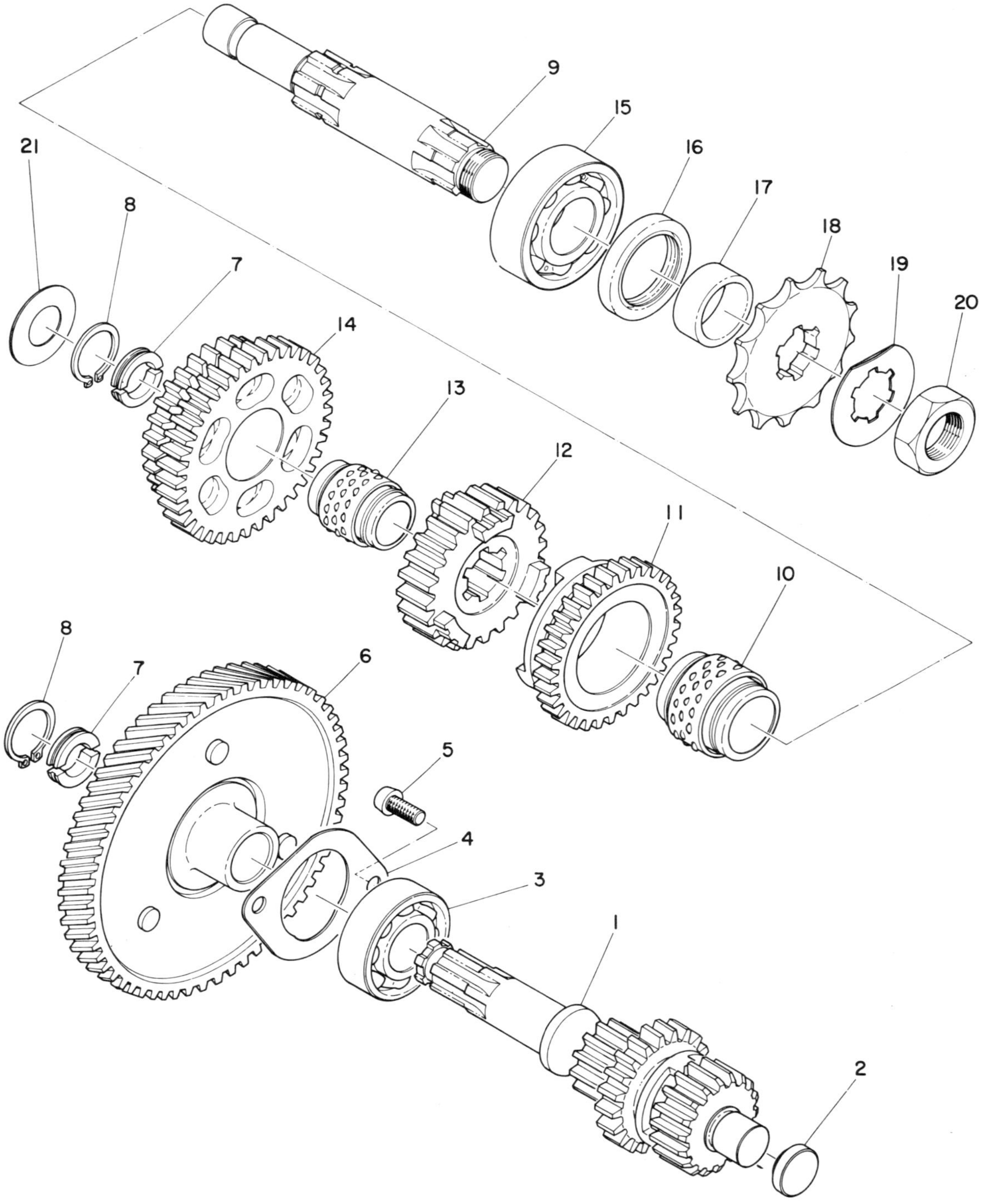

1 Mainshaft assembly
2 Plug
3 Bearing
4 Retaining plate
5 Screw – 2 off
6 Primary gear assembly
7 Half collet – 4 off
8 Circlip – 2 off
9 Output shaft
10 Slide bearing
11 Second gear pinion
12 Top gear pinion
13 Slide bearing
14 First gear pinion
15 Bearing
16 Oil seal
17 Spacer
18 Sprocket
19 Tab washer
20 Nut
21 Shim – 1 or 2 off

Fig. 1.8 Gearbox components (late models)

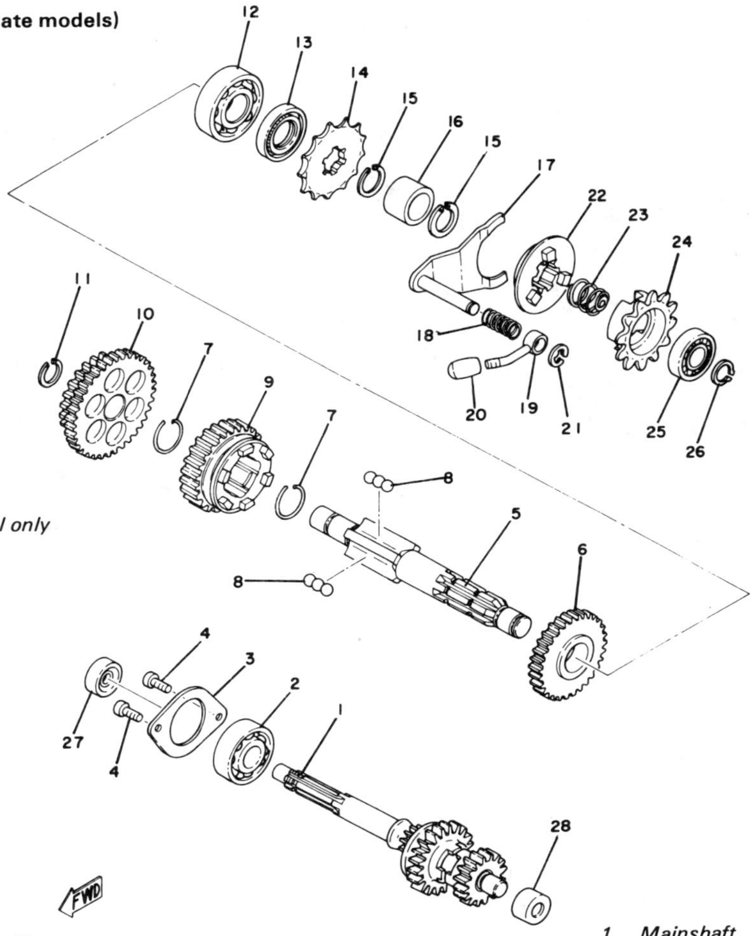

1 Mainshaft assembly
2 Bearing
3 Retaining plate
4 Screw – 2 off
5 Output shaft
6 Second gear pinion
7 Circlip – 2 off
8 Steel ball – 12 off
9 Top gear pinion
10 First gear pinion
11 Circlip
12 Bearing
13 Oil seal
14 Sprocket
15 Circlip – 1 or 2 off
16 Spacer
17 Selector fork
18 Spring
19 Selector lever
20 Knob
21 Circlip
22 Driving dog
23 Spring
24 Sprocket
25 Bearing
26 Circlip
27 Oil seal
28 Bearing

(16–26: V50P model only)

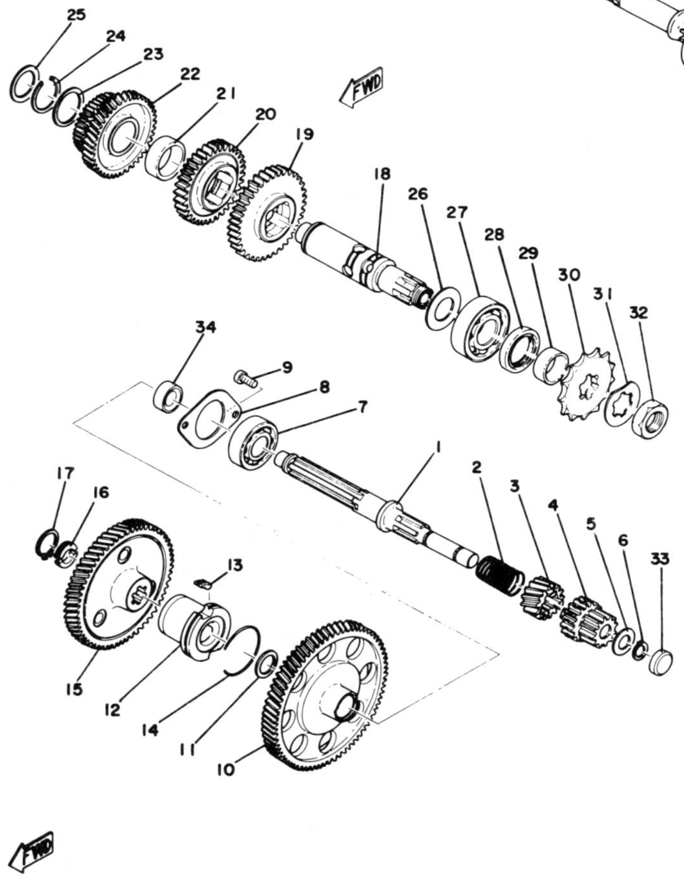

1 Mainshaft
2 Spring
3 Kickstart pinion
4 Gear pinion
5 Washer
6 Circlip
7 Bearing
8 Retaining plate
9 Screw – 2 off
10 Drive gear (low)
11 Washer
12 Pawl carrier
13 Pawl – 2 off
14 Pawl spring
15 Driven gear (high)
16 Half collet – 2 off
17 Circlip
18 Output shaft
19 First gear pinion
20 Second gear pinion
21 Spacer
22 Kickstart idler gear
23 Shim
24 Circlip
25 Washer
26 Thrust washer
27 Bearing
28 Oil seal
29 Spacer
30 Sprocket
31 Tab washer
32 Nut
33 Plug
34 Oil seal

Fig. 1.9 Gearbox components (automatic models)

37.3a Mesh the mainshaft and output shaft ...

37.3b ... and feed the cluster into the crankcase

39.1 Refit the neutral indicator switch

43 Kickstarter mechanism: refitting

1 Feed the kickstarter mechanism into the crankcase, ensuring that the ratchet spring and the plastic cover locate in their correct positions.
2 Rotate the kickstart shaft clockwise until it will go no further, and wind the kickstart return spring round until it hooks on the anchor lug.

44 Oil pump: refitting

1 If the oil pump has been removed, check the condition of the O rings that are fitted round the body, before feeding the oil pump back into position. Push the pump inwards to seat it securely and fix it with the two large screws.
2 On no account hammer the nut on the end of the pump to push it into position because this will ruin the pump.

41 Reed valve and inlet stub: refitting

1 Smear the joint faces with Golden Hermatite or other jointing compound and stick the gaskets in position.
2 Fit the reed valve assembly into the crankcase, position the inlet stub and fit the four screws to hold them securely.

42 Gearchange mechanism and index arm: refitting – manual change models only

1 Hook the index arm spring into the index arm and over the anchor pin and pull the index arm across to allow the shouldered bolt to screw into the crankcase.
2 Ensure that the gearchange return and pawl springs are in position. Feed the shaft through the crankcases, pulling the pawl clear of the selector drum whilst easing the gearchange return spring over its pin to allow the gearchange assembly to seat home.
3 On some models the spring pin is adjustable to ensure that the gearchange pawls locate correctly on the gearchange drum.
4 Replace washer and circlip on the gearshaft on the other side of the engine.

42.2 Refit the gearchange assembly and index arm

43.1 Ensure that the kickstart assembly locates on its boss

43.2 Wind up the return spring and hook it onto the anchor boss

44.1 Push the oil pump back into position

45 Clutch and primary drive: refitting

Early models

1 Ensure that the crankshaft oil seal spacer has been fitted and fit the O ring on the crankshaft.

2 Fit the drive pin for the oil pump gear into the crankshaft and slide the oil pump gear into position. It may be necessary to turn the oil pump to ensure that the gears mesh correctly.

3 Slide the primary gear pinion onto its splines, fit the two half collets and secure them with the circlip.

4 The primary drive gear assembly and bush already located within the clutch unit make an assembly that slides onto the splines of the crankshaft. Refit the central nut and washer and tighten to the recommended torque setting.

5 Smear the joint face with Golden Hermatite or other jointing compound and stick the gasket to the crankcase face.

6 Refit the side cover and retain it with its seven screws, noting that the long one fits in the front lower position, through one of the dowels.

Late models

7 Ensure that the crankshaft oil seal spacer has been fitted and fit the O ring on the crankshaft.

8 Fit the drive pin for the oil pump gear into the crankshaft and slide the oil pump gear into position. It may be necessary to turn the oil pump to ensure that the gears mesh correctly.

9 Fit the parallel key into the primary drive pinion and slide the pinion onto the crankshaft. Fit the nut and washer and tighten to the recommended torque setting.

10 Fit the thrust washer and bush onto the mainshaft followed by the clutch as a complete unit. Refit the central nut and washer and tighten to the recommended torque setting.

11 Smear the joint face with Golden Hermatite or other jointing compound and stick the gasket to the crankcase face.

12 Refit the side cover and retain it with its screws, noting that the long one fits in the front lower position, through one of the dowels.

Automatic models

13 Ensure that the crankshaft oil seal spacer has been fitted and fit the O ring on the crankshaft.

14 Fit the drive pin for the oil pump gear into the crankshaft and slide the oil pump gear into position. It may be necessary to turn the oil pump to ensure that the gears mesh correctly.

15 On to the mainshaft feed the bottom gear pinion followed by a thrust washer. Carefully feed the pawl carrier, complete with pawls, into position inside the bottom gear pinion.

16 Fit the thrust washer and bush onto the crankshaft followed by the clutch as a complete unit. Fit another thrust washer, a plain washer and the central nut, and tighten to the recommended torque setting.

17 Slide the top gear pinion onto its splines; fit the two half collets and secure them with the circlip.

18 Smear the joint face with Golden Hermatite or other jointing compound and stick the gasket to the crankcase face.

19 Refit the side cover and retain it with its screws, noting that the long one fits in the front lower position, through one of the dowels.

46 Final drive sprocket: refitting

1 For the early and the automatic models, ensure that the spacer is fitted in the oil seal and then fit the sprocket, the tab washer and the nut. Fully tighten the nut and lock it in position with the tab washer.

2 For the later models, fit the sprocket and retain it with a circlip.

3 For the V50P model, fit the sprocket, retain it with a circlip, fit the spacer and retain that with a second circlip.

45.7 Check the O ring on the crankshaft

45.8a Fit the drive pin ...

45.8b ... and slide the gear into position

45.9 Slide the drive pinion and parallel key onto the crankshaft

47 Cylinder head, cylinder barrel and piston: refitting

1 Raise the connecting rod to its highest point and pad the mouth of the crankcase with clean rag as a precaution against displaced parts falling into the crankcase. Replace the caged roller small end bearing. Fit the piston, complete with rings, after oiling both the gudgeon pin and the small end bearing. To aid replacement in the correct position, the piston crown is marked with an arrow head. This must face in the direction of the exhaust port or downward.

2 If the gudgeon pin is a tight fit, it may be necessary to warm the piston in order to expand the gudgeon pin bosses. Holding the piston under a stream of hot water will usually suffice, provided the water is quickly wiped off before reassembly commences. Push the pin home and replace both circlips, which should have been renewed. It is false economy to re-use the originals, which may become displaced and cause serious engine damage.

3 Check that both circlips are located in their grooves. Before the cylinder barrel is replaced, oil the piston and the inside of the cylinder barrel. Note that if the engine has been rebored it will probably be necessary to relieve the edges of the ports very slightly to prevent the rings from being trapped. Careful work with emery cloth and/or a fine file will remove any burrs or lips; make sure none of the abrasive material remains in the cylinder bore before it is wiped clean and coated with oil. Fit a new cylinder base gasket.

4 The piston will have two rings. Note that the ring grooves are fitted with a peg, which predetermines where the ring gaps will occur. This is essential, otherwise the ends of the rings will project into the ports, causing breakages and severe engine damage.

5 Smear the cylinder bore with clean oil and lower the cylinder barrel down the holding down studs until it can be engaged with the piston. Check that the piston rings are correctly lined up with the piston pegs and then compress the rings so that the piston can be inserted into the cylinder bore. The spigot of the cylinder barrel has a taper, to facilitate the entry of the piston rings. Do not use force; the piston rings are brittle and will break very easily if they become trapped.

6 It is permissible to use a piston ring clamp if this method is preferred, assuming care is taken to ensure each ring is located correctly with its peg.

7 When the piston and rings have passed into the cylinder bore, remove the crankcase padding and slide the cylinder barrel and piston downward until the spigot of the cylinder barrel enters the mouth of the crankcase and the flange seats correctly on the new cylinder base gasket.

8 Fit a new cylinder head gasket to the top flange of the

cylinder barrel.
9 Gasket cement is not required at the cylinder head joint.
10 Lower the cylinder head into position. Replace the four cylinder head nuts and washers and tighten them in a diagonal sequence, a little at a time, until the recommended torque wrench setting is achieved.
11 Before proceeding to the next stage of reassembly, check that the engine turns freely in either direction. Any tight spots must be investigated and remedied, even if it means removing the cylinder barrel and head again.

48 Flywheel generator: refitting

1 The Woodruff key should now be tapped into the crankshaft.
2 The stator and its two fixing screws should then be replaced, making sure that the wires feed out at the top of the engine so that the rubber grommet can be pushed back in its slot.
3 The neutral warning light switch can now be reconnected.
4 Before fitting the flywheel rotor, place a few drops of light oil on the felt wick which lubricates the contact breaker cam in the centre of the flywheel rotor.
5 It is advisable to check also whether the contact breaker points require attention at this stage, otherwise it will be necessary to withdraw the flywheel rotor again in order to gain access. Reference to Chapter 4 will show how the contact breaker points are renovated and adjusted.
6 Feed the rotor onto the crankshaft so that the slot lines up with the Woodruff key. The rotor may have to be turned to clear the heel of the contact breaker before it will slide fully home.
7 The washer and rotor nut can now be fitted and the nut fully tightened.

49 Refitting the engine/gearbox unit in the frame

1 If the engine mounting bushes have been removed, check that they are replaced before the engine is offered up.
2 Follow in reverse the procedure given in Section 5 of this Chapter.
3 When the engine is located temporarily on the engine bottom bolt, before being swung up into position, check that all the pipes, wires and cables are put into their correct places as there is very little room between the engine and the frame when completed. It is very annoying to have to remove the engine again simply because a wire was incorrectly placed.
4 Fit the spark plug as soon as the engine unit is lifted into the frame and the engine bolts are replaced, to prevent dirt and foreign matter from dropping into the engine.
5 Use a new ring gasket for the exhaust pipe joint. A leaktight exhaust system is essential for the correct running of the engine.
6 Refit the kickstarter and gear change levers so that they are positioned at the correct angles. These are easier to determine when the engine is in the frame. Make reference to the punch marks made during dismantling.
7 Remove the gearbox oil filler plug from the top of the right-hand crankcase and refill the gearbox with the recommended oil. The filler cap has an integral dipstick; oil should be added until it reaches the groove when the machine is standing on level ground. Do not overfill.
8 Remove the bleeder screw on the oil pump until the oil flows out with no bubbles, then replace the screw ensuring that the sealing washer is in good condition. A few kicks on the starter pedal before the ignition is switched on will pump the oil to the engine. Adjust the oil pump cable as described in the Routine Maintenance Section, if necessary.

47.1 The arrow must point to the exhaust port

47.3 Check that both circlips are located properly

47.9 Fit a new cylinder head gasket

47.11 Replace the cylinder head and secure with the nuts tightened in a diagonal sequence

48.3 Reconnect the neutral indicator switch

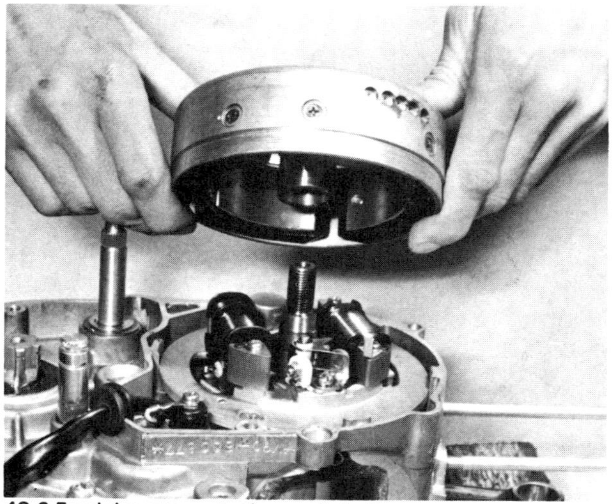

48.6 Feed the rotor onto the crankshaft

49.1 Refit the engine mounting bushes

49.3 Ensure that the wires and cables are correctly positioned before swinging the engine into position

49.5 Always use a new gasket for the exhaust pipe joint

49.6a The centre-pop marks aid assembly

49.6b Refit the gearchange lever in the correct position

49.7 Refill the engine with the correct grade of engine oil

49.8 Bleed the oil pump to remove any trapped air

50 Starting and running the rebuilt engine

1 When the initial start-up is made, run the engine slowly for the first few minutes, especially if the engine has been rebored. Check that all the controls function correctly and that there are no oil leaks before taking the machine on the road.
2 Remember that a good seal between the piston and the cylinder barrel is essential for the correct functioning of any two-stroke engine. In consequence, a rebored engine will require more careful running in than its four-stroke counterpart. There is a far greater risk of engine seizure during the first hundred miles if the engine is permitted to work hard.
3 Do not tamper with the exhaust system or run the engine without the baffles fitted to the silencer. Unwarranted changes in the exhaust system will have a very noticeable effect on engine performance, invariably for the worse.

Fault diagnosis Engine and Gearbox is given on Page 44.

51 Fault diagnosis: engine

Symptom	Cause	Remedy
Engine will not start	Defective spark plug	Remove plug and lay it on cylinder head. Check whether spark occurs when engine is kicked over.
	Dirty or closed contact breaker points	Check condition of points and whether gap is correct.
	Air leak at crankcase or worn oil seals around crankshaft	Flood carburettor and check whether mixture is reaching the spark plug.
Engine runs unevenly	Ignition and/or fuel system fault	Check systems as though engine will not start.
	Blowing cylinder head gasket	Leak should be evident from oil leakage where gas escapes.
	Incorrect ignition timing	Check timing and reset if necessary.
	Loose pin on which moving contact breaker point pivots	Renew defective parts.
Lack of power	Incorrect ignition timing	See above.
	Fault in fuel system	Check system and filler cap vent.
	Blowing head gasket	See above.
	Choked silencer	Clean out baffles.
High fuel/oil consumption	Cylinder barrel in need of rebore and o/s piston	Fit new rings and piston after rebore.
	Oil leaks or air leaks from damaged gaskets or oil seals	Trace source of leak and replace damaged gaskets or seals.
Excessive mechanical noise	Worn cylinder barrel (piston slap)	Rebore and fit oversize piston.
	Worn small end bearing (rattle)	Renew bearing and gudgeon pin.
	Worn big-end bearing (knock)	Fit new big-end bearing.
	Worn main bearings (rumble)	Fit new journal bearings and seals.
Engine overheats and fades	Pre-ignition and/or weak mixture	Check carburettor settings. Check also whether plug grade correct.
	Lubrication failure	Check oil pump and tank.

52 Fault diagnosis: gearbox

Symptom	Cause	Remedy
Difficulty in engaging gears	Broken gear selector pawl or cam	Renew.
	Deformed gear selector	Repair or renew.
Machine jumps out of gear	Worn sliding gears on mainshaft and layshaft	Renew.
	Distorted or worn gear selector fork	Repair or renew.
	Weak gearchange drum stop spring	Renew spring.
Gearchange lever fails to return to normal position	Broken or displaced gearchange return spring	Renew or repair.
Kickstart lever fails to return to normal position	Broken kickstart return spring	Renew spring.

Chapter 2 Clutch

For modifications, and information relating to later models, see Chapter 8

Contents

Specifications

Early models with clutch mounted on crankshaft

	V50	V75	V90
Number of roller assemblies	4	4	6
Number of friction plates	2	3	3
Number of clutch springs	5	5	6
Gap between clutch plates should be	1·8 mm – 2·2 mm (0·072 in – 0·088 in)		
Roller lock for starting with bob-weight release			

Later models with clutch mounted on gearbox mainshaft

	V50	V90
Number of roller assemblies	9	12
or ballweights	14	16
Number of friction plates	5	7
Number of clutch springs	8	8
Gap between clutch plates should be	1·8 mm – 2·2 mm (0·072 in – 0·088 in)	
Ratchet and pawl for starting with centrifugal release		

Automatic models with clutch mounted on crankshaft

Number of clutch carrier assemblies	2
Number of shoes in each assembly	3
Roller lock for starting with torsion spring release	

1 General description

There are various types of clutch fitted to the Yamaha 50, 75 and 90 models, but they are all of the centrifugal type, being engaged as the engine speed rises without any means of manual operation.

The early models have a multi-plate clutch operated by roller weights to force the clutch plates together. The later models have more weights due to the clutch being mounted on the gearbox mainshaft and hence not rotating as quickly as that of the early models. The automatic models have an expanding shoe clutch where the shoes are forced open by centrifugal force until they grip the clutch drum. The first set of shoes grip the drum as the engine speed rises to enable the rider to pull away, and the second set of shoes grip the drum as the road speed rises, effectively giving a higher gear ratio.

As the clutch is disengaged when the engine is stationary there is a device incorporated in the clutch to enable the kick-start to turn the engine. On the early models this is a roller lock which is released by the action of two bob-weights when the engine is running. The later models embody a ratchet and pawl device which, due to the design, retracts the pawl when the engine speed is sufficient. This helps reduce wear on the pawl and ratchet. The automatic models use a roller locking device similar to that used on the early models but with a torsion spring release in place of the bob-weights.

The clutch springs in the multi-plate clutch, sandwiched between the pressure plates, act in completely the opposite manner to normal clutch springs in that they relieve the pressure on the clutch plates when the weights start to act, and provide a cushion to ensure that the take off of the machine is smooth.

The small springs round the edges of the clutch plates ensure that the weights are pushed back to their starting positions and that the clutch plates are separated when the engine slows down or stops.

The automatic models have the ratchet and pawl device mounted on the gearbox mainshaft to enable the lower gear pinion to freewheel when the higher gears are driving the machine.

2 Clutch assembly: dismantling – early models

1 The clutch assembly complete can be removed by following the procedure detailed in Chapter 1, Section 10, Paragraphs 3 to 7.

2 The clutch centre assembly will lift straight out from the clutch, complete with the bearing sleeve. The sleeve will slide out for examination. Remove the circlip and unhook the spring on each bob-wieght before removing them. The roller cage, the six rollers and the splined boss will nowslide out of the clutch centre.

3 Compress the clutch plates slightly within the drum to enable the large circlip to be removed. Release the pressure and lift out the clutch plates, the pressure plates assembly and the centrifugal roller weights.

4 Compress the pressure plates assembly to enable the four small circlips to be removed. Release the pressure and separate the plates and springs.

3 Clutch assembly: dismantling - later models

1 The clutch assembly complete is removed by following the procedure detailed in Chapter 1, Section 10, Paragraphs 11 to 15.

2 Compress the clutch plates slightly within the drum to enable the large circlip to be removed. Release the pressure and lift out the pressure plates assembly, followed by the clutch plates. The clutch centre will now lift clear and the centrifugal roller assemblies or steel balls can be tipped out.

3 Compress the pressure plates assembly to enable the four small circlips to be removed. Release the pressure and separate the plates and springs.

4 The pawl carrier complete with the pawls will lift out of the clutch drum for inspection. If the ratchet ring is worn, releasing the circlip will allow its removal.

3.2a Remove the large circlip ...

3.2b ... the pressure plate assembly ...

3.2c ... the clutch plates ...

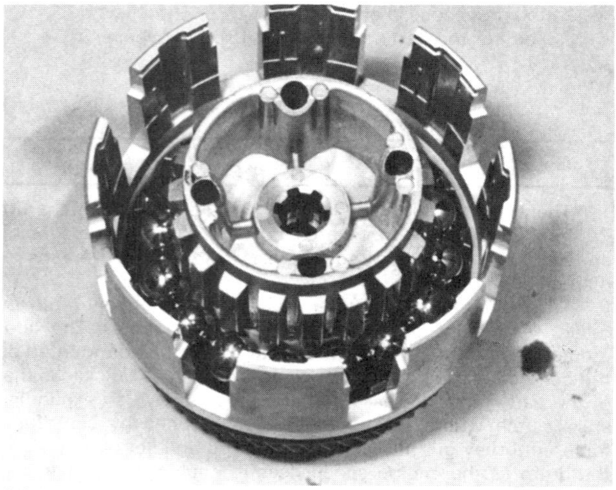

3.2d ... the clutch centre ...

3.2e ... and tip out the ball bearing weights

3.4 The circlip retains the ratchet ring

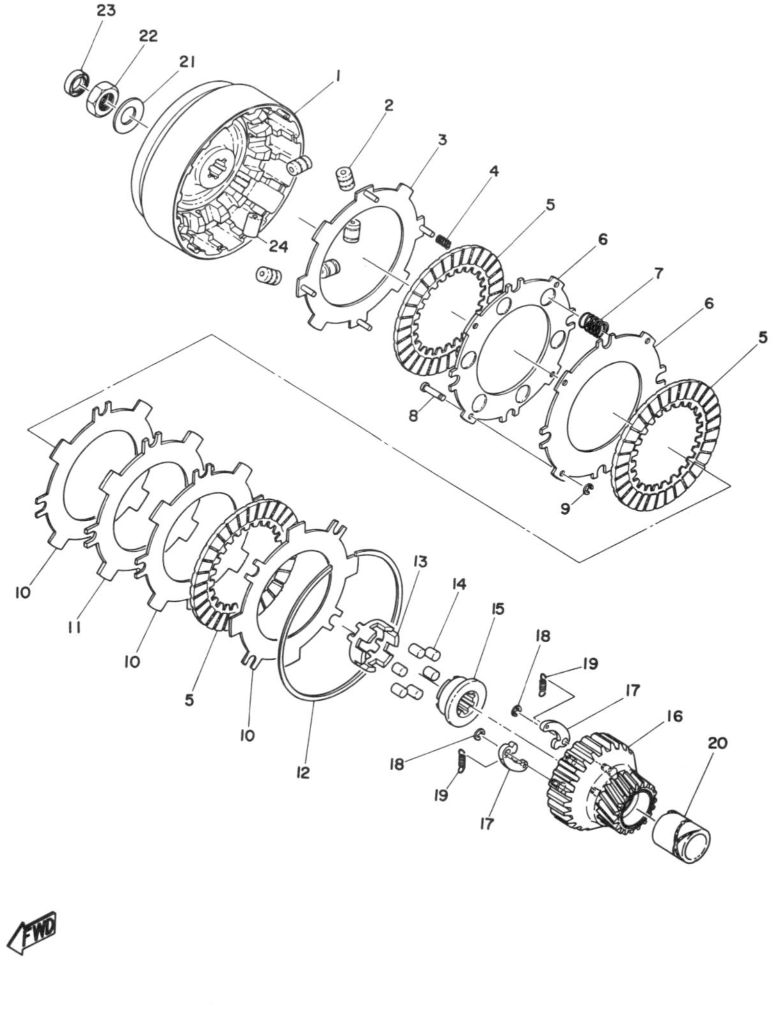

1 Clutch housing
2 Roller weight assembly – 4 or 5 off
3 Plate assembly
4 Spring – 4 off
5 Friction plate – 2 or 3 off
6 Pressure plate – 2 off
7 Clutch spring – 5 or 6 off
8 Pin – 4 off
9 Circlip – 4 off
10 Plain clutch plate – 1, 2 or 3 off
11 Clutch spacer plate (not V50 model)
12 Circlip
13 Cage
14 Roller – 6 off
15 Boss
16 Primary drive gear assembly
17 Bob-weight – 2 off
18 Circlip – 2 off
19 Spring – 2 off
20 Sleeve
21 Bellville washer
22 Locknut
23 Oil seal
24 Roller weight (V90 model only)

Fig. 2.1 Clutch assembly (early models)

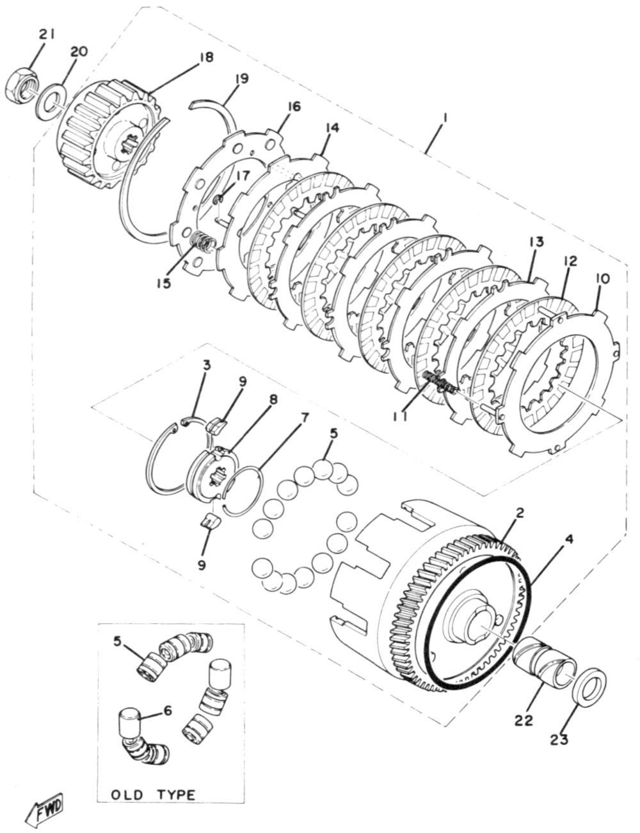

1 Clutch assembly
2 Clutch housing
3 Circlip
4 O ring
5 Steel ball – 14 off or roller weight assembly – 7 off
6 Roller weight – 2 off
7 Pawl spring
8 Boss
9 Pawl
10 Plate assembly
11 Spring – 4 off
12 Friction plate – 5 or 7 off
13 Plain clutch plate – 4 or 6 off
14 Pressure plate assembly
15 Spring – 8 off
16 Pressure plate
17 Circlip – 4 off
18 Clutch centre
19 Circlip
20 Washer
21 Nut
22 Sleeve
23 Thrust washer

Fig. 2.2 Clutch assembly (late models)

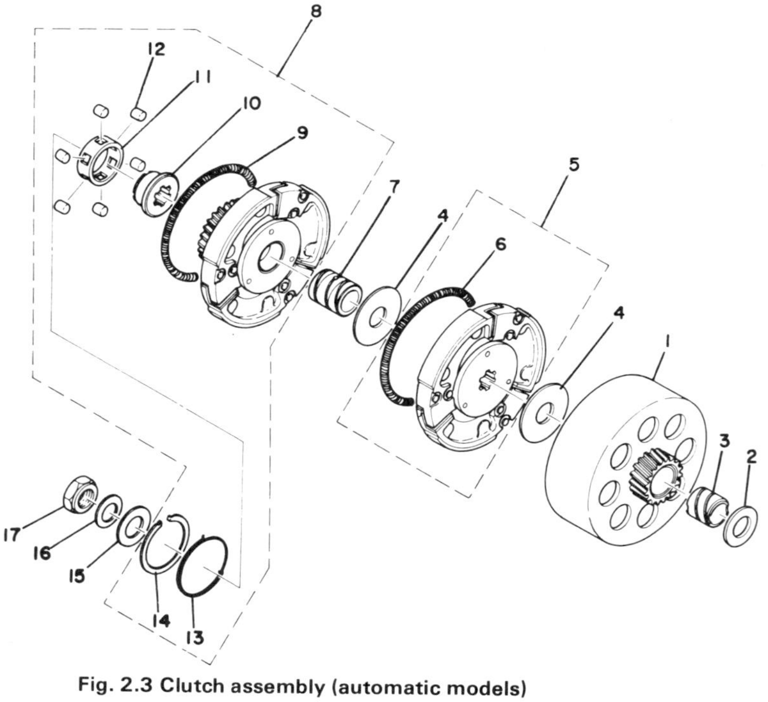

1 Clutch housing assembly
2 Thrust washer
3 Sleeve
4 Thrust washer
5 Carrier assembly
6 Spring
7 Sleeve
8 Carrier assembly
9 Spring
10 Boss
11 Cage
12 Roller – 6 off
13 Torsion spring
14 Circlip
15 Thrust washer
16 Washer
17 Nut

Fig. 2.3 Clutch assembly (automatic models)

4 Clutch assembly: dismantling - automatic models

1 The clutch assembly complete is removed by following the procedure detailed in Chapter 1, Section 10, Paragraphs 18 to 23.
2 Remove the outer thrust washers and the clutch drum bearing sleeve if these are still in position on the clutch.
3 Lift out the higher gear shoe sub-assembly, remove the bearing sleeve and the thrust washer, lift out the lower gear shoe sub-assembly and another thrust washer.
4 By removing the circlip on the higher gear shoe sub-assembly, the torsion spring roller cage, rollers and splined boss can be slid out.
5 The shoe return springs can be unhooked from their sub-assemblies

5 Clutch: examination and renovation

1 Check the conditions of the primary drive teeth and the internal splines to ensure the the parts are not chipped, broken or badly worn.
2 Give the plain and friction clutch plates or the shoes a wash with a paraffin/petrol mix and check that they are not buckled or distorted. Remove all traces of friction material debris, otherwise a gradual build up will affect clutch action.
3 Visual inspection will show whether the tongues of the clutch plates have become burred and whether indentations have formed in the slots with which they engage. Burrs should be removed with a file, which can also be used to dress the slots, provided the depth of the indentations is not great.
4 Check the friction clutch plates for wear, renewing them if they are well worn or if the clutch setting cannot be obtained.
5 Check the shoes for wear, renewing the sub-assembly if the shoes are worn excessively.
6 Check all the springs for signs of weakening or damage renewing any suspect springs. Springs that are used together should always be replaced in sets as the clutch depends on the plates being square for its smooth action.
7 Check the condition of the locking rollers or the pawls and ratchet to ensure that they are not chipped or badly worn and that when reassembled the mechanism operates freely.
8 Check the condition of the roller ramps in the clutch drum and the roller contact areas on the clutch plates. Excessive wear in these areas is often the cause of engine stalling, fierce clutch engagement and difficulty in gear changing. Replace the worn parts.
9 It is rarely necessary to renew the centrifugal roller assemblies or balls, this being only necessary if excessive wear is evident on the rollers, balls and clutch drum.

6 Clutch: reassembly and adjustment

1 Reassemble the clutch components by following the dismantling procedure in reverse but placing the clutch centre in position to ensure that the friction plates line up correctly on the multi-plate versions.
2 When the large circlip has been fitted in place, remove the clutch centre, and ensure that the gap between the friction plate and the end plain plate or pressure plates is between 1.8 mm (0.072 in) and 2.2 mm (0.088 in). Plain clutch plates of different thicknesses are available and the gap in the clutch can be adjusted by dismantling and rebuilding with different plates. If the allowed gap is not obtainable, it probably means that the friction plates are worn excessively, so the whole procedure needs repeating with new friction plates.
3 On the automatic models ensure that the correct tension spring is fitted to the shoe sub-assemblies.
4 The built-up clutch can then be refitted to the engine, following the engine reassembly procedure given in Chapter 1, Section 45.

7 Clutch: correct operation

1 As the special starting mechanism operates when starting the engine, clutch slip can only be detected when the machine is being ridden by the fact that the engine speed will increase with no increase in road speed.
2 Clutch drag is characterised by the engine having a tendency to stall or the machine starting to move forward, when first gear is engaged, with the engine running at tickover speed.
3 Refer to the fault diagnosis chart, Section 8, for possible causes for the above symptom.
4 Note that a fast tickover speed will cause the machine to snatch when first gear is engaged during the pullaway from a standstill.

5.2 Clean and check the clutch plates

5.7 Check the pawls and spring for any damage

8 Fault diagnosis: clutch

Symptom	Cause	Remedy
Clutch slips	Incorrect adjustment	Re-adjust.
	Worn or distorted pressure plate	Renew.
	Distorted clutch plates	Renew.
	Worn friction plates or shoes	Renew.
Knocking noise from clutch	Loose clutch centre	Renew clutch.
Clutch does not fully disengage	Incorrect adjustment	Re-adjust.
	Uneven clutch spring tension	Renew set.
	Distorted clutch plates	Renew.
	Broken shoe spring	Renew.
Clutch snatches	Weak clutch springs	Renew set.
	Worn roller ramps	Renew.
	Broken shoe spring	Renew.

Chapter 3 Fuel system and lubrication

For modifications, and information relating to later models, see Chapter 8

Contents

Specifications

Capacities

Petrol tank	5·3 litres (1·68 gallons)
Oil tank	1.4 litres (2.4 pints)
Gearbox oil	0.65 litres (1.14 pints)

Carburettor

	V50	V75	V90
Make		Mikuni Kogyo	
Type	VM14SC	VM15SC	VM16SC
Main jet	85 or 75	100	100
Needle	3G12–3 or 3E2–3	3G9–3	3G9–3 or 3H2–3
Needle jet	E8 or E6	E8	E8
Pilot jet	12·5	12·5	15·0
Throttle slide cut away	2·5	2·5 (1·5 on V75A)	2·5
Air screw setting	1$\frac{3}{4}$ turns (1 turn out on V50MA)	1$\frac{3}{4}$ turns (1 turn out on V75A)	1$\frac{1}{4}$ turns out
Idling speed	1200–1400 rpm	1200–1400 rpm (1250–1450 rpm on V75A)	1200–1400 rpm

Oil pump

Correct minimum stroke:

V50 models	0·15 mm – 0·20 mm (0·060 in – 0·080 in)
V75 and V90 models	0·25 mm – 0·29 mm (0·100 in – 0·116 in)

1 General description

The fuel system consists of a fuel tank from which petrol is fed by gravity to the float chamber of the carburettor. The open frame layout necessitates the use of a specially-shaped petrol tank that is located immediately below the nose of the dualseat. of the dualseat.

The petrol tap fitted in the bottom of the tank is automatically switched on when the engine is turning and has a reserve position when the main content of the tank has been used.

The carburettor fitted to the V50, 75 and 90 models is of the same type only the bore size differing. A handlebar control operates the choke and the carburettor uses a throttle slide and needle arrangement to control the petrol/air mixture supplied to the engine.

The engine lubrication is from a separate oil tank through an oil pump into the inlet tract via a control jet. The oil pump is driven by the crankshaft and the oil supply increases with either engine speed or carburettor opening. As there is no reserve in the oil tank a watch must be kept on the 'goggle eye' to ensure the machine is not run without oil.

The gearbox lubrication is by running the components in an oil bath, letting the gears splash lubricate themselves.

2 Legshields: removal

1 The plastic legshield assembly encloses the engine unit, to enhance the clean appearance of the machine. There are suitable holes and blanking discs to enable the simplest of the adjusting tasks to be carried out without necessitating removal of the legshields, but whenever access is required for more complex tasks, the legshield assembly must be removed.
2 Place the machine on the centre stand and make sure it is standing firmly, on level ground.
3 Remove the six screws and lift the legshields clear of the machine.

3 Dualseat: removal and replacement

1 The dualseat is hinged at the back and will lift up and be supported by a prop whilst any inspection work is done on the petrol or oil tanks. If any dismantling is to be undertaken the support prop must be disengaged so it is advisable to remove the dualseat completely.
2 Unhook the catch and lift the dualseat. Remove the bolt retaining the support prop and the two clips holding the hinge pins. The dualseat can be lifted clear when the pins are slid out.
3 Reassembly is straightforward, but ensure that the clips are properly located on the hinge pins.

4 Oil tank: removal and replacement

1 The oil tank is a special shaped plastic container mounted inside the frame of the machine. It needs to be removed when access inside the frame is required, or if the tank itself is suspect.
2 Ensure that the legshields and the dualseat have been removed as described in the previous Sections.
3 Remove the two bolts and the machine lifting handle.
4 Remove the oil pump cover and disconnect the oil feed pipe at the pump. Allow the oil to drain into a suitable container or plug the end of the pipe.
5 Remove the oil tank filler cap, ease up the cover plate sufficiently to enable the inspection light (where fitted) to be disconnected. Lift the cover plate clear of the machine and put it in a safe place to avoid smashing the bulb.
6 Remove the metal covers on the right-hand side of the machine to expose the battery and the oil feed pipe. Slide the battery out and disconnect the wires.
7 The oil tank will now lift out of the machine but ensure that the oil feed pipe does not get trapped and pulled off the oil tank.
8 Reassemble by reversing the above procedure but take care that the oil feed pipe is not trapped or pinched otherwise serious engine damage may result from lack of proper lubrication.

4.4 Disconnect the oil feed pipe from the pump

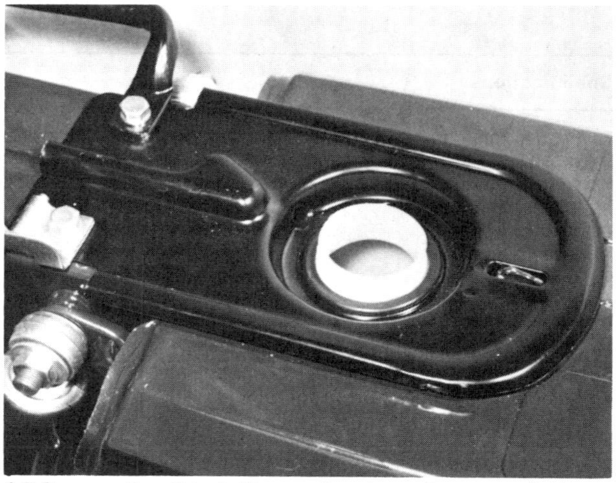
4.5 Remove the oil tank filler cap to release the cover plate

4.6 Remove the metal side cover to expose the pipe

4.7 Lift out the oil tank

5 Petrol tank: removal and replacement

1 It is unlikely that there will be need to remove the petrol tank completely unless the machine has been laid up and rust has formed inside or if it needs reconditioning. The engine/gear unit can be removed from the frame without having to detach the tank.
2 Ensure that the legshields, dualseat and oil tank have been removed as described in the previous Sections.
3 Ensure that the petrol tap is not in the 'prime' position, release the clips and pull the petrol pipe and the vacuum pipe off the petrol tap.
4 Remove the two bolts inside the frame, which were covered by the oil tank, loosen the nuts holding the top of each rear suspension unit and lift the tank clear of the machine.
5 Check the condition of the rubber pad on the bottom of the tank which rests on a bracket bolted to the frame.
6 To replace the tank, reverse the procedure described in the preceding paragraphs, ensuring that the petrol pipe and the vacuum pipe are connected the right way round.

5.4 Remove the two bolts from the inside

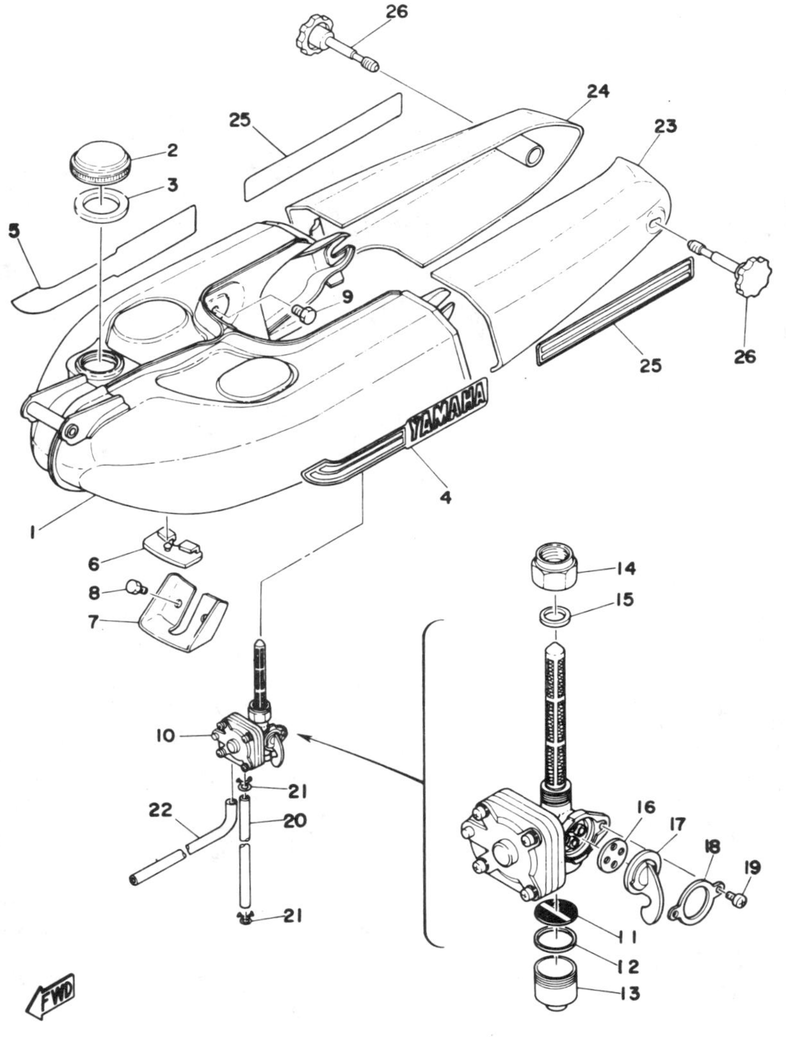

1 Petrol tank
2 Cap assembly
3 Sealing washer
4 Tank decal, LH
5 Tank decal, RH
6 Mounting rubber
7 Tank bracket
8 Bolt – 2 off
9 Bolt – 2 off
10 Petrol tap assembly
11 Filter
12 Sealing washer
13 Filter bowl
14 Union nut
15 Sealing washer
16 Valve plate
17 Lever
18 Retaining plate
19 Screw – 2 off
20 Feed hose
21 Hose clip – 2 off
22 Vacuum hose
23 Toolroll cover
24 RH cover
25 Side cover decal – 2 off
26 Knob – 2 off

Fig. 3.1 Petrol tank and tap

6 Petrol tap: removal, cleaning and reassembly

1 The petrol tap is a three position, on-reserve-prime type with a diaphragm-operated valve built in. When the engine is turning it draws air down the vacuum tube allowing the diaphragm to open the valve and petrol to flow to the carburettor. When the engine stops a spring closes the valve. The 'reserve' position, with the lever horizontal, is used when the tank is very low on fuel. The 'prime' position, with the lever vertically up, opens the valve against the spring pressure so that the petrol will flow if the engine is stopped or if the vacuum tube is damaged or leaking.
2 For routine cleaning unscrew the bowl on the bottom of the tap, remove the filter disc and the sealing ring. Clean off the filter disc and inside the filter bowl.
3 To remove the tap completely the tank must first be drained. Unscrew the union nut and withdraw the tap from the tank, taking care not to damage the filter tube.
4 To check the condition of the tap washer, remove the two screws, the retaining plate and the tap lever. The washer can then be removed for examination and, if necessary, renewed.
5 It is not advisable to dismantle the diaphragm assembly as no spare parts are available and even the smallest air leak when reassembled can stop the tap from working.
6 To refit the tap, reverse the procedure described in the preceding paragraphs, ensuring that the sealing washers are in good condition.

7 Petrol feed pipe and vacuum pipe: examination

1 The petrol feed pipe and vacuum pipe are made of synthetic rubber. From time to time check that they are not cracked or chafed, especially where they pass under the cover plate. Leaking petrol from the feed pipe can cause a fire and a leak in the vacuum pipe will stop the petrol tap working.
2 Release the screw and remove the left-hand side panel to thoroughly inspect the pipes. Ensure that the wire retaining clips on each end are present, in good condition, and properly located. Renew if any doubt is felt regarding the condition of any parts.

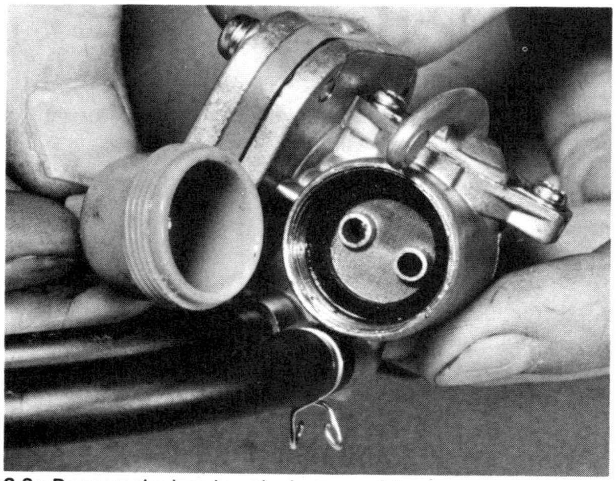
6.2a Remove the bowl on the bottom of the tap ...

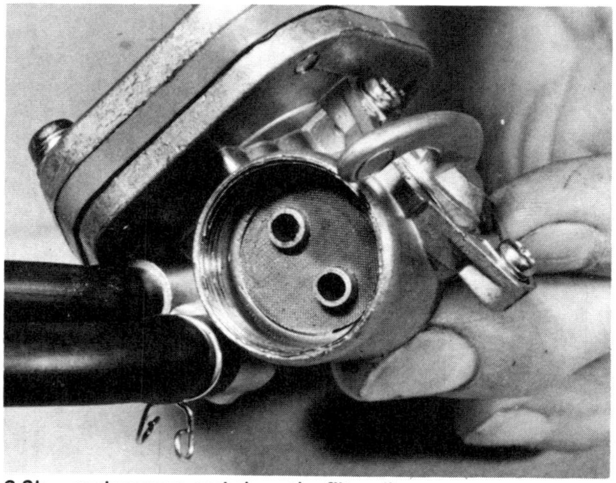
6.2b ... and remove and clean the filter disc

6.3 Drain the petrol tank before removing the tap

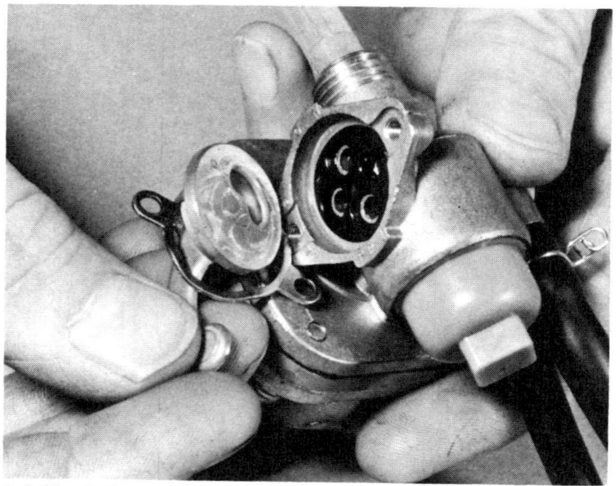
6.4 Check the condition of the tap washer under the tap lever

8 Carburettor: removal

Engine removed from the frame

1 If the engine has already been removed from the frame, the carburettor will be attached to the control cables, the petrol feed pipe and the vacuum pipe.

2 Ensure that the petrol tap is not in the 'prime' position, remove the clips and pull the pipes off the carburettor.

Engine still in the frame

3 Place the machine on the centre stand and make sure it is standing firmly on level ground. Remove the rear plastic side panel to obtain the toolkit.

4 Remove the six screws that retain the legshields and lift the legshields clear of the machine, thus allowing easy access to the carburettor.

5 Remove the spring clip and pull the intake hose off the carburettor.

6 Ensure that the petrol tap is not in the 'prime' position, remove the clips and pull the pipes off the carburettor.

7 Slacken off the pinch bolt and gently ease the carburettor off the inlet stub.

9 Carburettor: dismantling

1 At this stage, the carburettor is still attached to the control cables and to remove it completely the carburettor top has to be released, by removing two screws. The top, throttle slide and choke plunger will now pull out of the body.

2 Compress the choke return spring and unhook the choke cable. The choke plunger and spring can then be removed.

3 Compress the slide return spring and unhook the throttle cable. The slide, the needle with its spring clip, the W-shaped spring, the return spring and the carburettor top will then slide off the cable.

4 To separate the float chamber, remove the four screws and gently pull off the float chamber taking care not to damage the gasket. Remove the drain screw.

5 Push out the float pivot pin and remove the twin floats. The float needle will now tip out. Unscrew the float needle seat for thorough examination.

6 Remove the main jet from the centre of the needle jet and also remove the needle jet.

7 Remove the pilot jet which is between the float needle seat and the needle jet.

8 Remove the throttle stop screw and spring from the side of the carburettor and remove the slow running screw and spring which is at an angle close to the carburettor inlet.

9 The overflow and drain pipes can be pulled off the carburettor.

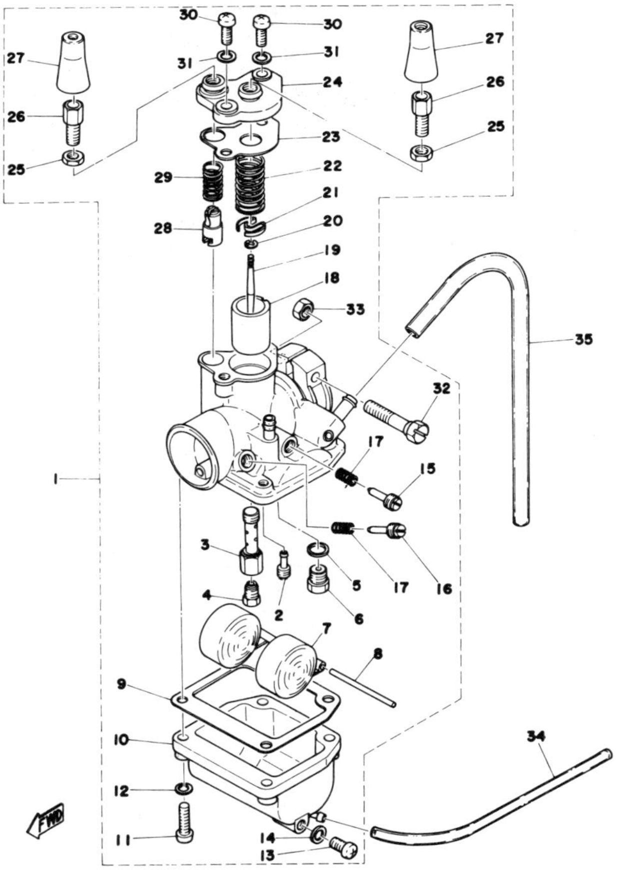

1 Carburettor assembly
2 Pilot jet
3 Needle jet
4 Main jet
5 Sealing washer
6 Valve seat assembly
7 Float
8 Float pivot pin
9 Gasket
10 Float chamber bowl
11 Screw – 4 off
12 Spring washer – 4 off
13 Screw
14 Sealing washer
15 Throttle stop screw
16 Slow running screw
17 Spring – 2 off
18 Throttle slide
19 Needle
20 Circlip
21 W-spring
22 Return spring
23 Gasket
24 Carburettor top
25 Nut – 2 off
26 Adjusting screw – 2 off
27 Rubber cap
28 Plunger
29 Plunger spring
30 Screw – 2 off
31 Spring washer – 2 off
32 Special bolt
33 Nut
34 Drain hose
35 Overflow hose

Fig. 3.2 Carburettor

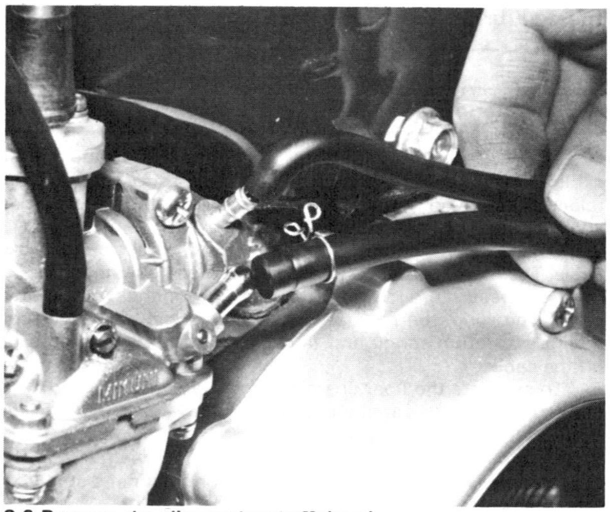
8.2 Remove the clips and pull off the pipes

8.7 Gently ease the carburettor off the inlet stub

9.1 Remove the top complete with the slides

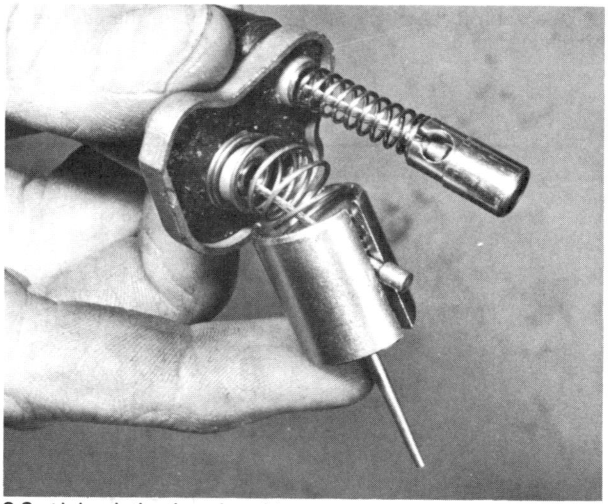
9.3a Unhook the throttle cable ...

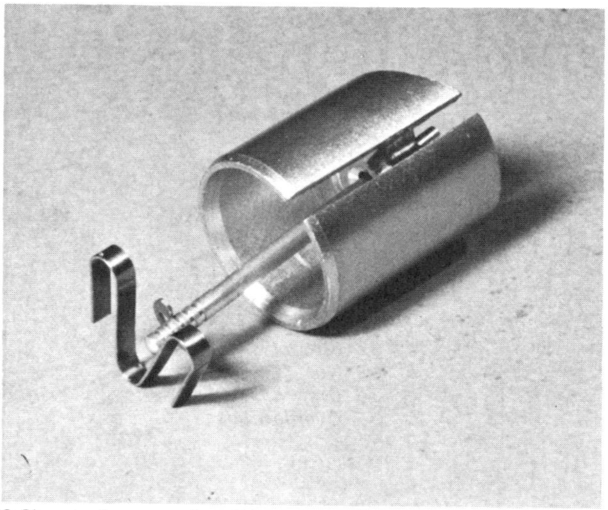
9.3b ... and remove the slide and needle

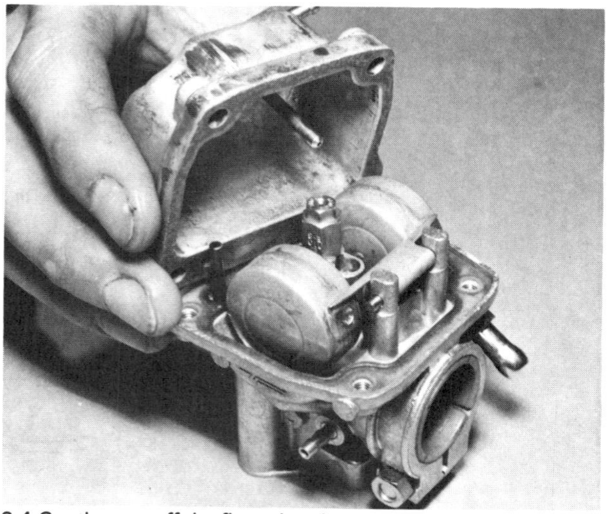
9.4 Gently ease off the float chamber

9.5a Push out the float pin and remove the floats

9.5b Tip out the float needle

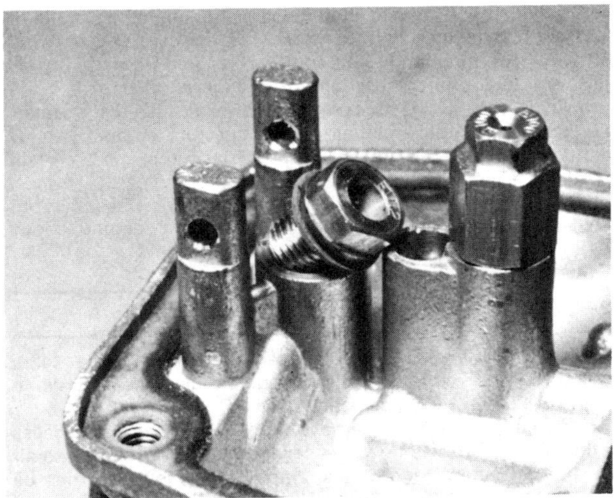

9.5c Remove and clean the float needle seat

9.6 Remove the main jet and needle jet

9.7 Remove the pilot jet

9.8a Remove the throttle stop screw and spring ...

9.8b ... and the slow running screw and spring

10 Carburettor: cleaning, examination and reassembling

1 Thoroughly clean all the parts paying particular attention to the internal passageways of the carburettor body, the bottom of the float chamber and any other places where sediment may collect.
2 Check that none of the springs are weak or broken.
3 Check for wear on the slide and carburettor body as air leaks round the slide can cause weak mixture problems.
4 Check for ridges on the conical seating portion of the float needle.
5 Check the condition of the float and shake it to see if there is any petrol inside. The float is non-repairable and should be renewed if damaged or punctured.
6 Check that all gaskets, sealing washers or rubber seals are in good condition. Preferably renew them when reassembling as leaking petrol can cause a fire.
7 When reassembling the carburettor, follow the dismantling instructions in reverse, ensuring that the needle clip is in its correct groove.
8 The various sizes of the jets, throttle slide and needle are predetermined by the manufacturer and should not require modification. Check with the Specifications list if there is any doubt about the values fitted.

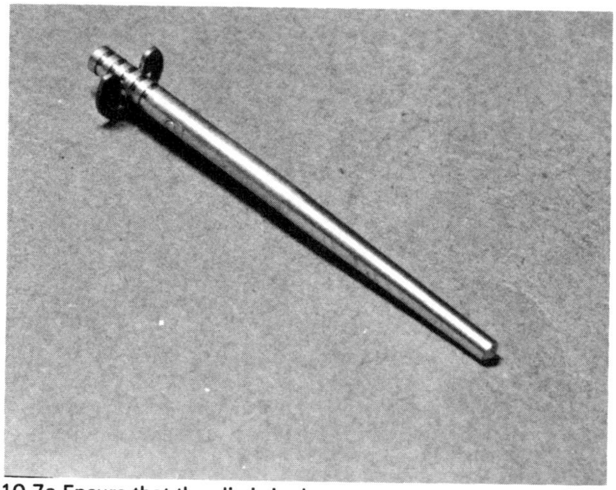

10.7a Ensure that the clip is in the correct groove

11 Carburettor: adjustments

1 All adjustments should be made when the engine is at normal working temperature.
2 To adjust the slow running speed the throttle cable should be slackened to ensure that it is the throttle stop screw that is holding the slide and not the cable. Set the throttle stop screw so that the engine runs at a fast tick-over speed.
3 Screw in or out the air screw until the engine runs evenly, without hunting or misfiring. Reduce the engine speed by unscrewing the throttle stop and re-adjust the air screw, if necessary. Do not arrive at a setting where the engine ticks over too slowly, otherwise there is risk that it may stall when the throttle is closed, during normal running.
4 As a rough guide, the air screw should be positioned from one to one and three quarter complete turns out from the fully closed position.
5 The amount of throttle slide cutaway, size of main jet, size of needle jet and size of slow running jet are pre-determined by the manufacturer and should be correct for the model in which they are used. The throttle needle position can be varied, by removing and replacing the needle clip. Under normal circumstances, the needle should be positioned in the second or third notch, measured from the top.
6 The slow running jet controls engine speed up to approximately $\frac{1}{8}$th throttle and the degree of throttle slide cutaway from $\frac{1}{8}$th to $\frac{1}{4}$ throttle. Thereafter the needle jet takes over, up to $\frac{3}{4}$ throttle, and main jet size controls the final $\frac{3}{4}$ to full throttle. These stages are only approximate; there is a certain amount of overlap.
7 Readjust the throttle cable to remove any excess play but leave a small amount of slack to avoid the engine speed increasing when the handlebars are turned.

12 Air filter: location and cleaning

1 The air filter is located under the main frame tube, immediately behind the steering head. It is clearly visible when the legshield assembly has been removed.
2 To clean the air filter, remove the legshields to gain access to the air filter box. Remove the centre nut and bolt from the air box and pull off the end plates. The filter element can then be pulled clear of the rubber intake hose and slid out of the air box. Accumulated dust can be removed from the element either by tapping it lightly and brushing with a soft brush or by using a vacuum cleaner on the outside, taking care not to damage the element as it is only made of paper. If it is torn or damaged, fit a replacement.

10.7b Align slot and projection to ensure carburettor is vertical

3 Oil or water will reduce the efficiency of the filter element and may upset the carburation. Renew any suspect element.
4 It is advisable to replace the element at less than the recommended 6000 miles if the machine is used in very dusty conditions. The usual signs of a filter element in need of replacement are reduced performance, misfiring and a tendency for the carburation to run rich.
5 On no account should the machine be run without the filter element in place because this will have an adverse effect on carburation.

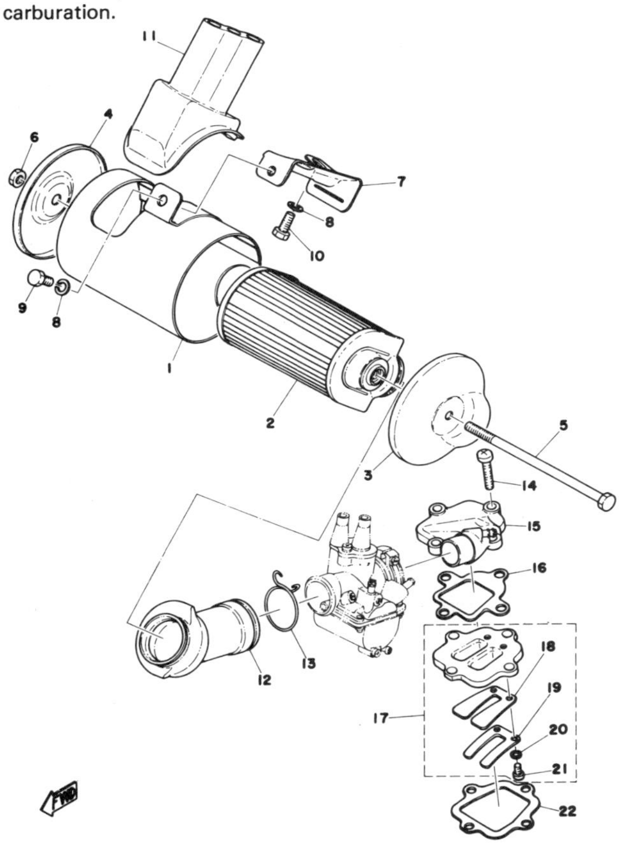

Fig. 3.3 Air cleaner and reed valve

1	*Air cleaner case*	12	*Connecting tube*
2	*Air cleaner element*	13	*Clip*
3	*Cover*	14	*Screw – 4 off*
4	*Cover*	15	*Manifold*
5	*Bolt*	16	*Gasket*
6	*Nut*	17	*Reed valve assembly*
7	*Bracket*	18	*Reed valve*
8	*Spring washer – 3 off*	19	*Limit stop*
9	*Bolt*	20	*Spring washer – 2 off*
10	*Bolt – 2 off*	21	*Screw – 2 off*
11	*Intake pipe*	22	*Gasket*

13 Exhaust system: cleaning

The exhaust system of any two-stroke engine requires quite frequent attention because the oily nature of the exhaust gases causes a build-up of sludge which will eventually partially block the system and cause serious back pressures.
2 The exhaust system is removed easily by following the procedure detailed in Chapter 1.5, Section 5, paragraph 5. The baffle tube is removed by unscrewing the retaining screw and sliding it out.
3 On early models the exhaust pipe and silencer are one unit and if a large amount of carbon has built up inside it is necessary to fill the silencer with a solution of caustic soda after

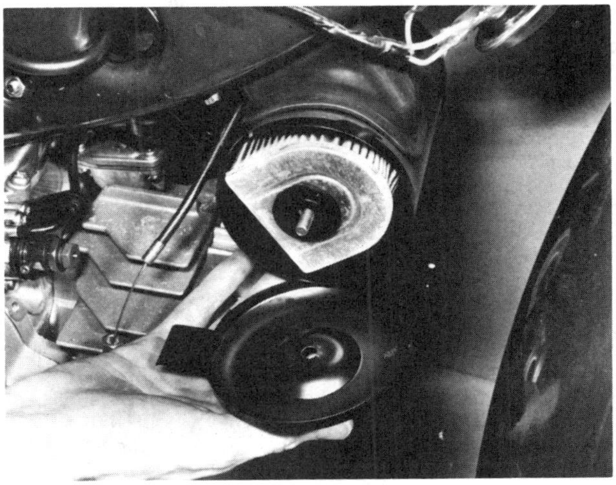

12.2a Remove the end plates ...

12.2b ... pull the element out of the intake hose ...

12.2c ... and carefully clean the element

blocking up one end. If possible, leave the caustic soda solution within the silencer overnight before draining off and washing out thoroughly with water.
4 Caustic soda is highly corrosive and every care should be taken when mixing and handling the solution. Keep the solution away from the skin and more particularly the eyes. The wearing of rubber gloves is advised whilst the solution is being mixed and used.
5 The solution is prepared by adding 3 lbs of caustic soda to 1 gallon of COLD water, whilst stirring. Add the caustic soda a little at a time and NEVER add the water to the chemical. The solution will become hot during the mixing process, which is why cold water must be used.
6 Make sure the used caustic soda solution is disposed of safely, preferably by diluting with a large amount of water. Do not allow the solution to come into contact with aluminium castings because it will react violently with this metal.
7 If the baffle assembly is heavily coated with a sludge of carbon and oil, it is permissible to burn this out with a blow lamp. Care should be taken that the felt of the baffle tube is not set alight.
8 Never tamper with the exhaust system, remove the baffles from the silencer or fit a quite different system. Although a louder exhaust note may give the illusion of greater speed, in nearly every case performance will be reduced and the rider may risk prosecution. It is difficult to improve on the manufacturer's original specification, which has been designed to match in with the characteristics of the engine. Speed and noise do not necessarily go hand in hand.
9 To reassemble the exhaust system reverse the dismantling procedure, using a new gasket to avoid any air leaks.

14 Oil pipes: examination

1 The oil pipes are made of synthetic rubber, and a check that they are not cracked or chafed, especially where they pass under the cover plates, should be made. Serious engine damage may occur if the oil pipes are damaged.
2 Ensure that the retaining clips on each pipe are present, in good condition, and properly located. Renew any doubtful parts.

13.2a The later models have a two piece exhaust system ...

13.2b ... with a special seal in the connecting nut

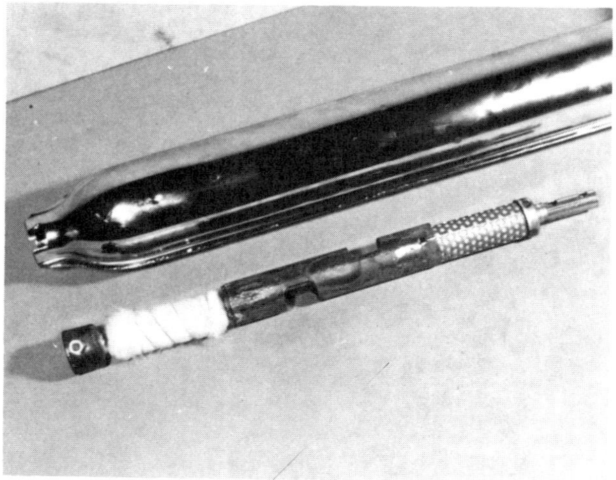

13.7 A nut on the stud holds the baffle assembly in place

13.9 Always use a new exhaust gasket

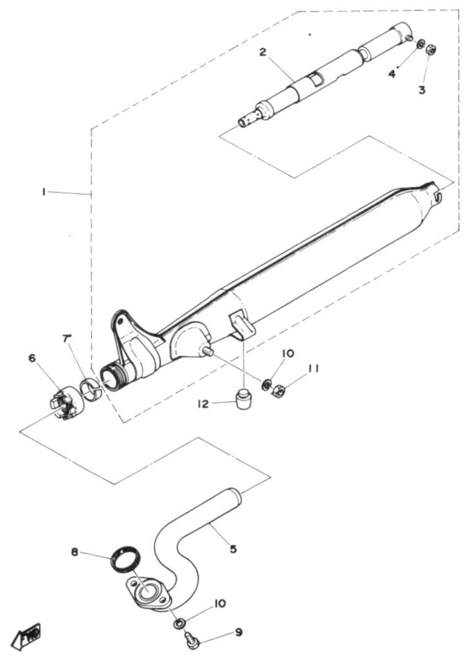

Fig. 3.4 Exhaust system (late models)

1	*Silencer assembly*	7	*Sealing ring*
2	*Baffle assembly*	8	*Exhaust gasket*
3	*Nut*	9	*Bolt – 2 off*
4	*Spring washer*	10	*Spring washer – 3 off*
5	*Exhaust pipe*	11	*Nut*
6	*Special ring nut*	12	*Rubber stop*

15 Oil pump: removal

1 Oil pump removal may be carried out as described in Chapter 1, Sections 5 and 11 when the engine is out of the frame for a major overhaul. If the engine is still in the frame, observe the following procedure.

2 Place the machine on the centre stand and make sure it is standing firmly on level ground. Remove the rear plastic side panel to obtain the toolkit.
3 Remove the six screws that retain the legshields and lift the legshields clear of the machine, thus allowing easy access to the oil pump.
4 Remove the two long headed bolts to release the oil pump cover from the right-hand side of the engine. Gently ease the cover off and disconnect the control cable from the pump pulley. Slide the spring clip up the oil feed pipe, prise the pipe off the pump and either plug the end or allow the oil to drain into a suitable container.On the later models the oil pipe between the pump and the inlet stub must be disconnected.
5 Remove the two large screws and gently ease the oil pump out of the engine casing.

16 Oil pump: dismantling and checking

1 The oil pump is set at the factory to deliver the correct amount of oil at all engine speeds. If oil pump trouble is suspected, your local dealer will be able to advise and repair, or reset the pump as necessary.
2 The only parts that can readily be replaced are the gearwheel on the end and the sealing O rings. A circlip retains the gear and care should be taken to avoid losing the drive pin.
3 The only check that can be done by the home mechanic is that the minimum stroke of the pump is within the limits set out in the Specifications. This dimension is measured between the control pulley and the adjusting nut or plate. The control wire should be disconnected and the engine turned over until the maximum gap is obtained and measured.

17 Oil pump: refitting and adjusting

1 When refitting the oil pump ensure that the O rings are in good condition. Refitting is the reverse of the dismantling procedure ensuring that the gear teeth mesh correctly.
2 Before fitting the oil pump cover remove the bleeder screw on the oil pump until the oil flows out with no bubbles, then replace the screw ensuring that the sealing washer is in good condition. A few kicks on the starter pedal before the ignition is switched on will pump the oil to the engine.
3 Adjust the oil pump cable so that the guide pin lines up with the pulley mark when the throttle cable slack is taken up, as described in the Routine Maintenance Section.

15.4 Remove the two long headed bolts and the cover

15.5 Gently ease the oil pump out

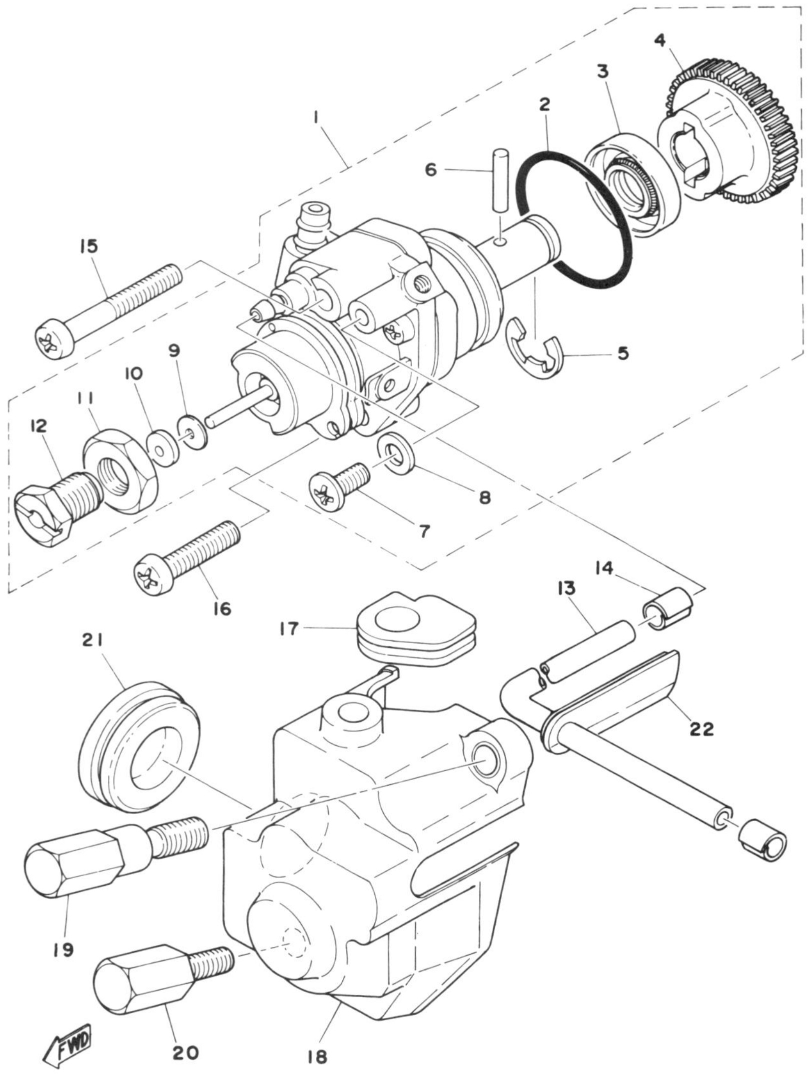

1 *Oil pump assembly*
2 *O ring*
3 *Oil seal*
4 *Gear pinion*
5 *Circlip*
6 *Drive pin*
7 *Screw*
8 *Sealing washer*
9 *Shim*
10 *Adjusting plate*
11 *Nut*
12 *Adjusting bolt*
13 *Delivery pipe*
14 *Pipe clip – 2 off*
15 *Screw*
16 *Screw*
17 *Feed pipe grommet*
18 *Cover*
19 *Special bolt*
20 *Special bolt*
21 *Grommet*
22 *Delivery pipe grommet*

Fig. 3.5 Oil pump

16.1 Oil pump: general view

16.2 Remove the circlip to release the gear

18 Fuel diagnosis: fuel system and lubrication

Symptom	Cause	Remedy
Excessive fuel consumption	Air cleaner choked or restricted	Clean.
	Fuel leaking from carburettor. Float sticking	Check all unions and gaskets. Float needle seat needs cleaning.
	Badly worn or distorted carburettor	Replace.
	Carburettor incorrectly adjusted	Tune and adjust as necessary.
	Incorrect silencer fitted to exhaust system	Do not deviate from manufacturer's original original silencer design.
Idling speed too high	Throttle stop screw in too far	Adjust screw.
	Carburettor top loose	Tighten top.
Engine does not respond to throttle	Back pressure in silencer	Check baffles in silencer.
	Float displaced or punctured	Check whether float is correctly located or has petrol inside.
	Use of incorrect silencer or baffles missing	See above. Do not run without baffles.
Engine dies after running for a short while	Blocked air hole in filler cap	Clean.
	Dirt or water in carburettor	Remove or clean out.
General lack of performance	Weak mixture; float needle stuck in seat	Remove float chamber or float and clean.
	Air leak at carburettor joint or in crankcase	Check joints to eliminate leakage.
Excessive white smoke from exhaust	Too much oil being pumped into engine	Check oil pump setting
Engine partially seizes	Lack of oil being pumped into engine	Check oil tank level. Fill. Check for air bubbles in oil pipes. Prime system. Check oil pump setting.

Chapter 4 Ignition system

For modifications, and information relating to later models, see Chapter 8

Contents

Specifications

	V50, V75 and late V90 models		Early V90 models	
Flywheel generator				
Type	F11–L43		F136–01	
Output:				
ignition	150–300 volts ac		12 volts ac	
lighting	6 volts ac		12 volts ac	
Contact breaker gap	0·3 – 0·4 mm (0·012 – 0·016 in)			
Ignition timing	1·8 mm (0·07 in) BTDC		1·8 mm (0·07 in) BTDC	
Capacitor (condenser)				
Capacitance	0·3 MicroFarad		0·18 MicroFarad	
Rectifier				
Type	Four-diode silicon			
Model	DS10HJ4–8 or CDC–H1/1E		SB4–5	
Ignition coil				
Type	CM61–20		CM11–04	
Spark plug				
Make	NGK	Motorcraft	NGK	Motorcraft
Type	B–7HS	AG2	B–7HS	AG2
Gap	0·5 – 0·6 mm (0·020 – 0·024 in)			

1 General description

All models use a flywheel generator, mounted on the extreme left-hand side of the crankshaft, to provide power for the ignition system and lighting system. On V50, V75 and the later V90 models the generator incorporates two separate and unconnected coils, one of which provides the charging current and the other the source power for the ignition. In this system power from the source coil is fed directly to the ignition coil. On early V90 models a two coil generator is used where the coils are interconnected and both feed the charging system. The source current for ignition is taken from the battery directly to the ignition coil.

In both systems a contact breaker and condenser are housed within the flywheel generator. As the flywheel rotates the contact breaker opens and closes by means of a cam incorporated in the flywheel centre boss. The opening of the points causes a break in the ignition source power – whether from the source coil or battery – which develops a high voltage in the ignition coil secondary windings. The current from the coil is fed to the spark plug to ignite the compressed air/fuel mixture in the combustion chamber. The condenser is incorporated in the system to prevent arcing across the contact breaker points and so reduce premature erosion or burning.

2 Legshield: removal

1 The plastic legshield assembly encloses the engine unit to enhance the clean appearance of the machine. There are suitable holes and blanking discs to enable the simplest of the adjusting tasks to be carried out without removing the legshield, but whenever access is required for more complex tasks the legshield assembly must be removed.
2 Place the machine on the centre stand and make sure it is standing firmly on level ground.
3 Remove the side panels to obtain the tool kit and reveal the battery. Unclip the fuse holder and remove the fuse to isolate the battery, eliminating all risks of electrical mishap.
4 Remove the six screws and lift the legshields clear of the machine.

3 Flywheel generator: checking output

The output from the flywheel generator can be checked only with specialised test equipment of the multi-meter type. It is unlikely that the average owner/rider will have access to this equipment or instruction in its use. In consequence, if the performance of the generator is suspect, it should be checked by a Yamaha agent or an auto-electrical expert.

4 Ignition coil: checking, removal and replacement

1 The ignition coil is a sealed unit, designed to give long service. If a weak spark and difficult starting cause its performance to be suspect, it should be tested by an auto-electrical expert. A faulty coil must be replaced; it is not practical to effect a repair.
2 To detach the coil, the engine must be removed from the frame as described in Chapter 1 Section 5. The coil is mounted inside the frame with no other means of access. Disconnect the wires at the snap connectors, and remove the spark plug cap from the plug and the end of the HT lead. Remove the two retaining nuts and slide the coil out of the frame.
3 Reassembly is the reverse of the removal procedure but it should be borne in mind that due to the large amount of work involved in replacing an ignition coil, all possibility of an electrical fault lying elsewhere should be eliminated.

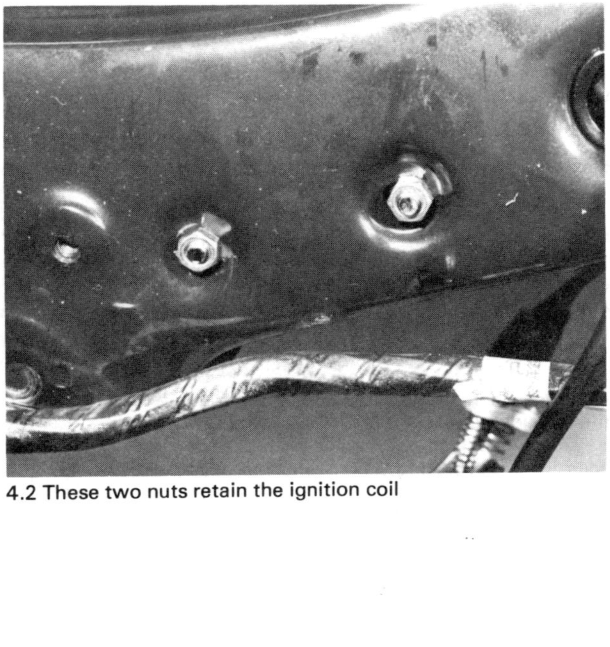

4.2 These two nuts retain the ignition coil

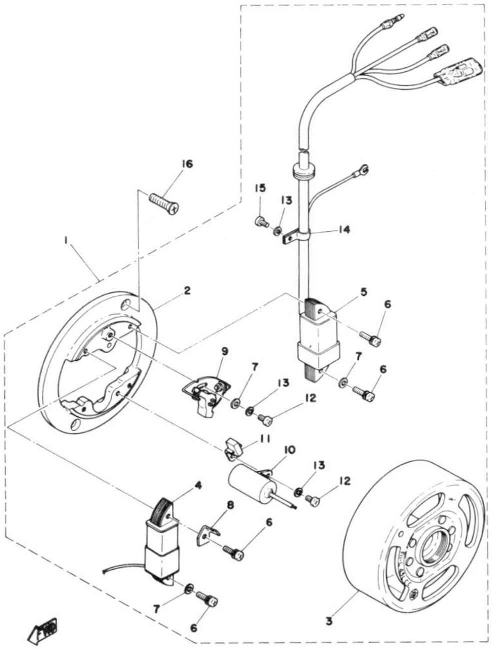

Fig. 4.1 Flywheel generator

1	*Flywheel generator assembly*	9	*Contact breaker assembly*
2	*Backplate*	10	*Condenser (capacitor)*
3	*Rotor assembly*	11	*Felt wick*
4	*Coil for ignition system*	12	*Screw – 2 off*
5	*Coil for lighting system*	13	*Spring washer – 3 off*
6	*Screw – 4 off*	14	*Clamp*
7	*Washer – 3 off*	15	*Screw*
8	*Timing plate*	16	*Screw – 2 off*

5 Contact breaker: adjustment

1 The V50, V75 and V90 models have fixed ignition timing, so the only means of adjusting the timing is by altering the contact breaker adjustment. The resulting maximum contact breaker gap should be between 0.3 mm and 0.4 mm (0.012 in and 0.016 in). If it is outside these limits, the contact breaker assembly should be renewed, since it is worn out. The ignition timing section describes the method of adjustment. If it should be necessary to remove the contact breaker assembly for further attention, or renewal, it will be necessary to withdraw the flywheel generator from the crankshaft, following the procedure described in Chapter 1, Section 7.
2 To gain access to the contact breaker assembly, remove the two screws which hold the flywheel generator cover in position and lift off the cover. The contact breaker points can be viewed through one of the apertures in the flywheel rotor.
3 Rotate the engine until the contact breaker is in its fully open position. Examine the faces of the contacts. If they are pitted or burnt it will be necessary to remove them for further attention, as described in Section 6 of this Chapter.
4 Check the contact breaker gap to see if it is between 0.3 mm and 0.4 mm (0.012 and 0.016 in). To adjust the contact breaker gap, slacken the screw that holds the contact breaker assembly and using a small screwdriver in the slot provided, ease the assembly to the correct position. Tighten the screw and recheck the gap to ensure that the assembly has not moved.
5 It is always advisable to check the ignition timing, especially if the contact breaker gap has been reset. It will almost certainly require readjustment in that case.

5.1 Check that the contact breaker gap is correct

6 Contact breaker assembly: removal, renovation and replacement

1 If the contact breaker points are burned, pitted or badly worn, they should be removed for dressing. If it is necessary to remove a substantial amount of material before the faces can be restored, the points should be renewed.
2 To remove the contact breaker assembly, access must be gained as described in the preceding Section. Slacken and remove the nut at the end of the moving contact return spring. Remove the spring and plain washer and detach the spring. Note that an insulating washer is located beneath the spring, to prevent the electrical current from being earthed.
3 Remove the spring clip from the moving contact pivot and the insulating washer. Withdraw the moving contact, which is integral with the fibre rocker arm.
4 Remove the screw that retains the fixed contact plate and withdraw the plate complete with contact.
5 The points should be dressed with an oilstone or fine emery cloth. Keep them absolutely square during the dressing operation, otherwise they will make angular contact when they are replaced and will quickly burn away.
6 Replace the contacts by reversing the dismantling procedure. Take particular care to replace the insulating washers in the correct sequence, otherwise the points will be isolated electrically and the ignition system will not function.

7.4 Remove the screw to release the condenser

7 Condenser: removal and replacement

1 A condenser is included in the contact breaker circuit to prevent arcing across the contact breaker points as they separate. It is connected in parallel with the points and if a fault develops, ignition failure will occur.
2 If the engine is difficult to start, or if misfiring occurs, it is possible that the condenser is at fault. To check whether the condenser has failed, remove the flywheel magneto cover and observe the points whilst the engine is running. If excessive sparking occurs across the points and they have a blackened or burnt appearance, it may be assumed the condenser is no longer serviceable.
3 The condenser is attached to the stator plate and it is first necessary to withdraw the flywheel rotor as described in Chapter 1, Section 7, to gain access.
4 Disconnect the condenser wire; the retaining screw can then be removed and the condenser and wick holder will pull clear.
5 Fit the new condenser and the wick holder and retain them with the screw. Reconnect the condenser wire.
6 Replace the flywheel rotor and lock it in position before tightening the centre retaining nut. Complete the reassembly by fitting the flywheel cover.

6.4 Remove the screw to release the contact breaker

8 Ignition timing: checking and re-setting

1 To check the ignition timing, remove the generator inspection cover.
2 If the ignition timing is correct, the contact breaker points will be about to separate when the line scribed on the rotor of the flywheel aligns exactly with the timing plate fixed to the stator plate. To verify the moment at which the points separate insert a cigarette paper between the points faces. As the points open they will release their grip on the paper.
3 The ignition timing is varied by adjusting the contact breaker gap. Slacken the screw holding the contact breaker assembly, and using a small screwdriver in the slot provided, ease the assembly to the correct position. Tighten the screw and recheck the ignition timing. Check that the contact breaker gap is between 0.3 mm and 0.4 mm (0.012 in and 0.016 in).
4 If, when the ignition timing is correct, the contact breaker gap is outside the specified range or if the ignition timing is incorrect when the gap has been adjusted to within the range, the contact breaker unit must be renewed.
5 After checking the timing, rotate the engine and check again before replacing the covers. The accuracy of the ignition timing is critical in terms of both engine performance and petrol consumption. Even a small error in setting will have a noticeable effect.

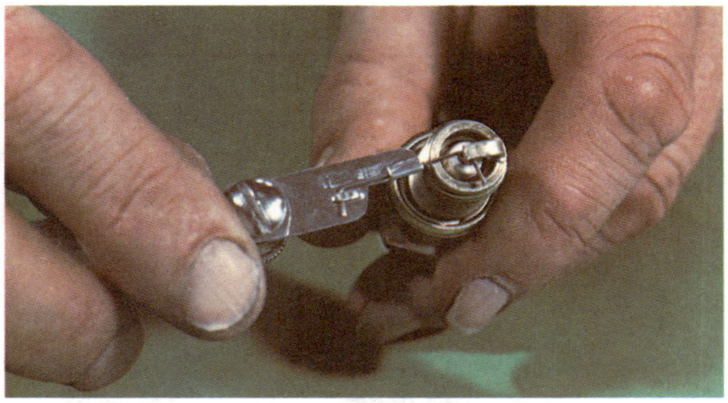

Spark plug maintenance: Checking plug gap with feeler gauges

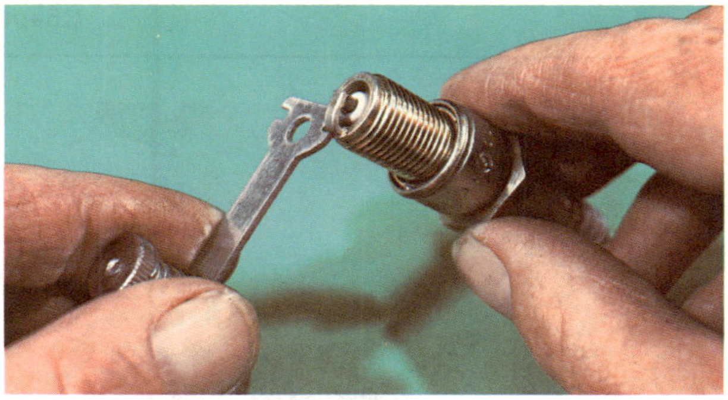

Altering the plug gap. Note use of correct tool

Spark plug conditions: A brown, tan or grey firing end is indicative of correct engine running conditions and the selection of the appropriate heat rating plug

White deposits have accumulated from excessive amounts of oil in the combustion chamber or through the use of low quality oil. Remove deposits or a hot spot may form

Black sooty deposits indicate an over-rich fuel/air mixture, or a malfunctioning ignition system. If no improvement is obtained, try one grade hotter plug

Wet, oily carbon deposits form an electrical leakage path along the insulator nose, resulting in a misfire. The cause may be a badly worn engine or a malfunctioning ignition system

A blistered white insulator or melted electrode indicates over-advanced ignition timing or a malfunctioning cooling system. If correction does not prove effective, try a colder grade plug

A worn spark plug not only wastes fuel but also overloads the whole ignition system because the increased gap requires higher voltage to initiate the spark. This condition can also affect air pollution

8.2a The line scribed on the rotor ...

8.2b ... should line up with the timing plate

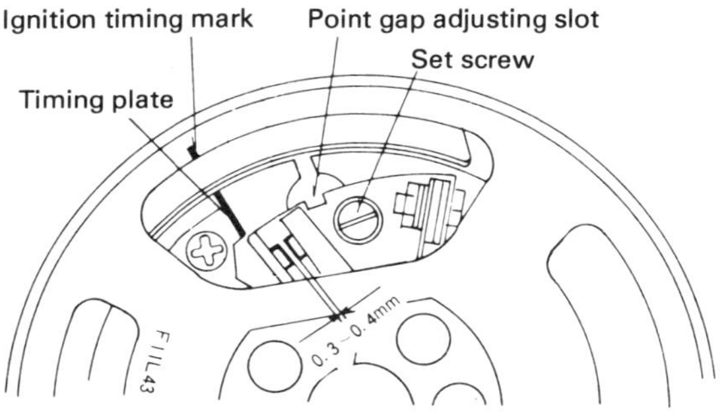

Fig. 4.2 Ignition timing marks

9 Spark plug: checking and resetting the gap

1 An NGK B-7HS plug is fitted as standard equipment to the Yamaha V50, V75 and V90 models.

2 The spark plug has a 14 mm thread. The recommended gap is 0.5 – 0.6 mm (0.020 – 0.024 inch). Always use the grade of plug recommended or the exact equivalent in another manufacturer's range.

3 Check the spark plug gap every six months or 1000 miles, whichever is sooner. To reset the gap, bend the outer electrode to bring it closer to the central electrode, otherwise the insulator will crack, causing engine damage if particles fall in whilst the engine is running.

4 Always carry a spare spark plug in the tool kit, wrapped so that the electrodes cannot become bent or dirt enter the electrode area. Two-stroke engines are more susceptible to plug troubles and may on occasion cause plug fouling or whiskering. A spare plug will enable the engine to be restarted promptly in the event of trouble, which invariably occurs at an ill-timed moment.

5 The condition of the spark plug electrodes and insulator can be used as a reliable guide to engine operating conditions. See accompanying diagrams.

6 Never overtighten a spark plug, otherwise there is danger of stripping the threads from the cylinder head, particularly those cast in light alloy. The plug should be sufficiently tight to seat firmly on copper sealing washer. Use a spanner which is a good fit, otherwise the spanner may slip and break the ceramic insulator.

7 If the thread within the cylinder head does strip, it can be repaired permanently and economically by the use of a Helicoil thread insert. Many dealers have facilities for effecting this type of repair at a fraction of the cost of a replacement cylinder head.

8 Make sure that the plug insulating cap is a good fit. This cap contains the suppressor which eliminates radio and TV interference.

10 Fault diagnosis: ignition system

Symptom	Cause	Remedy
Engine will not start	No spark at plug	Try replacement plug if gap correct. Check whether contact breaker points are opening and closing, also whether they are clean. Check whether points arc badly when separated. If so, renew the condenser. Check ignition switch and ignition coil. Battery discharged (early V90 models).
Engine starts but runs erratically	Intermittent or weak spark	Try replacement plug. Check whether points are arcing. If so, replace condenser. Check accuracy of ignition timing. Low output from flywheel magneto generator or imminent breakdown of ignition coil.

Chapter 5 Frame and forks

For modifications, and information relating to later models, see Chapter 8

Contents

Specifications

Frame	Spine type, scooter style
Front suspension	Hydraulically damped leading link forks
Rear suspension	Pressed steel swinging arm controlled by hydraulically damped suspension units
Caster angle	63°
Trail	80 mm (3·15 inch)

1 General description

The frame used on these models is of the scooter style spine type ie. it has a single tube holding the steering head mounted low enough to step over. This is why the models are sometimes referred to as step-thru models. The forks are of the leading link variety, with hydraulic damping. The rear suspension is of the swinging arm type, controlled by two suspension units also with hydraulic damping.

2 Front forks: removal from frame

1 It is extremely unlikely that the front forks will need to be removed from the frame as a unit unless the steering head bearings give trouble or the forks are damaged in an accident.
2 Commence operations by placing the machine on the centre stand.
3 Remove front wheel as described in Chapter 6, Section 3.
4 Although not essential, it is advisable to remove the front mudguard for ease of handling. Remove the two nuts and their washers from the suspension top bolts and remove the two nuts from the rear pivot bolts. Pull the mudguard off the pivot bolts and clear of the machine, ensuring that the front brake and speedometer cables slide out of the slot.
5 Remove the screw and the headlamp unit. Disconnect the headlamp wires and put the headlamp in a safe place.
6 Disconnect the throttle cable at the handlebar end. To do this the two screws in the clamp must be removed allowing the twistgrip to slide off the handlebar. Lift out the cable block and the cable stop and disconnect the cable. It is worth tying a piece of string to the cable so that the cable can be pulled back into place when reassembling.
7 Dismantle the choke lever and disconnect the choke cable. Disconnect the front brake cable.
8 Remove the centre screw on the front panel. Lift the panel clear to reveal four screws that hold the front moulding in place. Remove the screws and the front moulding and disconnect the pilot light wire.
9 Remove the two screws at the front and the two screws and the two nuts and their washers from the underside of the handlebar fairing. The handlebars can now be eased up to allow the remainder of the wires to be disconnected at their snap connectors. All the wires are colour coded, to make reconnection easy. Disconnect the speedometer cable and lift the handlebars clear.
10 Remove the two nuts and the single bolt with their washers to release the steering bracket. The handlebar lower cover can be lifted clear. Remove the slotted nut to release the steering plate.
11 Remove the two screws and the bracket which on the early models supports the flasher unit. Pull the speedometer and brake cables clear.

12 Support the fork legs, to prevent their dropping permaturely, and remove the steering head column nut and dust cover.
13 Remove the top cone to reveal 22 ball bearings in the top race, which can then be lifted out with a magnet or a greased screwdriver.
14 As the forks are now lowered, the 22 ball bearings in the lower race will be displaced and once these have been collected, the fork assembly can be pulled clear of the frame.
15 The bottom cone, the dust seal and the dust seal holder, can be removed from the fork assembly, if required.

3 Front forks: dismantling

1 If only the fork leading links and suspension units are to be removed, without disturbing the head races, remove the front wheel as described in Chapter 6, Section 3.
2 As all the fixings for the mudguard will be removed to release the suspension units, it is advantageous to remove the mudguard completely. Remove the two nuts and their washers from the top suspension bolts and remove the two nuts from the rear pivot bolts. Pull the mudguard off the pivot bolts and clear of the machine, ensuring that the speedometer and brake cables slide out of the slot.
3 Continue from here for further dismantling, irrespective of whether the forks are on or off the machine. Remove the bottom pivot bolt that was fitted with the nut. Remove the bolts, from the top of the suspension unit, and pull the link and suspension unit out of the forks. Repeat for the second unit.
4 To detach the bottom link from the suspension unit, remove the pivot bolt and nut.
5 If play is evident between any of the pivot pins and their respective bushes, both components will need to be renewed.
6 The dust seals and covers will need to be removed to gain access to the bushes and where the arm is peened over to retain the cover, care should be taken not to destroy the latter.
7 The bush is a press fit in the pivot eye, and the new bush can be used to press out the old one.
8 Note the damper units are sealed and cannot be further dismantled. If the units leak or if the damping action is lost, replacement of the units is the only satisfactory answer.

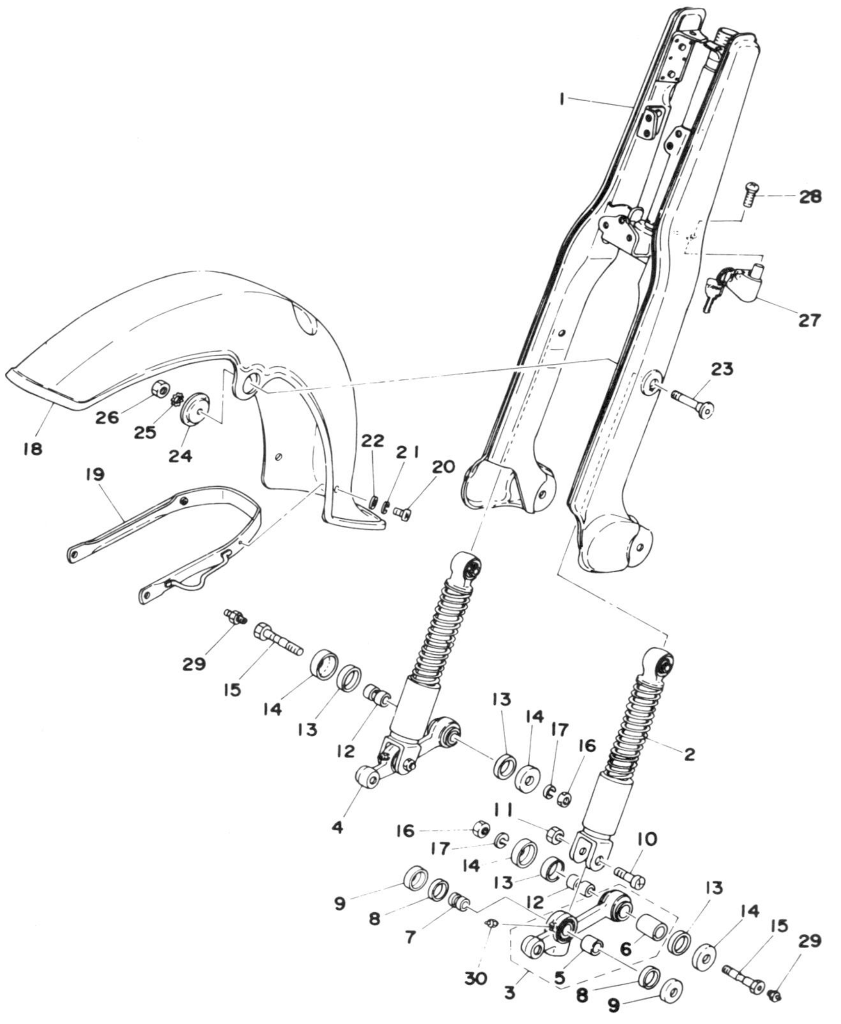

1 Front forks
2 Suspension unit – 2 off
3 LH pivot arm assembly
4 RH pivot arm assembly
5 Bush – 2 off
6 Bush – 2 off
7 Pivot pin – 2 off
8 Dust seal – 4 off
9 Dust seal cover – 4 off
10 Screw – 2 off
11 Nut – 2 off
12 Pivot pin – 2 off
13 Dust seal – 4 off
14 Dust seal cover – 4 off
15 Special bolt – 2 off
16 Nut – 2 off
17 Spring washer – 2 off
18 Front mudguard
19 Mudguard stay
20 Screw – 2 off
21 Spring washer – 2 off
22 Washer – 2 off
23 Special bolt – 2 off
24 Special washer – 2 off
25 Toothed washer – 2 off
26 Nut – 2 off
27 Steering lock assembly
28 Screw – 2 off
29 Grease nipple – 2 off
30 Grease nipple – 2 off

Fig. 5.1 Front forks

Fig. 5.2 Handlebar assembly

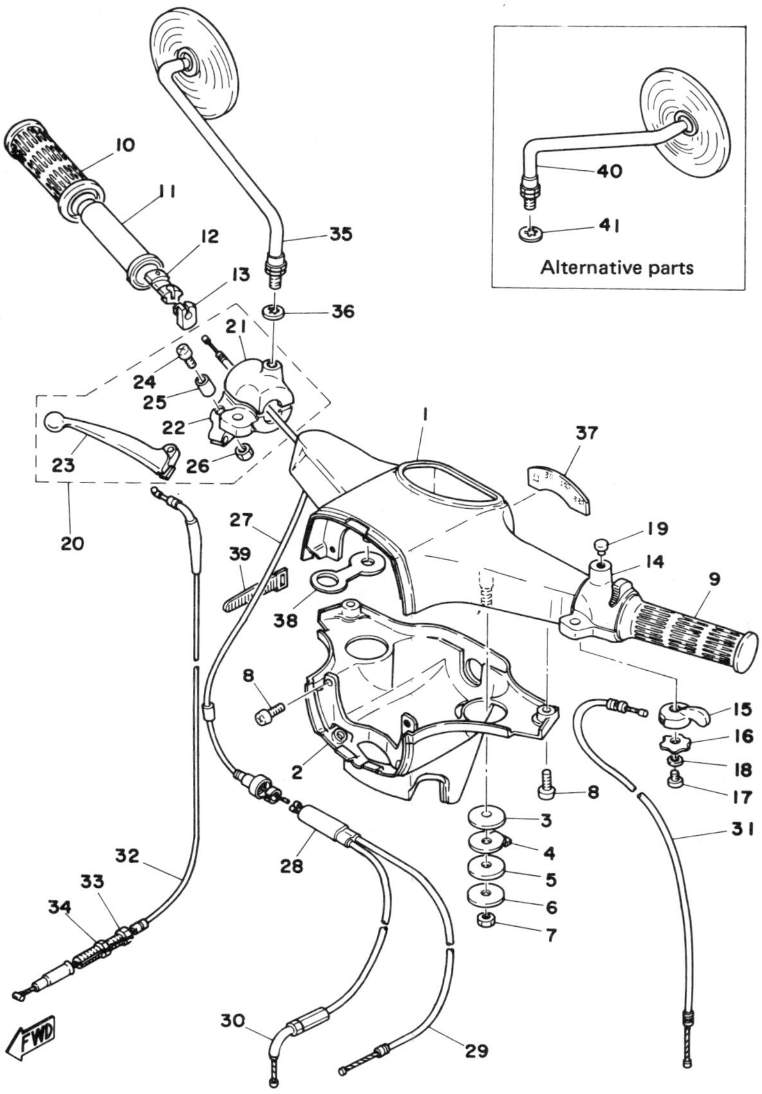

1 Handlebar top section
2 Handlebar bottom section
3 Shock absorbing washer – 2 off
4 Locking washer – 2 off
5 Shock absorbing washer – 2 off
6 Special washer – 2 off
7 Nut – 2 off
8 Screw – 4 off
9 Left-hand grip
10 Right-hand grip
11 Twistgrip sleeve
12 Sliding block
13 Cable stop block
14 Left-hand control assembly
15 Choke lever
16 Special washer
17 Bolt
18 Washer
19 Plug
20 Right-hand control assembly
21 Top half of control assembly
22 Bottom half of control assembly
23 Front brake lever
24 Screw
25 Pivot bush
26 Nut
27 Throttle cable (top part)
28 Junction box
29 Throttle cable (bottom part)
30 Oil pump cable
31 Choke cable
32 Brake cable
33 Adjusting bolt
34 Locking nut
35 Rear view mirror RH
36 Toothed washer
37 Switch decal
38 Earthing plate
39 Cable clip
40 Rear view mirror LH
41 Toothed washer

2.4 Remove the nuts and washers to release the mudguard

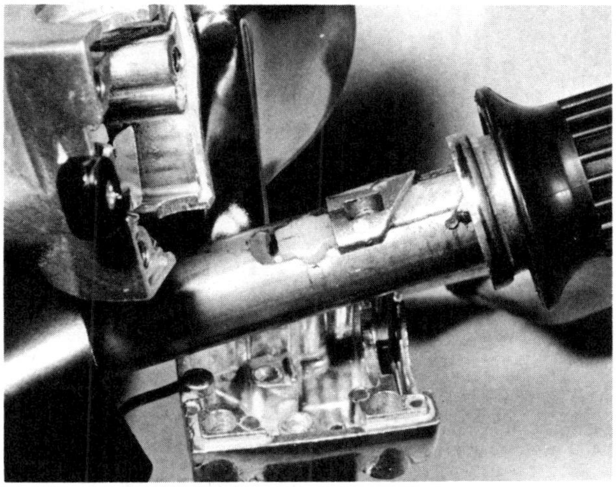

2.6 Disconnect the throttle cable

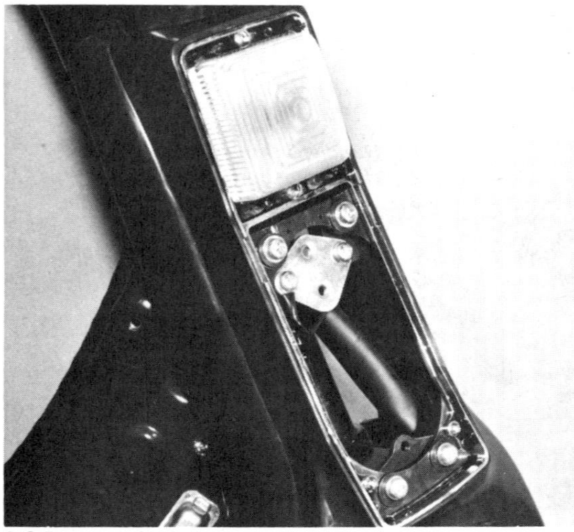
2.8 Remove the four screws and the front moulding

2.10 Remove the bolt to release the steering bracket

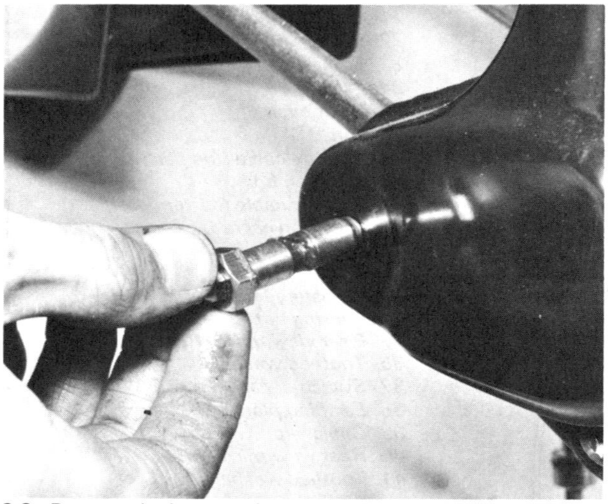
3.3a Remove the bottom pivot bolt ...

3.3b ... and the bolt from the top of the suspension unit

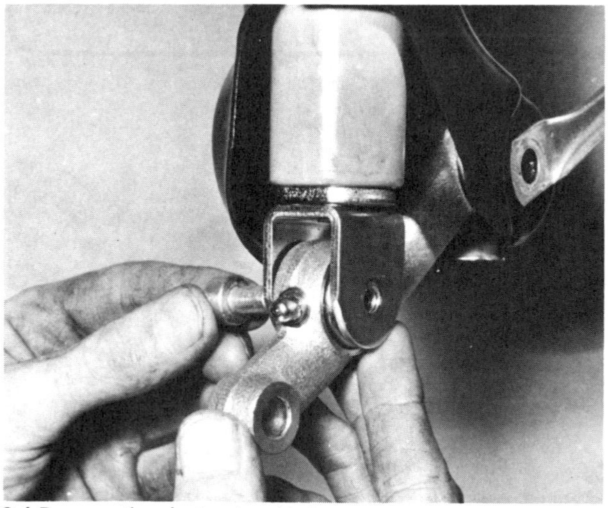
3.4 Remove the pivot nut and bolt

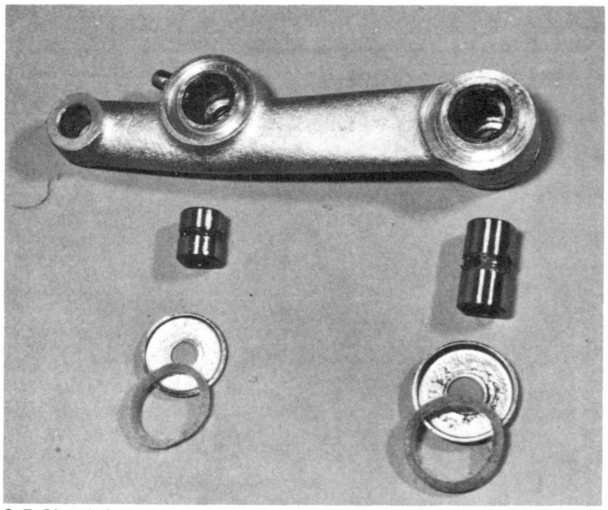
3.5 Check for wear on the pins or in the bushes

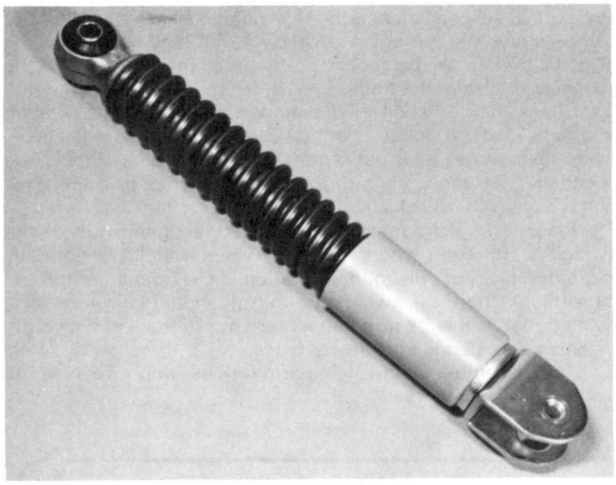

3.8 Check the suspension unit for leaks

5.1 The steering lock is located behind the steering head

4 Steering head bearings: examination and renovation

1 Before commencing to reassemble the forks, inspect the steering head races. The ball bearing tracks should be polished and free from indentations or cracks. If signs of wear or damage are evident, the cups and cones must be replaced. They are a tight push fit and need to be drifted out of position.

2 Ball bearings are cheap. Each race has 22 x $\frac{3}{16}$ inch ball bearings, which should be renewed if the originals are marked or discoloured. To hold the steel balls in position during the reattachment of the forks, pack the bearings with grease.

3 The forks can be reassembled and attached to the frame by following a reversal of the dismantling procedure. Do not over-tighten the steering head bearings, otherwise the handling characteristics of the machine will be affected. It is possible to over-tighten and create a load of several tons on the steering head bearings, even though the handlebars appear to turn with relative ease. As a guide, only very slight pressure should be needed to start the front wheel turning to either side under its own weight, when it is raised clear of the ground. Check also that the bearings are not too slack; there should be no discernible movement of the forks, in the fore and aft direction.

5 Steering head lock

A steering head lock is attached to the lower fork yoke by two crosshead screws. The tongue of the lock engages with a hole drilled in a plate attached to the steering head column, so that the machine can be left unattended with the handlebars on full left lock. If the lock malfunctions, it must be renewed.

6 Frame assembly: inspection and renovation

1 The frame assembly is unlikely to require attention unless it has been damaged in an accident. Replacement of the complete unit is the only satisfactory course of action when the frame is out of alignment, if only because the special jigs and mandrels essential for resetting the frame will not be available.

2 After a machine has covered an extensive mileage, it is advisable to inspect the frame for signs of cracking or splitting in the vicinity of the engine mounting points. Repairs can be effected by welding.

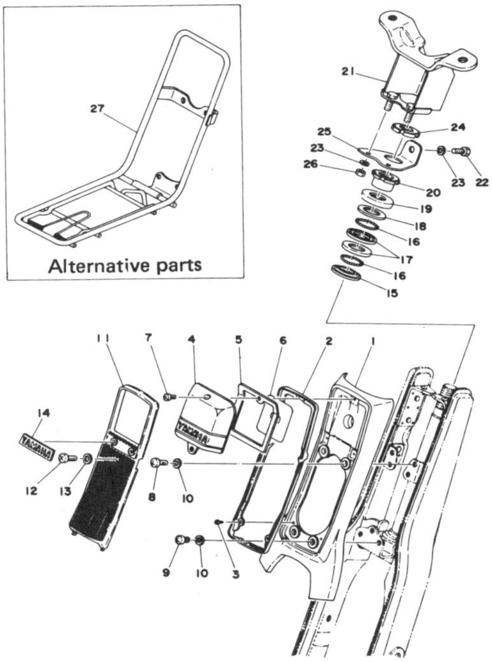

Fig. 5.3 Steering head and front panel

1 Inner front panel
2 Weatherproof moulding
3 Special screw – 4 off
4 Parking light lens
5 Sealing strip
6 Reflector
7 Screw – 2 off
8 Screw – 2 off
9 Screw – 2 off
10 Washer – 4 off
11 Outer front panel
12 Screw
13 Washer
14 Nameplate
15 Bottom bearing cone
16 Steel ball – 44 off
17 Bearing cup – 2 off
18 Top bearing cone
19 Bearing cover
20 Adjusting nut
21 Handlebar bracket
22 Bolt
23 Spring washer – 3 off
24 Special locking nut
25 Plate
26 Nut – 2 off
27 Front carrier assembly

7 Swinging arm rear fork: dismantling, inspection and reassembly

1 The rear fork of the frame assembly pivots on the rear fork pivot bolt which is carried in rubber bushes. Its action is controlled by two hydraulically-damped rear suspension units that each carry a compression spring, connected between the swinging arm fork and the frame, one on each side of the machine.

2 To detach the rear fork, remove the rear wheel, as described in Chapter 6. Remove the upper and lower halves of the rear chaincase and remove the final drive chain. Remove the final drive sprocket as described in Chapter 6.

3 On the V50P model the pedalling gear must be removed as described in Chapter 6, whilst on the other models the brake light switch must be removed and the wires disconnected and pulled out of the swinging arm. A single screw retains the switch in the right-hand end of the crossmember.

4 Remove the domed nuts and the bolts that secure the lower eye of each suspension unit to the swinging arm.

5 Unscrew the swinging arm pivot nut and withdraw the pivot bolt. Unhook the rubber protection band and remove the swinging arm from the frame.

6 Check the condition of the rubber bushes in the swinging arm fork pivot. A rubber bonded bush is fitted to each side, which can be pressed out if renewal is necesary. Renew the bushes if they show signs of damage or ageing, or if the pivot bolt is a slack fit. Check also the pivot bolt.

7 Place a straight metal rod across the open ends of the swinging arm fork, where the rear wheel spindle is normally located. Check for twist or deformation. If the amount of twist is more than 1 mm, the swinging arm fork should be renewed. A twisted rear fork will throw the wheels out of track and give the machine poor handling characteristics.

8 To reassemble the swinging arm fork assembly, reverse the dismantling procedure.

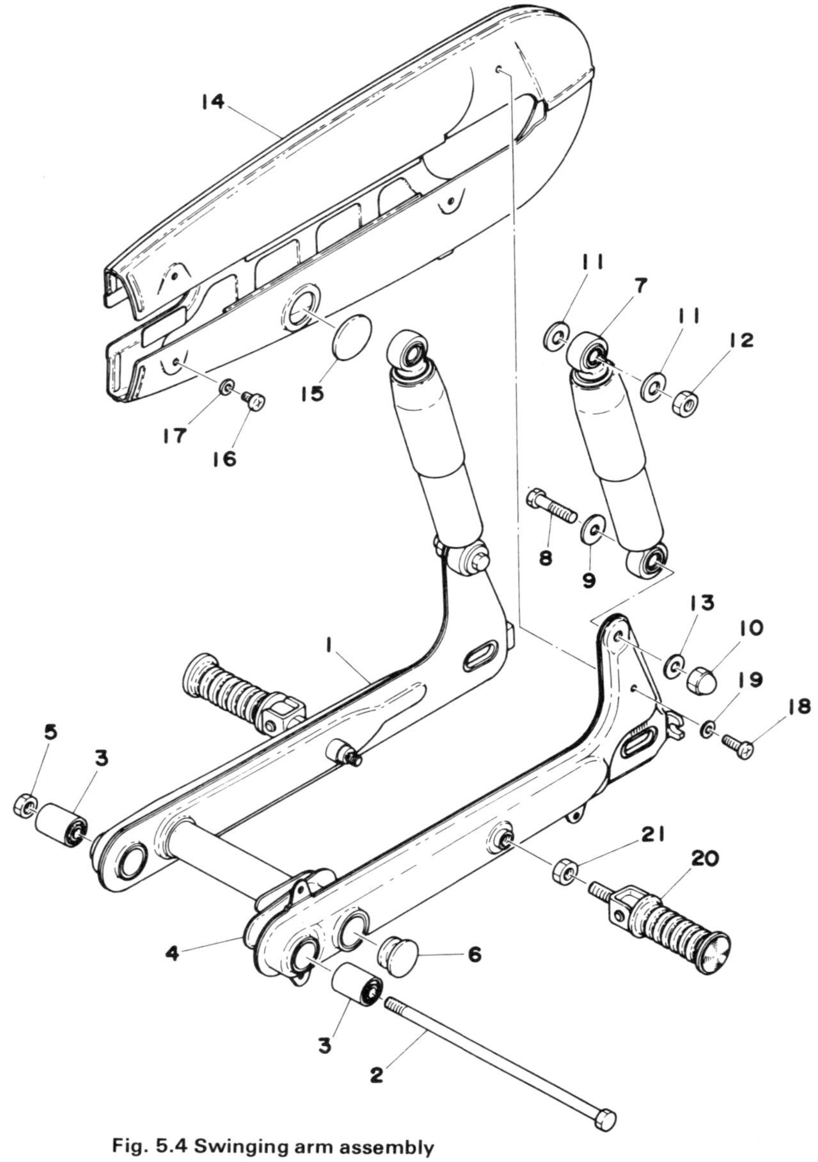

1 *Swinging arm*
2 *Pivot bolt*
3 *Silentbloc bush – 2 off*
4 *Rubber guard*
5 *Nut*
6 *Cap (not V50P)*
7 *Rear suspension unit – 2 off*
8 *Bolt – 2 off*
9 *Washer – 2 off*
10 *Domed nut – 2 off*
11 *Washer – 4 off*
12 *Nut – 2 off*
13 *Washer – 2 off*
14 *Chaincase assembly*
15 *Inspection cap*
16 *Screw – 3 off*
17 *Washer – 3 off*
18 *Screw*
19 *Washer*
20 *Rear footrest assembly – 2 off*
21 *Nut – 2 off*

Fig. 5.4 Swinging arm assembly

7.2 Remove the chaincase halves

7.3a Remove the brake light switch ...

7.3b ... and remove the wires

7.4a Remove the domed nuts ...

7.4b ... and the suspension bolts

7.5a Remove the pivot bolt ...

7.5b ... unhook the protection band ...

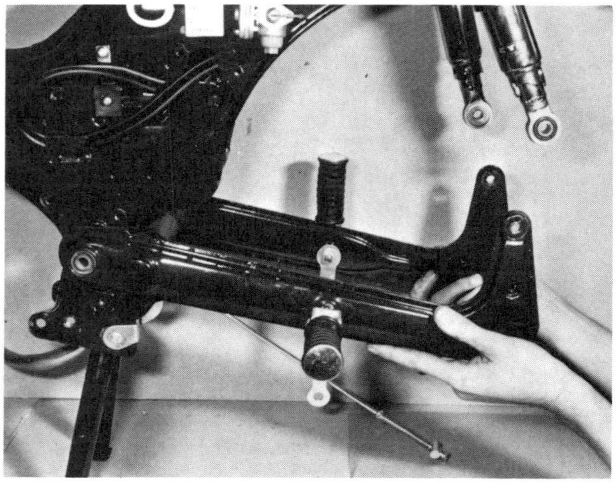

7.5c ... and remove the swinging arm

7.6 Check the condition of the silentbloc bushes

8 Rear suspension units: removal and inspection

1 Place the machine on its centre stand so that it is standing firmly on level ground. Put weight on the front of the machine to ensure that the front wheel stops on the ground.
2 Remove the plastic side panels and the nut and washer securing the top of the suspension units.
3 Remove the domed nut and the bolt from the bottom of each suspension unit and allow the rear wheel to rest on the ground. Pull the suspension units off their top mounting.
4 If the suspension units show signs of leakage or if the damping action is no longer evident, the units should be renewed. Always renew both, as a matched pair, in the interests of good roadholding. The damper unit is sealed and cannot be repaired.
5 Reassembly is the reverse of the dismantling procedure.
6 On V90 models the suspension units are adjustable to three different positions to cater for different load carrying conditons. Adjustment is made by rotating the stepped seat at the bottom of each unit. Always ensure that both units are set to the same position.

8.2 Remove the top nut and washer

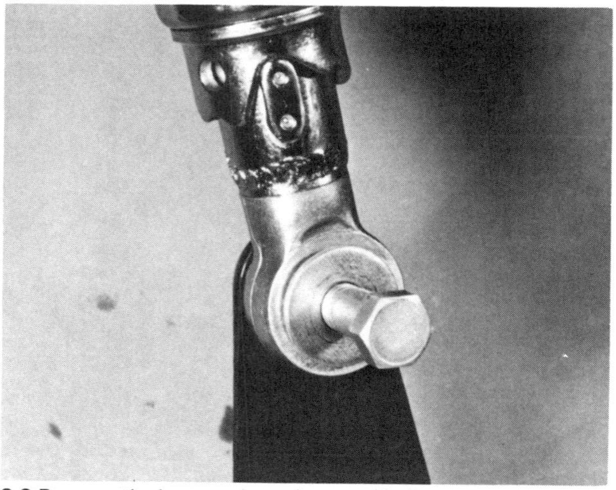

8.3 Remove the bottom domed nut and bolt

8.6 Ensure that both units are on the same setting

9 Centre stand and prop stand: inspection

1 The centre stand is atached to the lower extremities of the frame unit, to provide a convenient means of parking the machine on level ground. It pivots on the rod that carries the rear brake pedal, which is retained in position by a circlip. A return spring retracts the stand when the machine is pushed forward, so that it can be wheeled prior to riding.
2 There is a prop stand fitted onto the footrest bar, also with a return spring.
3 The condition of the return springs and their return action should be checked regularly. If a stand falls whist the machine is in motion, it may catch in some obstacle in the road and unseat the rider.

10 Footrests: inspection and renovation

1 The footrest bar is atached to the bottom of the frame by three bolts and is rubber mounted. The bar is malleable and is likely to become bent if the machine is dropped.
2 To straighten the bar first remove it from the machine and detach the footrest rubbers. It can then be bent straight in a vice, using a blow lamp to warm the tube if the bend is severe. Never attempt to straighten the bar whilst it is still attached to the frame otherwise damage to the mounting may result.

11 Speedometer: removal and replacement

1 A speedometer of the magnetic type is fitted to the Yamaha V50, V75 and V90 models. It contains also the odometer for recording the total mileage covered by the machine, a small bulb for illuminating the dial during the hours of darkness, and the neutral indicator lamp.
2 The speedometer is held in place by a clamp and a single nut and washer. To remove the speedometer, remove the screw and the headlamp unit, unscrew the speedometer cable, remove the nut and washer to release the clamp and lift the speedometer out of the top.
3 Although a speedometer on a machine of less than 100 cc capacity is not a statutory requirement in the UK, if one is fitted it must be in good working order. Reference to the mileage reading shown on the odometer is a good way of keeping pace with the routine maintenance schedules.
4 Apart from defects in the speedometer drive or in the drive cable itself, a speedometer that malfunctions is difficult to repair. Fit a replacement or alternatively entrust the repair to an instrument repair specialist.

12 Speedometer cable: inspection and maintenance

1 It is advisable to detach the speedometer drive cable from time to time, in order to check whether it is adequately lubricated and whether the outer covering is compressed or damaged at any point along its run. A jerky or sluggish speedometer movement can often be attributed to a cable fault.
2 To grease the cable, withdraw the inner cable. After removing the old grease, clean with a petrol soaked rag and examine the cable for broken strands or other damage.
3 Regrease the cable with high melting point grease, taking care not to grease the last six inches at the point where the cable enters the speedometer head. If this precaution is not observed, grease will work into the speedometer head and immobilise the movement.
4 If the speedometer and odometer stop working, it is probable that the speedometer cable has broken. The inner and outer cables must be renewed together; they are not supplied as separate parts.

10.1a Two of the bolts hold the footrest assembly ...

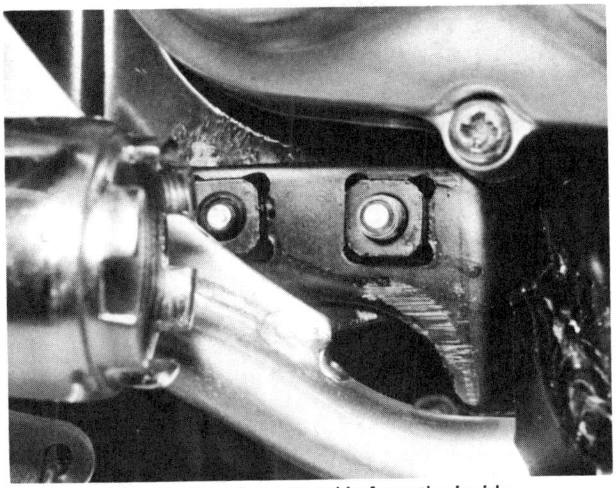
10.1b ... whilst the third is screwed in from the inside

11.2 Speedometer is secured by clamp and single nut

13 Dualseat: removal

1 To remove the dualseat, unhook the catch and lift the dual-seat. Remove the bolt retaining the support prop and the two clips holding the seat hinge pins. The dualseat can be lifted clear when the pins are slid out.

2 A single bolt retains the catch onto the petrol tank.

3 Reassembly is the reverse of the dismantling procedure. Ensure that the clips are properly located on the hinge pins.

14 Cleaning the plastic mouldings

1 The moulded plastic cycle parts, such as the front mudguard, and legshield cover, will not respond to cleaning in the same way as the other metal parts as they are moulded in rigid polyethylene. It is best to wash these parts with a household detergent solution, which will remove oil and grease in a most effective manner.

2 Avoid the use of scouring powder as much as possible because this will score the surface of the mouldings and make them more receptive to dirt.

15 Cleaning: general

1 After removing all surface dirt with a rag or sponge that is washed frequently in clean water, the application of car polish or wax will give a good finish to the cycle parts of the machine, after they have dried thoroughly. The plated parts should require only a wipe over with a damp rag.

2 If possible, the machine should be wiped over immediately after it has been used in the wet, so that it is not garaged in damp conditions that will promote rusting. Remember there is little chance of water entering the control cables if they are lubricated regularly, as recommended in the Routine Maintenance Section.

13.1 Remove the two clips to release the hinge pins

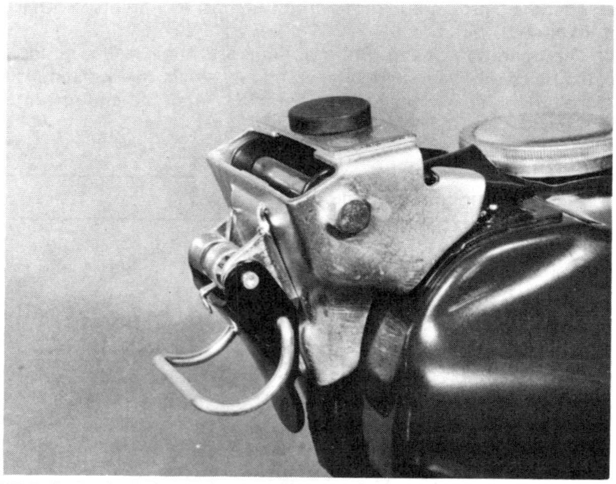

13.2 A single bolt retains catch onto the petrol tank

16 Fault diagnosis: frame and fork assembly

Symptom	Cause	Remedy
Machine is unduly sensitive to road surface irregularities	Fork and/or rear suspension units damping ineffective	Renew suspension units.
Machine rolls at low speeds	Steering head bearings overtight or damaged	Slacken bearing adjustment. If no improvement, dismantle and inspect head bearings.
Machine tends to wander; steering is imprecise	Worn swinging arm suspension bearings	Check and if necessary renew pivot bolt and bushes.
Fork action stiff	Fork legs have twisted	Check alignment.
Forks judder when front brake is applied	Worn bushes in fork assembly Steering head bearings too slack	Strip forks and renew bushes. Re-adjust to take up play.
Wheels seem out of alignment	Frame distorted as result of accident damage	Check frame after stripping out. If bent, replacement frame is necessary.

Chapter 6 Wheels, brakes and tyres

For modifications, and information relating to later models, see Chapter 8

Contents

Specifications

Wheels	17 inch diameter front and rear
Tyres	2·25 inch x 17 inch front and rear (V50 and V75 models) 2·50 inch x 17 inch front and rear (V90 model)
Tyre pressures	
Front	20 psi
Rear	28 psi
Increase by 4 psi when carrying a pillion passenger	
Brakes	Internally expanding drum brakes front and rear
Engine sprocket	
V50	13 teeth
V75	13 or 14 teeth
V90	14 or 15 teeth
Rear wheel sprocket	
V50	39 teeth
V75	36 or 37 teeth
V90	35 or 36 teeth
Final drive chain	
Number of links	99, 100 or 102 depending on sprockets fitted
Chain size	$\frac{1}{2}$ x $\frac{1}{4}$ inch all models

1 General description

Both wheels are of 17 inch diameter and carry tyres of 2·25 inch section (2·50 inch section, V90 models), a ribbed tyre at the front and a block tread at the rear. Steel wheel rims are used in conjunction with cast aluminium alloy hubs, each hub containing a 110 mm internal expanding brake. The wheels are not interchangeable because the rear wheel incorporates a special cush drive arrangement to act as a transmission shock absorber. Both wheels are quickly detachable; the rear wheel can be removed from the frame without disturbing the rear wheel sprocket or the final drive chain.

2 Front wheel: examination and renovation

1 Place the machine on the centre stand so that the front-wheel is raised clear of the ground. Spin the wheel and check the rim alignment for run-out. Small irregularities can be corrected by tightening the spokes in the area affected, although a certain amount of experience is advisable if over-correction is to be avoided.
2 Any flats in the wheel rim should be evident at the same time. These are much more difficult to remove and in most cases the wheel will need to be rebuilt on a new rim. Apart from the effect on stability, there is greater risk of damage to the tyre bead and walls if the machine is run with a deformed wheel. In an extreme case the tyre can even separate from the rim.
3 Check for loose or broken spokes. Tapping the spokes is the best guide to tension. A loose spoke will produce a quite different sound. Always recheck for run-out by spinning the wheel again.
4 If it is necessary to turn a spoke nipple an excessive amount to restore tension, it is advisable to remove the tyre and tube so that the end of the spoke that now protrudes into the wheel rim can be ground flush. If this precaution is not taken, there is danger of the spoke end chafing the inner tube and causing a puncture.

3 Front wheel: removal

1 Commence operations by placing the machine on the centre stand, on level ground.
2 Disconnect the speedometer cable by removing the spring clip and pulling the cable out of the backplate.
3 Slacken the front brake adjuster, pull the rubber boot off the adjuster and slide the cable out of the slot in the adjuster and unhook the cable from the brake arm.
4 Remove the split pin and the nut from the brake anchor point and withdraw the bolt to free the back plate.
5 Withdraw the split pin from the front wheel spindle nut and remove the nut and washer. The front wheel spindle can now be pulled out, releasing the wheel complete with brake assembly. Ensure that the machine is well supported so that it does not topple forward once the wheel is removed.

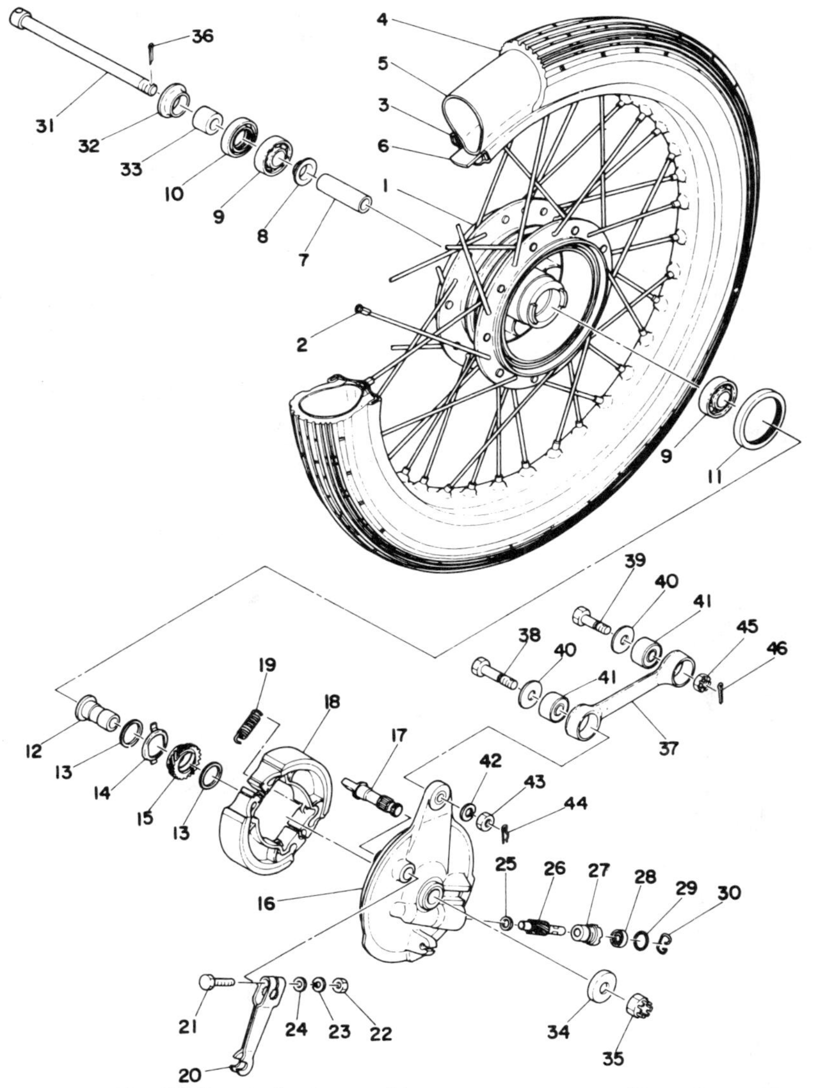

1 Hub
2 Spoke set
3 Rim
4 Tyre
5 Inner tube
6 Rim tape
7 Spacer
8 Flange
9 Bearing – 2 off
10 Oil seal
11 Oil seal
12 Pivot bush
13 Washer – 2 off
14 Driving dog
15 Speedometer gear
16 Brake backplate
17 Brake cam
18 Brake shoe assembly – 2 off
19 Pull-off spring – 2 off
20 Brake lever arm
21 Bolt
22 Nut
23 Spring washer
24 Washer
25 Washer
26 Speedometer worm
27 Bush
28 Oil seal
29 O ring
30 Retaining ring
31 Wheel spindle
32 Dust cover
33 Spacer
34 Dust cover
35 Castle nut
36 Split pin
37 Anchor arm
38 Bolt
39 Bolt
40 Washer – 2 off
41 Rubber bush
42 Spring washer
43 Nut
44 Spring slip
45 Slotted nut
46 Split pin

Fig. 6.1 Front wheel assembly

Note: *items 37 to 46 are fitted to the V90 model only*

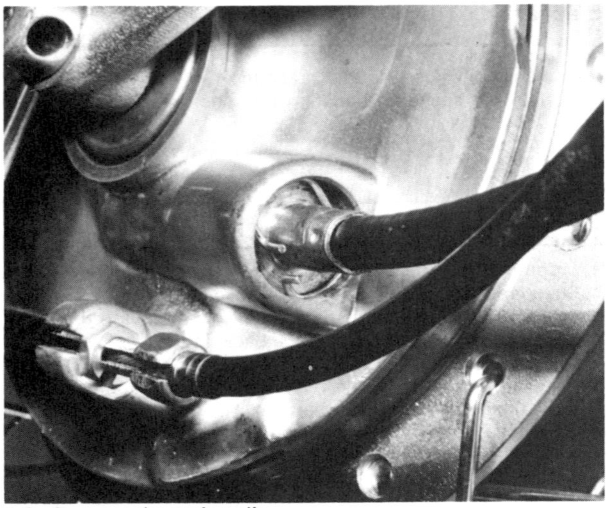

3.2a Remove the spring clip ...

3.2b ... to release the speedometer cable

3.3a Slacken the adjuster and pull off the rubber boot and slide the cable out of the slot ...

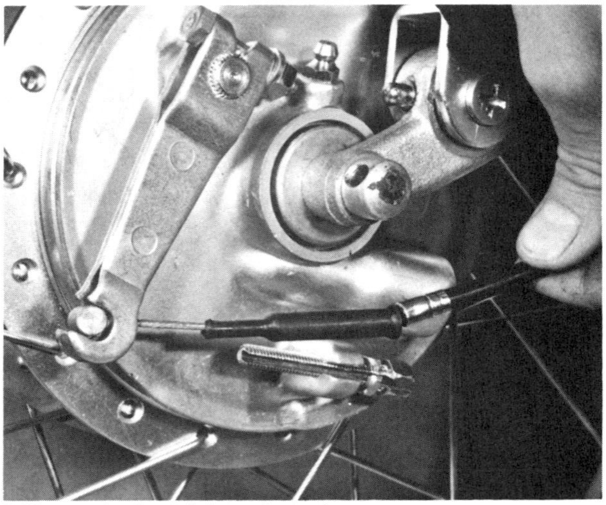

3.3b ... and unhook it from the brake arm

3.4 Remove the split pin and anchor nut and bolt

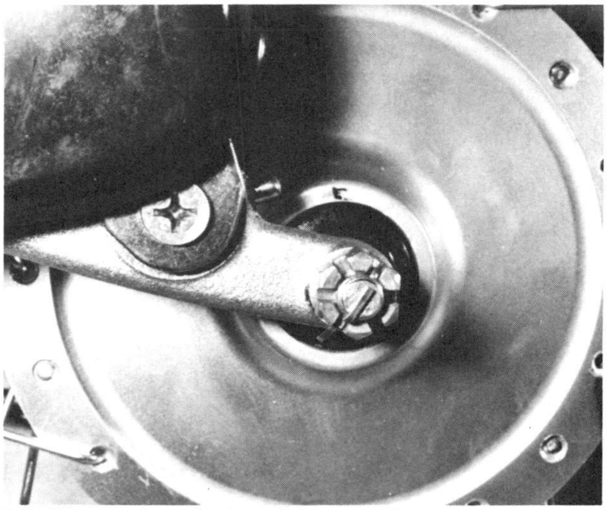

3.5a Remove the split pin and the nut and ...

3.5b ... slide out the spindle

4 Front brake assembly: examination, renovation and reassembly

1 To remove the brake assembly, the backplate lifts straight out of the brake drum.
2 Examine the brake linings. If they are wearing thin or unevenly, the brake shoes should be renewed. The linings are bonded on and cannot be replaced as a separate item.
3 To remove the brake shoes from the brake plate assembly, arrange the operating lever so that the brakes are in the 'full on' position and then pull the shoes apart whilst lifting them upward in the form of a 'V'. When they are clear of the brake plate, the return springs can be removed and the shoes separated.
4 Before replacing the brake shoes, check that the brake operating cam is working smoothly and is not binding in its pivot. The cam can be removed by withdrawing the retaining bolt in the operating arm and pulling the arm off the shaft. Before removing the arm, it is advisable to mark its position in relation to the shaft, so that it can be relocated correctly. The shaft should be greased prior to reassembly and also a light smear of grease placed on the faces of the operating cam.
5 Check the inner surface of the brake drum on which the brake shoes bear. The surface should be smooth and free from score marks or indentations, otherwise reduced braking efficiency will be inevitable. Remove all traces of brake lining dust and wipe with a clean rag soaked in petrol to remove any traces of grease or oil.
6 If the brake drum has become scored, special attention is required. It is possible to skim a brake drum in a lathe provided the score marks are not too deep. Under these circumstances, packing will have to be added to the ends of the brake shoes, to compensate for the amount of metal removed from the surface of the drum.
7 To reassemble the brake shoes on the brake plate, fit the return springs first and then force the shoes apart, holding them in a 'V' formation. If they are now located with the brake operating cam and pivot they can usually be snapped into position by pressing downward. Never use excessive force, otherwise there is risk of distorting the shoes permanently.

5 Front wheel bearings: examination and replacement

1 The front wheel bearings are of the ball journal type and are not adjustable. If the bearings are worn, indicated by side play at the wheel rim, the bearings must be renewed.
2 Access to the wheel bearings is gained when the brake plate has been removed from the front wheel.
3 The wheel bearings are a drive fit in the hub. Use a double diameter drift to displace the bearings from the hub, working from each side of the hub. When the first bearing emerges from the hub the hollow distance collar that separates them can be removed.
4 Remove all the old grease from the hub and bearings, giving the latter a final wash in petrol. Check the bearings for play or signs of roughness when they are turned. If there is any doubt about their condition, renew them.
5 Before replacing the bearings, first pack the hub with new grease. Then grease both bearings and drive them back into position with the same double diameter drift, not forgetting the distance collar that separates them.

6 Speedometer drive gears: examination and replacement

1 The speedometer drive gears are housed in the front brake backplate and are driven by two tongues that engage with dogs in the hub.
2 The drive gears should be checked for wear or broken teeth and renewed if necessary.
3 The large gear with its two drive tongues simply lifts out of the backplate, complete with its headed bush that retains it when the brake is assembled.
4 To renew the small worm gear in the brake plate it is necessary to prise out the small oil seal, unscrew the bush and withdraw the worm gear.
5 Reassembly of the gears is by reversing the above procedure, ensuring that the gear tongues engage with the hub slots. Thoroughly grease the gears and ensure that the oil seal is in good condition.

7 Front wheel: replacement

1 To replace the front wheel, reverse the removal procedure and ensure that the anchor arm is fixed securely. This cannot be overstressed as failure to anchor the brake plate will cause the brake to lock on when it is first applied.
2 Adjust the front brake and check that the brake functions correctly, especially if the adjustment has been altered or the brake operating arm has been removed and replaced during the dismantling operation.

8 Rear wheel: examination and renovation

1 Place the machine on the centre stand, so that the rear wheel is clear of the ground. Check the wheel for rim alignment, damage to the rim or loose or broken spokes, by following the procedure adopted for the front wheel in Section 2 of this Chapter.

9 Rear wheel: removal

1 To remove the rear wheel, place the machine on the centre stand so that the wheel is raised clear of the ground. Remove the brake adjusting nut and separate the brake rod from the operating arm of the rear brake. Remove the clip, slacken and remove the nut and bolt from the rear brake torque arm, at the brake plate anchorage.
2 Remove the split pin, the centre of the two rear wheel spindle nuts and pull the spindle from the hub. Remove the distance pieces if they have not fallen clear and disengage the hub from the cush drive assembly by pulling the wheel towards the right-hand side of the machine. The wheel can now be removed from the frame complete with the rear brake assembly, leaving the rear sprocket and final drive chain in position.

4.1 The brake assembly lifts out of the drum

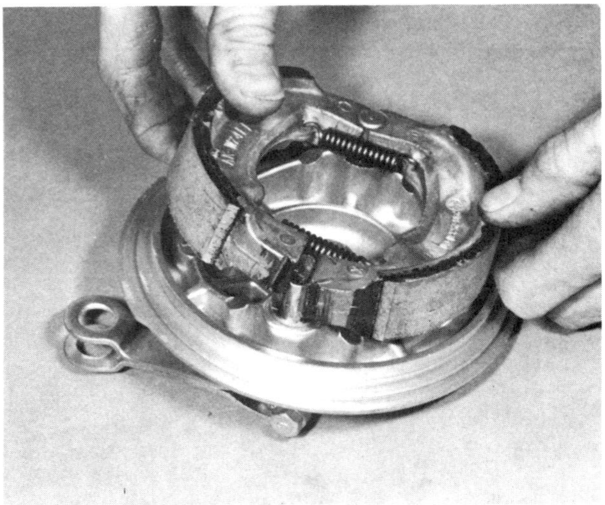

4.7 Place the shoes in a V-formation before snapping them into position

5.3a Drive out the bearings ...

5.3b ... and remove the distance collar

6.3a The large drive gear ...

6.3b ... is retained by a headed bush ...

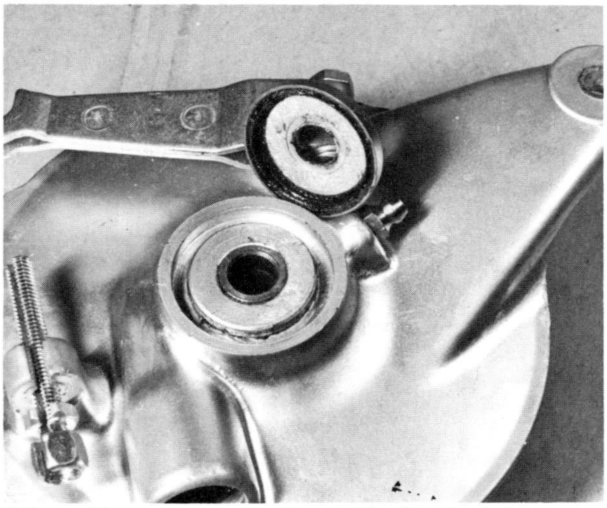

6.3c ... with a grease seal on the outside of the backplate

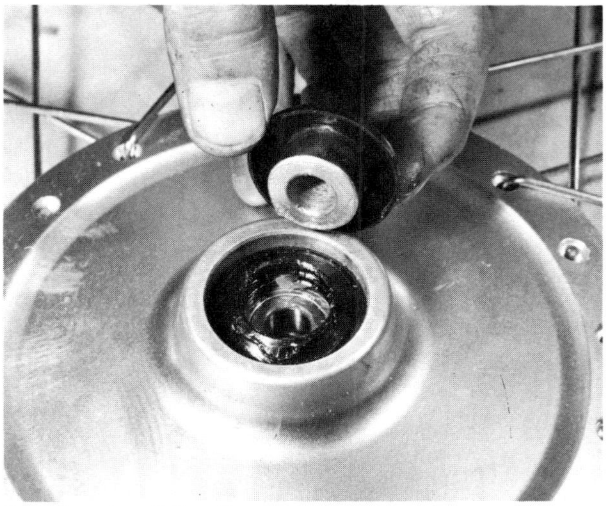

7.1a Do not omit the oil seal spacer ...

7.1b ... and ensure that the anchor arm is fitted securely

9.1 Remove the clip and the anchor nut and bolt

9.2a Remove the distance piece ...

9.2b ... and disengage the rear wheel from the shock absorber assembly

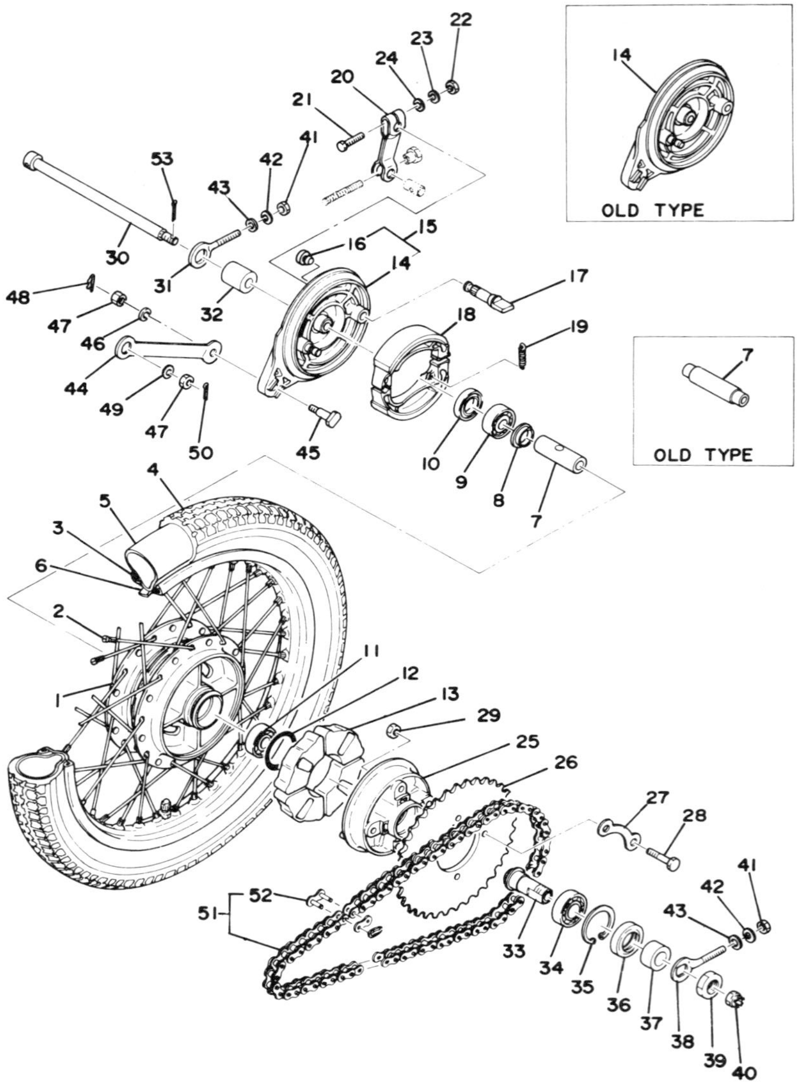

Fig. 6.2 Rear wheel assembly

1 *Hub*
2 *Spoke set*
3 *Rim*
4 *Tyre*
5 *Inner tube*
6 *Rim tape*
7 *Spacer*
8 *Flange*
9 *Bearing*
10 *Oil seal*
11 *Bearing*
12 *O ring*
13 *Shock absorber rubber – 4 off*
14 *Brake backplate*
15 *Backplate assembly*
16 *Inspection grommet*
17 *Brake cam*
18 *Brake shoe assembly – 2 off*
19 *Pull-off spring – 2 off*
20 *Brake lever arm*
21 *Bolt*
22 *Nut*
23 *Spring washer*
24 *Washer*
25 *Shock absorber hub*
26 *Sprocket*
27 *Tab washer – 2 off*
28 *Bolt – 4 off*
29 *Nut – 4 off*
30 *Wheel spindle*
31 *RH chain adjuster*
32 *Spacer*
33 *Stub axle*
34 *Bearing*
35 *Circlip*
36 *Oil seal*
37 *Spacer*
38 *LH chain adjuster*
39 *Nut*
40 *Castle nut*
41 *Nut – 2 off*
42 *Spring washer – 2 off*
43 *Washer – 2 off*
44 *Anchor arm*
45 *Special bolt*
46 *Spring washer*
47 *Nut – 2 off*
48 *Spring clip*
49 *Washer*
50 *Split pin*
51 *Chain*
52 *Spring link*
53 *Split pin*

Tyre removal: Deflate inner tube and insert lever in close proximity to tyre valve

Use two levers to work bead over the edge of rim

When first bead is clear, remove tyre as shown

Tyre fitting: Inflate inner tube and insert in tyre

Lay tyre on rim and feed valve through hole in rim

Work first bead over rim, using lever in final section

Use similar technique for second bead, finish at tyre valve position

Push valve and tube up into tyre when fitting final section, to avoid trapping

10 Rear brake assembly: examination, renovation and reassembly

As the rear brake is identical to the front brake, the advice given in Section 4 of this Chapter will apply.

11 Rear wheel bearings: examination and replacement

As the bearing layout for the hubs is identical, the procedure described in Section 5 of this Chapter will apply for each model except that there is an oil seal in front of the bearing on the brake drum side, to prevent grease from reaching the brake operating parts. This seal should be prised out of position and a new replacement obtained.

12 Rear wheel sprocket: removal, examination and replacement

1 It is unlikely that the sprocket will require renewal until a very substantial mileage has been covered. The usual signs of wear occur when the teeth assume a hooked or very shallow formation that will cause rapid wear of the chain. A worn sprocket must be renewed, together with the gearbox final drive sprocket and the chain. Always renew the final drive assembly as a complete set, otherwise rapid wear will occur as the result of running old and new parts together.

2 As the sprocket is left attached to the machine when the rear wheel is removed, the chainguard halves must be removed for access. Remove the two bolts on each half and pull the top half clear first.

3 Disconnect the chain at the spring link and pull it clear of the rear sprocket. Remove the stub axle nut and washer and pull the sprocket assembly clear of the machine. Prise down the two double tab washers, remove the four fixing bolts and lift the sprocket off.

4 To refit the sprocket, reverse the dismantling procedure.

10.1 The brake assembly lifts out of the drum

11.1a Prise out the oil seal and then ...

11.1b ... knock out the first bearing ...

11.1c ... followed by the second bearing

12.1 Check the condition of the sprocket teeth

12.2 Remove the chainguard halves

12.3a Remove the stub axle nut to release the shock absorber assembly

12.3b Prise down the tab washers, remove the bolts and lift off the sprocket

13 Rear wheel shock absorber assembly: examination and replacement

1 The shock absorber assembly is removed from the machine as described in the preceding Section.
2 The shock absorber assembly has a ball journal bearing and if worn the following procedure should be followed.
3 Tap out the stub axle, remove the spacer from the centre of the oil seal, prise out the oil seal, remove the circlip and drive the bearing out of the housing.
4 To replace the bearing, reverse the above procedure, ensuring that the bearing is well greased and the oil seal is in good condition.
5 The shock absorber rubbers should be checked for any damage or deterioration. All oil or grease should be wiped away as this may cause premature deterioration.
6 To refit the shock absorber assembly reverse the dismantling procedure described in Sections 9 and 12.

14 Rear wheel: reassembly

1 To refit the rear wheel, reverse the removal procedure, ensuring that the brake anchor arm is securely fitted. If the anchor arm becomes detached, the rear brake will lock in the full-on position immediately it is applied and may give rise to a serious accident.
2 Before fully tightening all the nuts, ensure that the final chain tension and the brake adjustment is correct.
3 Check also whether the wheel alignment is correct. See diagram on page 91.
4 Do not omit to replace the split pin that passes through the rear wheel spindle nut.

13.3a Tap out the stub axle ...

13.3b ... prise out the oil seal

13.3c Remove the circlip and drive out the bearing

13.5 Ensure that the shock absorber rubbers are free of oil and grease

14.1 Ensure that the anchor arm is fitted securely

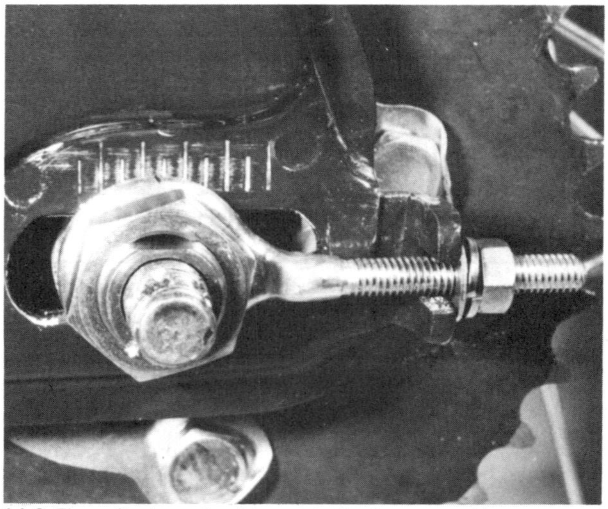

14.3 The adjusters should match the frame markings on each side

15 Front and rear brakes: adjustment

1 The front brake adjuster is located on the front brake cable. The brake should be adjusted so that the wheel is free to revolve before pressure is applied to the handlebar lever, and is applied fully before the handlebar lever touches the handlebar.
2 The rear brake is adjusted by means of the adjusting nut on the end of the brake cable or rod. Adjustment is largely a matter of personal choice, but excessive travel of the footbrake pedal should not be necessary before the brake is applied fully.
3 Efficient brakes depend on good leverage of the operating arm. The angle between the brake operating arm and the cable or rod should never exceed 90° when the brake is fully applied.
4 Check that the brakes pull off correctly when the lever and pedal are released. Sluggish action can usually be traced to a broken return spring on the brake shoes or a tendency for the operating cam to bind in its bush.

16 Final drive chain: examination and lubrication

1 The final drive chain is fully enclosed within a chaincase. Periodically, the tension of the chain will need to be adjusted, to compensate for wear. This is accomplished by sliding the rear wheel backwards in the ends of the rear fork, using the drawbolt adjusters provided. The rear wheel spindle nuts must be slackened before the drawbolts can be turned; also the torque arm bolt on the rear brake plate.
2 The chain is in correct adjustment if there is from 1 – 2 cm free play in the middle of the lower run. An inspection plug in the lower section of the full chaincase permits access to the chain to check whether the tension is correct.
3 Always adjust an identical amount, otherwise the rear wheel will be thrown out of alignment. If desired, wheel alignment can be checked by running a plank of wood parallel to the machine, so that it touches the sides of the rear tyre. If wheel alignment is correct, the plank will be equidistant from each side of the front wheel tyre, when tested on both sides of the rear wheel.
4 After a period of running, the chain will require lubrication. Lack of oil will accelerate the rate of wear of both chain and sprockets, leading to harsh transmission. The application of engine oil from an oil can will serve as a satisfactory lubricant, but it is preferable to remove the chain at regular intervals and immerse it in a molten lubricant such as Linklyfe, after it has been cleaned in a paraffin bath. This latter type of lubricant achieves better penetration of the chain links and rollers and is less likely to be thrown off when the chain is in motion. An equally effective and less messy alternative is a spray-on lubricant of the aerosol type, such as Castrol Chain Lubricant.
5 The chain fitted as standard is of Japanese manufacture. When renewal is necessary, it should be noted that a Renold equivalent of British manufacture is available as an alternative. The size and length of chain is stated in the Specifications Section.
6 To check whether the chain requires replacement, lay it lengthwise in a straight line and compress it so that all play is taken up. Anchor one end and then pull on the other end to take up the end play in the other direction. If the chain extends by more than the distance between two adjacent rollers, it should be renewed in conjunction with the two sprockets. Note that this check should be made after the chain has been washed but before any lubricant is applied, otherwise the lubricant will take up some of the play.
7 When replacing the chain, make sure the spring link is correctly seated, with the closed end facing the direction of chain travel. Also make sure the chaincase is firmly secured, and the drain vent is clear.

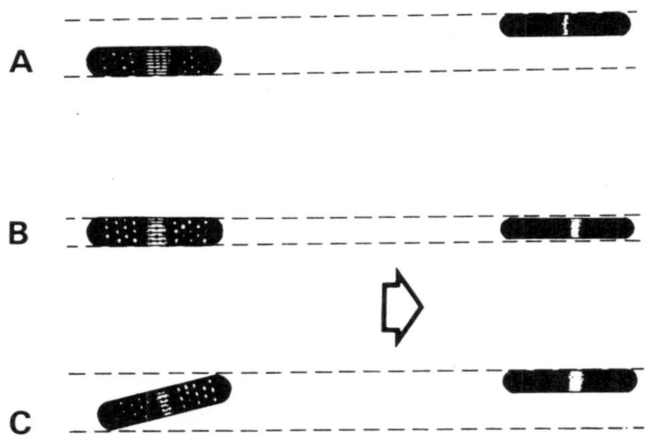

Fig. 6.3 Checking wheel alignment
A and C – Incorrect *B – Correct*

16.7a Closed end of spring link must face direction of travel

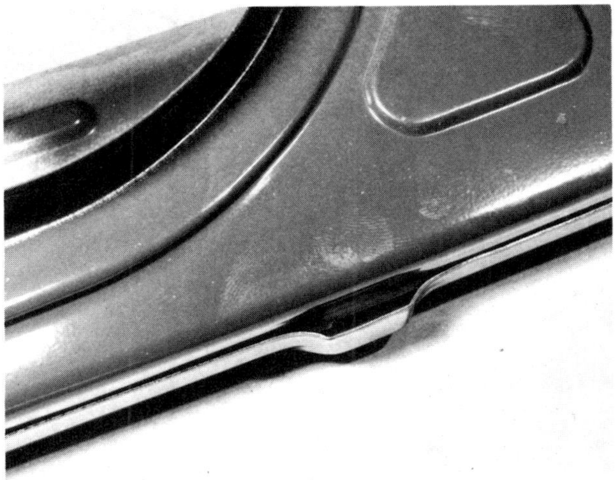

16.7b Check that the chaincase drain vent is clear

17 Pedalling gear chain: inspection and lubrication – V50P only

1 The same advice given in the preceding Section applies to the pedalling gear chain, although this chain is only in occasional use and will not be subjected to anything like the same amount of wear.
2 The pedalling gear chain does not require checking for tension because it is not adjustable. If it is badly worn, it must be renewed.

18 Pedal assembly: examination and replacement – V50P only

1 As pedals are fitted to this machine to make it legal for 16 year olds to ride, there should be very little wear and parts should only need replacing due to accidental damage.
2 The pedals are normal bicycle pedals which can be unscrewed and new ones screwed in if necessary. Note that the right-hand pedal has a left-hand thread.
3 If the left-hand crank and chainwheel need renewing, the procedure is found in Chapter 1, Section 5, paragraph 12.
4 If the right-hand crank needs renewing, the rubber boot should be pulled up the crank to expose a circlip on the shaft, which retains the crank. There is a slot in the crank into which the peg in the shaft must go to allow the crank to slide off.
5 To replace the spring it is easiest to remove the shaft from the machine prior to detaching the small circlip and spring.
6 If either crank is bent, renewal is advised. They are difficult to straighten without risk of a fracture occurring.

19 Tyres: removal and replacement

1 At some time or other the need will arise to remove and replace the tyres, either as the result of a puncture or because a replacement is required to offset wear. To the inexperienced, tyre changing represents a formidable task, yet if a few simple rules are observed and the technique learned, the whole operation is surprisingly simple.
2 To remove the tyre from either wheel, first detach the wheel from the machine by following the procedure in Sections 3 or 9, depending on whether the front or the rear wheel is involved. Deflate the tyre by removing the valve insert and when it is fully deflated, push the bead of the tyre away from the wheel rim on both sides so that the bead enters the centre well of the rim. Remove the locking cap and push the tyre valve into the tyre itself.
3 Insert a tyre lever close to the valve and lever the edge of the tyre over the outside of the wheel rim. Very little force should be necessary; if resistance is encountered it is probably due to the fact that the tyre beads have not entered the well of the wheel rim all the way round the tyre.
4 Once the tyre has been edged over the wheel rim, it is easy to work around the wheel rim so that the tyre is completely free on one side. At this stage, the inner tube can be removed.
5 Working from the other side of the wheel, ease the other edge of the tyre over the outside of the wheel rim that is furthest away. Continue to work around the rim until the tyre is free completely from the rim.
6 If a puncture has necessitated the removal of the tyre, reinflate the inner tube and immerse it in a bowl of water to trace the source of the leak. Mark its position and deflate the

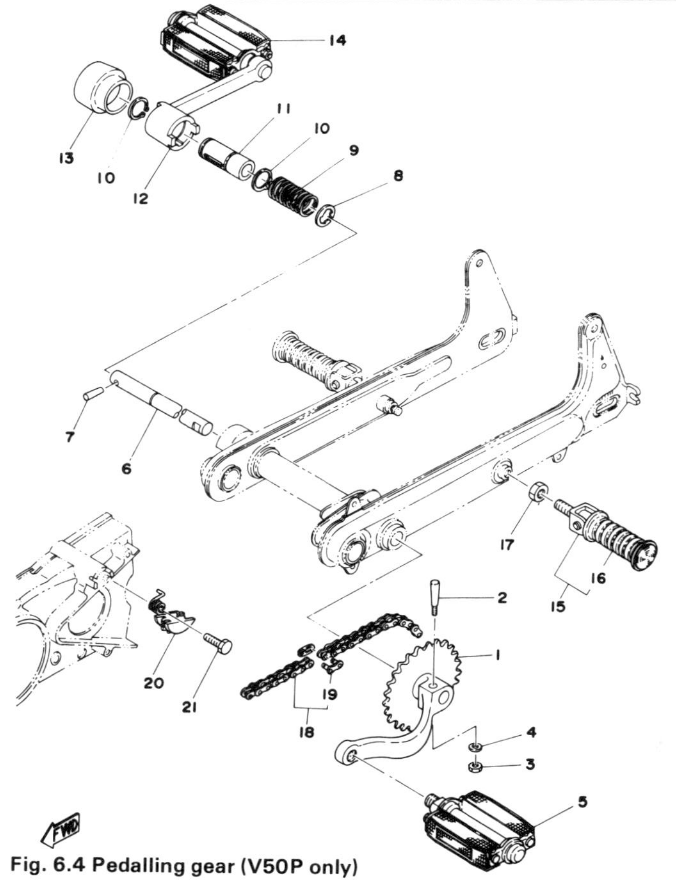

1 Pedal crank assembly
2 Cotter pin
3 Nut
4 Washer
5 LH pedal assembly
6 Pedal spindle
7 Pin
8 Circlip
9 Spring
10 Circlip – 2 off
11 Sleeve
12 RH pedal crank
13 Rubber cover
14 Pedal assembly RH
15 Rear footrest assembly – 2 off
16 Footrest rubber – 2 off
17 Nut – 2 off
18 Chain
19 Spring link
20 Chain tensioner
21 Bolt

Fig. 6.4 Pedalling gear (V50P only)

tube. Dry the tube and clean the area around the puncture with a petrol-soaked rag. When the surface has dried, apply the rubber solution and allow this to dry before removing the backing from the patch and applying the patch to the surface.
7 It is best to use a patch of the self-vulcanising type, which will form a very permanent repair.Note that it may be necessary to remove a protective covering from the top surface of the patch after it has sealed in position. Inner tubes made from synthetic rubber may require a special type of patch and adhesive, if a satisfactory bond is to be achieved.
8 Before replacing the tyre, check the inside to make sure the agent that caused the puncture is not trapped. Check also the outside of the tyre, particularly the tread area, to make sure nothing is trapped that may cause a further puncture.
9 If the inner tube has been patched on a number of past occasions, or if there is a tear or large hole, it is preferable to discard it and fit a replacement. Sudden deflation may cause an accident, particularly if it occurs with the front wheel.
10 To replace the tyre, inflate the inner tube sufficiently for it to assume a circular shape but only just. Then push it into the tyre so that it is enclosed completely. Lay the tyre on the wheel at an angle and insert the valve through the rim tape and the hole in the wheel rim. Attach the locking cap on the first few threads, sufficient to hold the valve captive in its correct location.
11 Starting at the point furthest from the valve, push the tyre bead over the edge of the wheel rim until it is located in the central well. Continue to work around the tyre in this fashion until the whole of one side of the tyre is on the rim. It may be necessary to use a tyre lever during the final stages.
12 Make sure there is no pull on the tyre valve and again commencing with the area furthest from the valve, ease the other bead of the tyre over the edge of the rim. Finish with the area close to the valve, pushing the valve up into the tyre until the locking cap touches the rim. This will ensure the inner tube is not trapped when the last section of the bead is edged over the rim with a tyre lever.
13 Check that the inner tube is not trapped at any point. Reinflate the inner tube, and check that the tyre is seating correctly around the wheel rim. There should be a thin rib moulded around the wall of the tyre on both sides, which should be equidistant from the wheel rim at all points. If the tyre is unevenly located on the rim, try bouncing the wheel when the tyre is at the recommended pressure. It is probable that one of the beads has not pulled clear of the centre well.
14 Always run the tyres at the recommended pressures and never under or over-inflate. The correct pressures for solo use are given in the Specifications Section of this Chapter. If a pillion passenger is carried, increase the rear tyre pressure only.
15 Tyre replacement is aided by dusting the side walls, particularly in the vicinity of the beads, with a liberal coating of French chalk. Washing-up liquid can also be used to good effect, but this has the disadvantage of causing the inner surfaces of the wheel rim to rust.
16 Never replace the inner tube and tyre without the rim tape in position. If this precaution is overlooked there is a good chance of the ends of the spoke nipples chafing the inner tube and causing a crop of punctures.
17 Never fit a tyre that has a damaged tread or side walls. Apart from the legal aspects, there is a very great risk of a blowout, which can have serious consequences on any two wheel vehicle.
18 Tyre valves rarely give trouble, but it is always advisable to check whether the valve itself is leaking before removing the tyre. Do not forget to fit the dust cap, which forms an effective second seal.

20 Fault diagnosis: wheels, brakes and tyres

Symptom	Cause	Remedy
Handlebars oscillate at low speeds	Buckle or flat in wheel rim, most probably front wheel	Check rim alignment by spinning wheel. Correct by retensioning spokes or by having wheel rebuilt on new rim.
	Tyre not straight on rim	Check tyre alignment.
Machine lacks power and accelerates poorly	Brakes binding	Warm brake drums provide best evidence. Re-adjust brakes.
Brakes grab when applied gently	Ends of brake shoes not chamfered Elliptical brake drum	Chamfer with file. Lightly skim in lathe (specialist attention) needed).
Brake pull-off sluggish	Brake cam binding in housing Weak brake shoe springs	Free and grease. Renew if springs not displaced.
Harsh transmission	Worn or badly adjusted chain Hooked or badly worn sprockets	Adjust or renew as necessary. Renew as a pair.
Tyres wear more rapidly in middle of tread	Over inflation	Check pressures and run at recommended settings.
Tyres wear rapidly at outer edges of tread	Under inflation	Ditto.

Chapter 7 Electrical system

For modifications, and information relating to later models, see Chapter 8

Contents

Specifications

	V50, 75 and late 90 models	early V90 models
Flywheel generator		
Type	F11–L43	F136–01
Output	6 volts ac	12 volts ac
Silicon rectifier		
Type	DS10 HJ4–8 or CDC–H1/1E	SB4–5
Battery		
Type	6N4–2A–2	AYT2–12
Capacity	6 volts 4 Ah	12 volts 5·5 Ah
Fuse rating	10 amp	10 amp

Bulbs	early V50 and 75	late V50 and 75	early V90	late V90
Voltage	6	6	12	6
Headlamp	15/15W	18/18W	15/15W	25/25W
Tail/stop lamp	3/10W	5/21W	3/10W	5·3/17W
Speedometer lamp	3W	3W	3W	3W
Flashing indicator	8W	8W	8W	8W
Pilot light	5W	5W	5W	5W
Oil level light	3W	3W	3W	—
Neutral indicator	3W	3W	3W	3W

1 General description

The electrical systems vary greatly between the models in this range so care should be taken to ensure that the correct components of the right value are fitted when any replacement is necessary. As there is an overlap in model specifications it is advisable to take the defective item to your dealer for positive identification before purchasing any spares.

The system used on the V50, V75 and some of the later V90 models has a flywheel generator producing 6 volt alternating current, which is rectified to charge the battery or delivered directly to the lighting system through the mainswitch.

The early V90 models use a flywheel generator to produce 12 volt alternating current, which is rectified to charge the battery, which then supplies the electrical system.

2 Flywheel generator: checking the output

1 As explained in Chapter 4, the output can be checked only with specialist test equipment of the multi-meter type. If the generator is suspect, it should be checked by either a Yamaha agent or an auto-electrical expert.

3 Battery: examination and maintenance

1 Maintenance is normally limited to keeping the electrolyte level just above the plates and separators. Modern batteries have translucent plastic cases, which makes the check of electrolyte level much easier.
2 Unless acid is split, which may occur if the machine falls over, the electrolyte should always be topped up with distilled water until the correct level is restored. If acid is split on any part of the machine, it should be neutralised with an alkali such as washing soda and washed away with plenty of water, otherwise serious corrosion will occur. Top up with sulphuric acid of the correct specific gravity (1.260 to 1.280) ONLY when spillage has occurred.
3 It is seldom practicable to repair a cracked battery case because the acid already in the joint will prevent the formation of an effective seal. It is always best to replace a cracked battery, especially in view of the corrosion that will be caused by the leakage of acid.

4 Battery:charging procedure

1 Whilst the machine is running, it is unlikely that the battery will require attention other than routine maintenance because the generator will keep it charged. However, if the machine is used for a succession of short journeys only, it is possible that the output from the generator will not be able to keep pace with the heavy electrical demand. Under these circumstances it will be necessary to remove the battery from time to time to have it charged independently.
2 The normal charging rate is 1 amp. A more rapid charge can be given in an emergency, but this should be avoided if possible because it will shorten the working life of the battery.
3 When the battery has been removed from a machine that has been laid up, a 'refresher' charge should be given every six weeks if the battery is to be maintained in good condition.

5 Silicon rectifier: general description

1 The function of the silicon rectifier is to convert the ac produced by the generator to dc so that it can be used to charge the battery and operate the lighting circuit etc. The usual symptom of a defective rectifier is a battery which discharges rapidly because it is receiving no charge from the generator.
2 The rectifier is located behind the left hand side cover next to the battery. The rectifier is unlikely to give trouble during normal operating conditions. It is not practicable to repair a damaged rectifier; replacement is the only satisfactory solution. One of the most frequent causes of rectifier failure is the inadvertent connection of the battery in reverse.
3 Damage to the rectifier is also liable to occur if the machine is run without a battery for any period of time. A high voltage will develop in the absence of any load on the coil which will cause a reverse flow of current and consequent damage to the rectifier cells.
4 It is not possible to check whether the rectifier is functioning correctly without the appropriate test equipment. A Yamaha agent or an auto-electrical expert is best qualified to advise in such cases.
5 Do not loosen the rectifier locking nut or bend, cut, scratch or rotate the wafer. Any such action will cause the electrode alloy coating to peel and destroy the working action.

6 Headlamp: replacing bulbs and adjusting beam height

1 To remove the headlamp rim, unscrew the screw at the right-hand side of the lower handlebar cover. The rim will then pull off, complete with the reflector unit and bulbs.

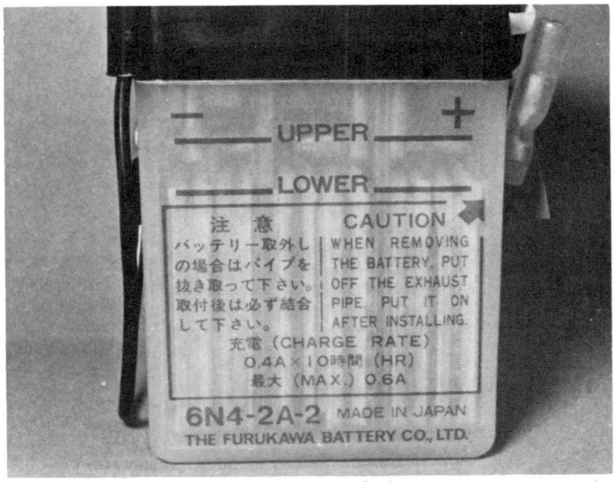

3.1 The acid level can be seen through the case

2 The reflector unit contains a double-filament bulb which provides the main and dipped headlamp beams. It is controlled from a dipswitch mounted on the handlebars.
3 It is not necessary to refocus the headlamp when a new bulb is fitted because the bulbs are of the prefocus type. To release the bulb holder from the reflector, twist and pull.
4 Beam height is adjusted by turning the small screw at the bottom of the headlamp rim. Adjustments should always be made with the rider normally seated.
5 UK lighting regulations stipulate that the lighting system must be arranged so that the light will not dazzle a person standing in the same horizontal plane as the vehicle at a distance greater than 25 feet from the lamp, whose eye level is not less than 3 feet 6 inches above that plane. It is easy to approximate this setting by placing the machine 25 feet away from a wall, on a level road, and setting the beam height so that it is concentrated at the same height as the distance from the centre of the headlamp to the ground. The rider must be seated normally during this operation and also the pillion passenger, if one is carried regularly.

7 Tail/stop lamp: replacing bulb

1 The moulded plastic cover of the rear lamp is retained by two screws. When these screws are removed, the cover can be removed and the bulb exposed.
2 To release the bulb from its holder, press it inwards, turn to the left and pull out. Press in the new bulb, turn to the right and pull downwards so that the stops locate. Refit the cover, making sure that the rubber moulding which surrounds the cover is located correctly to exclude water.
3 Make sure that the flexible contact makes a good connection with the bottom contact of the bulb, otherwise the bulb may work only intermittently and eventually 'blow'.

8 Speedometer bulbs: replacement

1 To replace the speedometer bulb or the neutral indicator bulb the headlamp reflector must first be removed.
2 The bulb holders are a push fit in the speedometer head. After the holder is pulled clear the bulbs can be replaced in the same manner as the tail light bulb. The holders are then pushed back into the speedometer head, and the reflector unit replaced.

5.2 The rectifier is located under the left-hand side panel

6.1 Remove the headlamp retaining screw

6.3a Twist and pull to remove the bulb holder ...

6.3b ... and lift the bulb out of the reflector

7.1 Remove two screws to release the lens cover

9 Flasher bulbs: replacement

1 The moulded plastic cover of the flasher lamp is retained by two screws. When these screws are removed, the cover can be removed and the bulb exposed.

2 To release the bulb from its holder, press it inwards, turn to the left and pull out. Press in the new bulb, turn to the right and pull downwards so that the stops locate. Refit the cover making sure the rubber moulding that surrounds the cover is located correctly to exclude water.

10 Pilot light bulb: replacement

1 To replace the pilot light bulb the front panel retained with one screw must be removed. This will expose the screw that retains the plastic lens. Remove this screw and the lens to gain access to the bulb.

2 To release the bulb, press it in, turn to the left and pull it out.

3 Reassembly is the reverse of the dismantling procedure but ensures that the rubber surround is fitted correctly to exclude water.

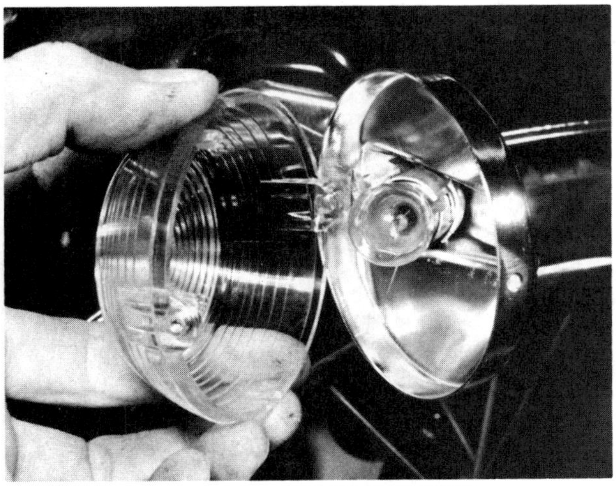
9.1 Remove two screws to release the lens cover

10.1 Remove a screw to release the lens cover

11 Oil level inspection light: replacing bulb

1 The oil level inspection light is similar to the speedometer light in that its holder is a push fit into the oil tank retaining plate under the dualseat.
2 Pull the holder out of the plate, remove the bulb by pressing it in, rotating it to the left and pulling it out.
3 Reassembly is the reverse of the dismantling procedure.

12 Resistance unit: general description

1 A resistance unit is mounted alongside the air cleaner. Its function is to protect the pilot and tail light bulbs from a surge of power when the engine is started, with the parking lights on.
2 To remove the resistance unit, the legshield assembly must first be detached, the wires disconnected at the snap connectors and the mounting nut and bolt removed.
3 A simple continuity test and a short circuit test are the only checks that can be applied, usually with a bulb and a battery.

13 Flasher unit: location and replacement

1 On the early models, the flasher unit is located behind the front panel with its single screw fixing. It is mounted on its own plate.
2 On the later models the unit is located under the right-hand plastic side cover retained by a single screw.
3 A series of audible clicks will be heard if the flasher unit is functioning correctly. If the unit malfunctions, the usual symptom is one initial flash before the unit goes dead. It will be necessary to replace the flasher unit complete if the fault cannot be attributed to either a burnt out indicator bulb or a blown fuse. Take care in handling the unit because it is easily damaged, if dropped.

14 Horn: location and adjustment

1 The horn is mounted on a bracket attached to the frame, behind the steering head and above the air cleaner box.
2 There is means of adjusting the horn note at the rear of the horn body. If the horn note is weak, the adjusting screw should be turned anti-clockwise to increase the volume.

15 Fuse: location and replacement

1 A fuse is incorporated in the electrical system to give protection from a sudden overload, such as may occur during a short circuit. The fuse is located within the fuse holder attached to the positive lead of the battery.
2 If a fuse blows it should be replaced, after checking to ensure that no obvious short circuit has occurred. If the second fuse blows shortly afterwards, the electrical circuit should be checked in order to trace the fault.
3 When a fuse blows whilst running the machine and no spare is available, a 'get you home' dodge is to remove the blown fuse and wrap it in silver paper before replacing it in the fuse holder. The silver paper will restore the electrical continuity by bridging the broken fuse wire. This expedient should never be used if there is evidence of a short circuit, otherwise more serious damage will be caused. Replace the blown fuse at the earliest possible opportunity, to restore the full circuit protection.

12.2 The resistance unit is mounted behind the steering head

13.2 On later models the flasher unit is mounted under the right-hand plastic cover

14.1 The horn is mounted above the air cleaner box

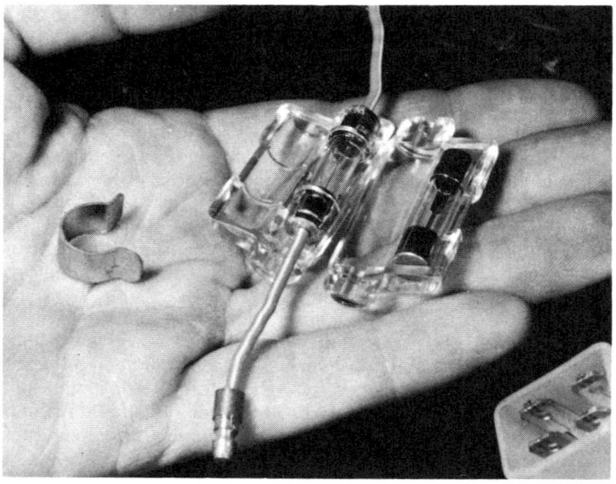

15.1 The fuse holder halves are secured by spring clip

16 Ignition and lighting switch: general description

1 The same key operated switch is used for ignition and lighting. This switch is not repairable and if found faulty must be replaced.
2 New keys are not available so if both keys are lost a new switch must be fitted.
3 On no account oil the switch or the oil will spread across the internal contacts and form an effective insulator.

17 Lighting switch and indicator switch: general description

1 The switches are mounted on the handlebars and are not repairable. If any are faulty or damaged they must be renewed as a complete unit.
2 On no account oil the switches or the oil will spread across the internal contacts and form an effective insulator.

18 Stop lamp switch: location and adjustment

1 The stop lamp switch is located in the swinging arm cross-member except in the case of the V50P where the cross-member carries the pedalling gear. On the V50P the switch is mounted on a small bracket attached by one of the engine mounting bolts.
2 The switch should operate when the rear brake pedal is depressed.
3 If the switch is late in operating it should be adjusted. The V50P model switch has a threaded body and adjustment of the locknuts will ensure that the switch operates at the correct time. On the other models judicious bending of the operating lever will again ensure that the switch operates at the correct time.

19 Wiring: layout and inspection

1 The wiring harness is colour-coded and will correspond with the accompanying wiring diagrams.
2 Visual inspection will show whether any breaks or frayed outer coverings are giving rise to short circuits. Another source of trouble may be the snap connectors, particularly where the connector has not been pushed home fully in the outer casing.
3 Intermittent short circuits can often be traced to a chafed wire which passes through or close to a metal component, such as a frame member. Avoid tight bends in the wire or situations where the wire can become trapped or stretched between casings.

17.1a The indicator switch and ...

17.1b ... the dipswitch must be renewed if faulty

18.1 The stop light switch is mounted in the swinging arm cross-member

20 Fault diagnosis: electrical system

Symptom	Cause	Remedy
Complete electrical failure	Blown fuse	Locate fault and renew fuse.
	Broken wire from generator	Reconnect.
	Lighting switch faulty	Renew switch.
	Generator not charging	Check output.
Dim lights	Bad connections	Renovate, paying particular attention to earth connections.
Constantly 'blowing' bulbs	Vibration	Check bulb holders are secure.
	Poor earth connections	Renovate.
Indicators not working	Flat battery	Recharge battery and check generator output.
	Blown fuse	Check wiring before renewing fuse.
	Isolated battery	Check battery connections. Clean any corrosion.
	Indicator switch faulty	Renew switch.
Battery not charging	Damaged rectifier	Renew.

Left-hand view of the V80 MDL model

Engine/transmission unit of the V80 MDL model

Chapter 8 The 1979 to 1986 models

Contents

Specifications

The Specifications shown below relate to the V50 and V80 models covered by this update Chapter. The specifications are given according to the model codes. These can be summarized as follows:

Model	Year	Code
V50 MA	1979-83	2J6
V50 MDL	1983-86	19M
V80	1979-83	3K3
V80 MDL	1983-86	19N

Specifications relating to Chapters 1 and 2

Engine

Type	Air-cooled reed valve two-stroke
Bore:	
2J6, 19M	40.0 mm (1.575 in)
3K3, 19N	47.0 mm (1.850 in)
Stroke:	
2J6, 19M	39.7 mm (1.563 in)
3K3, 19N	45.6 mm (1.795 in)
Capacity:	
2J6, 19M	49 cc (2.99 cu in)
3K3, 19N	79 cc (4.82 cu in)
Compression ratio:	
2J6, 3K3	6.6 : 1
19M	5.7 : 1
19N	6.9 : 1

Cylinder barrel

Type	Cast iron
Bore size:	
2J6, 19M	40.00 – 40.02 mm (1.5750 – 1.5758 in)
3K3, 19N	47.00 – 47.02 mm (1.8500 – 1.8508 in)
Maximum taper:	
2J6, 3K3	0.05 mm (0.002 in)
19M, 19N	0.004 mm (0.0002 in)
Maximum ovality:	
2J6, 3K3	0.01 mm (0.0004 in)
19M, 19N	0.0025 mm (0.0001 in)

Piston

Piston to bore clearance:	
2J6	0.025 – 0.030 mm (0.0010 – 0.0012 in)
3K3	0.035 – 0.040 mm (0.0014 – 0.0016 in)
19M	0.028 – 0.036 mm (0.0011 – 0.0014 in)
19N	0.032 – 0.040 mm (0.0013 – 0.0016 in)
Piston oversizes:	
2J6, 3K3	+0.25, +0.50, +0.75, +1.00 mm (+0.010, +0.020, +0.030, +0.040 in)
19M, 19N	+0.25, +0.50 mm (+0.010, +0.020 in)

Piston rings

Type (Top & 2nd)	Keystone
Ring end gap (Top & 2nd, Installed)	0.15 – 0.35 mm (0.006 – 0.014 in)
Ring to groove clearance (Top & 2nd):	
2J6, 3K3	0.03 – 0.05 mm (0.001 – 0.002 in)
19M, 19N	Not available

Crankshaft

Big-end bearing	Needle roller
Small-end bearing	Needle roller
Crankshaft width (across flywheel outer faces):	
2J6, 19M	37.90 – 37.95 mm (1.496 – 1.498 in)
3K3, 19N	47.90 – 47.95 mm (1.886 – 1.888 in)
Crankshaft runout (maximum)	0.03 mm (0.0012 in)
Big-end side clearance:	
2J6, 19M	0.2 – 0.5 mm (0.008 – 0.020 in)
3K3, 19N	0.3 – 0.8 mm (0.012 – 0.030 in)
Connecting rod deflection (measured at small-end):	
2J6, 3K3	2.0 mm (0.08 in)
19M, 19N	Not available

Clutch – V50 models

Type	Automatic centrifugal
Lining thickness	2.5 mm (0.10 in)
Service limit (2J6)	Not available
Service limit (19M)	2.0 mm (0.08 in)
Return spring tension:	
2J6	7.4 – 8.6 kg @ 248 mm (16.3 – 19.0 lbs @ 9.76 in)
19M	Not available
Return spring free length:	
2J6	Not available
19M	181 mm (7.13 in)
Clutch commences engagement at:	
2J6	2150 – 2450 rpm
19M	2400 rpm
Clutch fully engaged at:	
2J6	2700 – 3200 rpm
19M	3000 rpm
Primary drive backlash tolerances (2J6):	
1st	131 – 133
2nd	60 – 62

Clutch – V80 models

Type	Wet multiplate, centrifugal
Primary drive type	Gear
Primary reduction ratio	3.143 : 1 (66/21)
Primary drive backlash tolerance:	
3K3	143 ± 1
19N	Not available
Friction plate thickness	3.0 mm (0.118 in)
Service limit:	
3K3	2.7 mm (0.106 in)
19N	2.5 mm (0.098 in)
Plain plate thickness	1.2 – 1.6 mm (0.047 – 0.063 in)
Service limit (3K3)	0.06 mm (0.002 in)
Warpage limit (19N)	0.4 mm (0.02 in)
Clutch spring free length	12.9 mm (0.508 in)
Pull-off spring free length:	
3K3	29.9 mm (1.177 in)
19N	Not available

Transmission

Type:		
2J6, 19M	2-speed constant mesh, automatic	
3K3, 19N	3-speed constant mesh, manual	
Reduction ratios	**2J6, 19M**	**3K3, 19N**
1st	3.833 : 1 (69/18)	3.250 : 1 (39/12)
2nd	2.109 : 1 (59/28)	1.813 : 1 (29/16)
3rd	Not applicable	1.200 : 1 (24/20)
Secondary reduction method	Chain	
Secondary reduction ratio:		
2J6, 19M	3.077 : 1 (40/13)	
3K3, 19N	2.923 : 1 (38/13)	
Sub-transmission gear ratios (2J6, 19M):		
Low	3.250 : 1 (39/12)	
High	2.188 : 1 (35/16)	

Torque wrench settings

Component	kgf m	lbf ft
Cylinder head nuts	1.0	7.0
Spark plug:		
2J6, 3K3	2.0	14.0
19M, 19N	2.5	18.0
Primary drive gear:		
2J6, 3K3	4.0	29.0
19M, 19N	5.0	36.0
Clutch boss:		
2J6, 3K3	4.0	29.0
19M, 19N	5.0	36.0
Kickstart lever:		
2J6, 3K3	1.0	7.0
19M, 19N	1.2	8.7
Crankcase oil seal stopper:		
2J6, 3K3	Not available	
19M, 19N	1.6	11.0
Input shaft bearing stopper:		
2J6, 3K3	Not available	
19M, 19N	0.8	5.8 (Use Loctite)
Selector drum stopper:		
2J6, 3K3	Not available	
19M, 19N	0.8	5.8 (Use Loctite)
Selector drum stopper lever:		
2J6, 3K3	Not available	
19M, 19N	1.4	10.0 (Use Loctite)
Gearchange pedal:		
2J6, 3K3	Not available	
19M, 19N	1.5	11.0
Transmission drain plug:		
2J6, 3K3	Not available	
19M, 19N	2.0	14.0
Carburettor mounting:		
2J6, 3K3	Not available	
19M, 19N	0.6	4.3
Neutral switch:		
2J6, 3K3	Not available	
19M, 19N	0.4	2.9

Specifications relating to Chapter 3

Capacities

Fuel tank	5.3 litres (1.68 Imp gallons)
Reserve capacity	0.7 litre (0.15 Imp gallon)
Oil tank	1.2 litres (2.2 Imp pints)
Transmission:	
Dry	700 cc (1.24 Imp pints)
Oil change	650 cc (1.14 Imp pints)

Carburettor

	2J6	19M	3K3	19N
Make	Mikuni	Mikuni	Mikuni	Mikuni
Type	VM14SC	VM14SC	VM15SC	VM15SC
ID mark	3E400	19M00	3E500	18E00
Main jet	80	75	110	80
Air jet	2.5	2.5	2.5	2.5
Jet needle	3F11	3T10	3E3	3X8

Clip position	4th	3rd	3rd	4th
Needle jet	E-2	E-8	E-4	D-8
Cutaway	2.5	3.0	2.5	2.5
Pilot jet	15	15	15	15
Pilot air jet	N/app	1.7	N/app	1.3
Air screw (turns out)	1 1/4	N/app	1 1/2	N/app
Starter jet	50	35	30	35
Float level:				
2J6, 3K3	22.5 ± 2.5 mm (0.89 ± 0.100 in)			
19M, 19N	22.0 ± 1.0 mm (0.87 ± 0.040 in)			
Idle speed:				
2J6, 3K3	1250 – 1450 rpm			
19M, 19N	1500 rpm			

Oil pump

Pump colour code:	
2J6	White
3K3, 19M, 19N	Brown
Minimum stroke:	
2J6, 19M	0.25 – 0.30 mm (0.010 – 0.012 in)
3K3, 19N	0.40 – 0.45 mm (0.016 – 0.018 in)
Maximum stroke:	
2J6, 3K3	Not available
19M	0.60 – 0.70 mm (0.024 – 0.028 in)
19N	1.00 – 1.10 mm (0.039 – 0.043 in)
Min. output per 200 strokes:	
2J6, 3K3	Not available
19M	0.53 ± 0.05 cc (0.019 ± 0.002 oz)
19N	0.82 ± 0.05 cc (0.029 ± 0.002 oz)
Max. output per 200 strokes:	
2J6, 3K3	Not available
19M	1.25 ± 0.10 cc (0.044 ± 0.004 oz)
19N	2.02 ± 0.10 cc (0.071 ± 0.004 oz)

Specifications relating to Chapter 4

Ignition system

Type	CDI (capacitor discharge ignition)
Flywheel generator:	
Make	Yamaha
Type:	
2J6	F3E4
3K3	F3E5
19M, 19N	F4F8
Voltage	6 volt
Charge coil resistance:	
2J6, 3K3	295 ohms ± 10% (black lead to red lead)
19M, 19N	330 ohms ± 10% (black/red lead to black lead)
Pulser coil resistance	20 ohms ± 10% (white/red lead to black lead)

Ignition timing

Static setting (piston position BTDC):	
2J6, 3K3	1.8 ± 0.15 mm (0.071 ± 0.006 in)
19M, 19N	Not available
Ignition timing:	
2J6, 3K3	Not available
19M, 19N	22° BTDC at 5000 rpm

Ignition coil

Make	Yamaha
Model	C2T4
Minimum spark gap	7 mm (0.28 in)
Primary winding resistance	1.6 ohms ± 10% at 20°C (68°F)
Secondary winding resistance	6.6 K ohms ± 10% at 20°C (68°F)

CDI unit

Make	Yamaha
Model:	
2J6, 3K3	2E9
19M, 19N	5G3

Spark plug

Make	**NGK**	**ND**
Type:		
2J6, 3K3	B6HS	N/app
19M	BR6ES	W20ESR-U
19N	BPR6HS	W20FPR-U
Gap:		
2J6, 3K3	0.5 – 0.6 mm (0.020 – 0.024 in)	
19M, 19N	0.6 – 0.7 mm (0.024 – 0.028 in)	

Specifications relating to Chapter 5

Frame

Type	Pressed steel spine

Front suspension

Type	Leading link fork

Steering

Caster angle:	
2J6, 3K3	27° from vertical (67° from horizontal)
19M, 19N	Not available
Trail:	
2J6, 3K3	80 mm (3.15 in)
19M, 19N	Not available
Steering head bearings:	
Size of balls	3/16 in
No. of balls	22 per race
Steering lock angle:	
2J6, 3K3	94°
19M, 19N	Not available

Rear suspension

Type	Pressed steel swinging arm, coil spring suspension units
Maximum swinging arm play	1.0 mm (0.04 in)

Torque wrench settings

	2J6 and 3K3		19M and 19N	
Component	**kgf m**	**lbf ft**	**kgf m**	**lbf ft**
Swinging arm pivot shaft	4.0	29.0	5.6	40.0
Suspension unit mountings:				
Upper	3.0	22.0	3.0	22.0
Lower	5.5	40.0	5.6	40.0
Handlebar/bracket bolts	1.5	11.0	1.6	11.0
Front wheel spindle nut	4.0	29.0	4.0	29.0
Rear wheel spindle nut	6.0	43.0	6.0	43.0
Rear wheel sprocket stub axle nut	8.0	58.0	8.0	58.0
Rear brake torque arm:				
Front	1.5	11.0	1.6	11.0
Rear	2.5	18.0	2.6	19.0

Specifications relating to Chapter 6

Wheels

Type	Chromium plated steel rims, wire spokes
Diameter	17 in front and rear
Section:	
2J6 and 3K3	1.20 (1.40 3K3 rear)
19M and 19N	1.40
Maximum runout (front and rear):	
Vertical	2.0 mm (0.08 in)
Lateral	2.0 mm (0.08 in)

Tyres

Sizes:	
2J6, front and rear	2.25-17-4PR
3K3	front: 2.25-17-4PR rear: 2.50-17-4PR
19M, 19N front and rear	2.50-17-4PR
Pressures:	
Front	1.5 kg cm^2 (22 psi)
Rear	2.0 kg cm^2 (28 psi)

Brakes

Type (front and rear)	Internal expanding drum brake, single leading shoe (sls) type
Drum diameter (front and rear)	110 mm (4.33 in)
Shoe diameter and width	110 x 25 mm (4.33 x 0.98 in)
Lining thickness:	
Nominal	4.0 mm (0.16 in)
Service limit	2.0 mm (0.08 in)

Sprocket sizes

Engine	13 teeth
Rear wheel:	
V50	40 teeth
V80	38 teeth

Final drive chain

Type:	
2J6, 3K3	DK420
19M, 19N	Not available
Number of links:	
2J6, 3K3	98 plus joining link
19M, 19N	100
Chain free play	20 mm (0.8 in)

Specifications relating to Chapter 7

Flywheel generator

Make	Yamaha
Type:	
2J6, 3K3	2E9
19M, 19N	F4F8
Charging commences at (2J6 and 3K3):	
Day	2500 rpm
Night	3000 rpm
Charging output (2J6 and 3K3):	
Day	3.0 – 4.5 amp @ 8000 rpm
Night	1.0 amp @ 8000 rpm
Charging current (19M and 19N):	
Day/night	0.8 amp or more @ 3000 rpm 2.0 amp or less @ 8000 rpm
Charge coil resistance (2J6 and 3K3):	
Day	0.9 ohms ± 10%
Night	1.5 ohms ± 10%
Charge coil resistance:	
19M and 19N	0.31 ohms ± 20%
Lighting coil output (2J6 and 3K3):	
Day	5.3 volts or more @ 2500 rpm
Night	8.0 volts or less @ 8000 rpm
Lighting coil output:	
19M and 19N	6.2 volts or more @ 3000 rpm 8.0 volts or more @ 8000 rpm
Lighting coil resistance:	
2J6, 3K3	1.3 ohms ± 10%
19M, 19N	Not available

Rectifier

Make	Stanley	Matsushita
Model:		
2J6, 3K3	DE4505	N/App
19M, 19N	SU229	EHU-01TR02
Type	Silicon	Silicon
Capacity	4 amps	4 amps
Withstand voltage	400 volt	120 volt

Battery

Make	GS, FB or YB
Type	6N4-2A-2
Capacity	6 volt 4 AH
Charge rate	0.4 A for 10 hours
Electrolyte specific gravity	1.260

	2J6	3K3	19M	19N
Bulb wattages (all 6 volt)				
Headlamp	25/25	25/25	25/25	25/25
Stop/tail	5.3/17	5.3/17	5/21	5/21
Turn signal lamp	10	15	10	15
Instrument panel lamp	3	3	3	3
Parking lamp	3	3	3	3
Neutral lamp	N/app	3	N/app	3

Horn

Type	MF-6 or GF-6
Maximum amperage	1.5 amp

Turn signal relay

Type	Hot wire
Model	FR-9T10, FR-9T20 or FR-9T30
Frequency	90 cpm

Fuse

Rating	10 amp

1 Introduction

The preceding Chapters of this manual cover the Yamaha V50, V75 and V90 models produced between 1971 and 1979. To aid model identification a summary of the various models covered during that period is given below. Note that the model suffix shown in brackets is a code which allows more precise identification than is possible from the model and year alone, and this should be quoted when ordering spare parts, along with the engine and frame numbers.

Models covered in preceding Chapters

Model	Code	Introduced	Discontinued
V50	(544)	August 1971	June 1976
V50 P	(1E9)	January 1976	July 1977
V50 MA	(3K6)	January 1977	During 1979
V75	(545)	June 1975	July 1975
V75 A	(595)	August 1975	January 1979
V90	(546)	November 1971	January 1979

In 1979 the V50 MA (3K6) model was dropped in favour of a revised automatic transmission model, the V50 MA (2J6). This model featured CDI ignition, a self-adjusting oil pump cable mechanism and a restyled headlamp nacelle and instrument panel. In most other respects it was similar to the machine it replaced. The V50 MA (2J6) was itself replaced in April 1983 by the V50 MDL (19M). This model retained the improvements of its predecessor, with the addition of a fuel gauge mounted in the instrument panel face and an oil warning lamp. Production continues at the time of writing.

The V75 and V90 models were both discontinued in January 1979 (though dealers' stocks may well have been sold and registered some months after this date). The two models were replaced in May 1979 by a new model, the V80 (3K3). This was generally similar to the V90 (546) model which it superseded, though with a number of detail changes to the engine and transmission components. Like the V50 MA (2J6) model, the new V80 featured CDI ignition, a self-adjusting oil pump cable mechanism and styling changes to the headlamp nacelle and instrument panel. In April 1983 the V80 (3K3) model was replaced by the V80 MDL (19N) model. This embodied similar modifications to the V50 MDL (19M) model which appeared at the same time, namely the introduction of the fuel gauge and oil warning lamp. This model remains in production at the time of writing.

In the interests of clarity, a summary of the models produced between 1979 and 1986 and covered in this update Chapter is shown below.

Models covered in this Chapter

Model	Code	Introduced	Discontinued
V50 MA	(2J6)	During 1979	April 1983
V50 MDL	(19M)	April 1983	During 1986
V80	(3K3)	May 1979	April 1983
V80 MDL	(19N)	April 1983	During 1986

2 Engine modifications: general description

V50 MA (2J6) and MDL (19M) models

1 In most respects, the above models resemble closely the V50 MA (3K6), and for all practical purposes the text covering the late automatic models in Chapter 1 can be followed. Note that the pawl carrier (item 12 in Fig. 1.9) has been modified on later machines and is now supplied in two pieces.

V80 (3K3) and V80 MDL (19N) models

2 The V80 engine unit is based on the earlier V90 unit and is generally similar in design. Some of the internal components have been modified or redesigned, and these are described below. The right-hand end of the crankshaft has been altered to accept the splined spacer and primary drive pinion. This arrangement replaces the Woodruff key type fitted to the V90. The clutch has also received minor modifications, and the accompanying line drawing should be compared with Figs 1.5 and 2.2.

3 The V80 gearbox arrangement is generally similar to that of the V90, but there have been a few detail changes. Compare the accompanying line drawing, Fig. 8.2 with Fig. 1.8. A revised gearchange mechanism, shown in Fig. 8.3, dispenses with the earlier three-fork arrangement shown in Fig. 1.2.

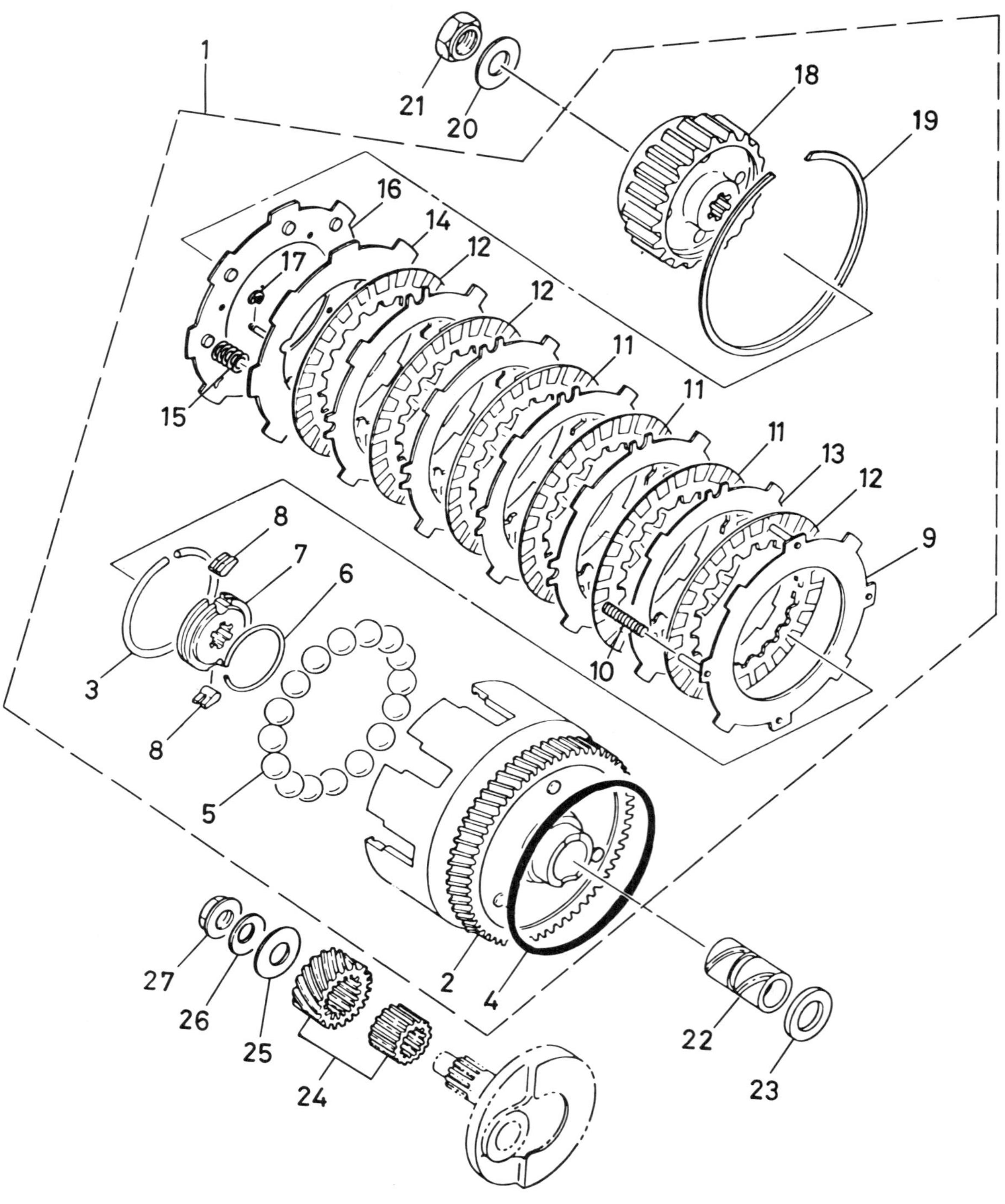

Fig. 8.1 Clutch and primary drive pinion assembly – V80 models

1 Clutch assembly
2 Clutch housing
3 Circlip
4 O-ring
5 Steel ball – 6 off
6 Circlip
7 Boss
8 Pawl – 2 off
9 Plate
10 Spring – 4 off
11 Friction plate – 3 off
12 Friction plate – 3 off
13 Plain plate – 5 off
14 Pressure plate
15 Spring – 8 off
16 Pressure plate
17 Circlip – 4 off
18 Clutch centre
19 Circlip
20 Washer
21 Nut
22 Sleeve
23 Thrust washer
24 Primary drive pinion assembly
25 Washer
26 Special washer
27 Nut

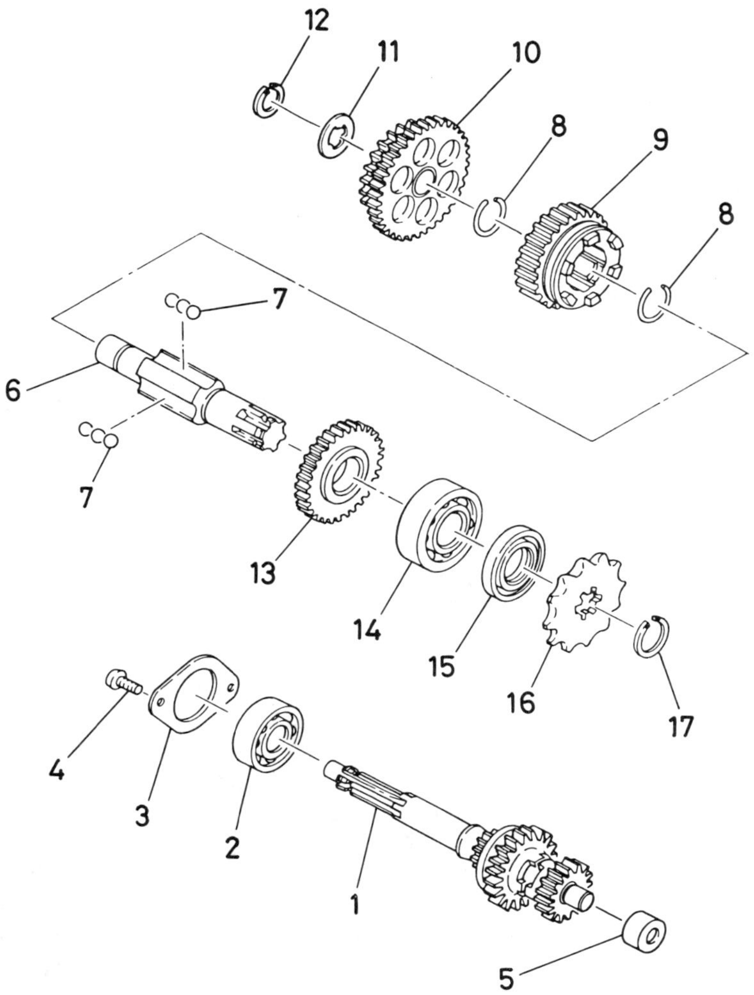

Fig. 8.2 Gearbox components – V80 models

1 Mainshaft assembly
2 Bearing
3 Retaining plate
4 Screw – 2 off
5 Bearing
6 Output shaft
7 Steel ball – 9 off
8 Circlip – 2 off
9 Top gear pinion
10 First gear pinion
11 Washer
12 Circlip
13 Second gear pinion
14 Bearing
15 Oil seal
16 Sprocket
17 Circlip

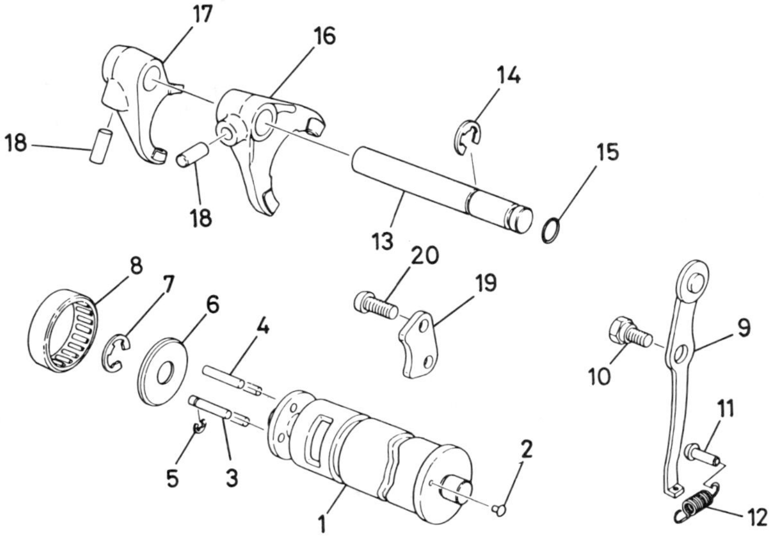

Fig. 8.3 Gear selector mechanism – V80 models

1 Barrel cam
2 Neutral contact
3 Pin
4 Pin – 3 off
5 Circlip
6 Plate
7 Circlip
8 Bearing
9 Positive stop arm
10 Pivot bolt
11 Spring anchor
12 Spring
13 Selector fork shaft
14 Circlip
15 O-ring
16 Selector fork
17 Selector fork
18 Cam follower pin – 2 off
19 Retaining plate
20 Screw – 2 off

3 Self-adjusting throttle/oil pump cable junction box: general description and maintenance

1 All models featured in this Chapter make use of a modified junction box between the throttle and oil pump cables. In the earlier arrangement, a single cable ran from the throttle twistgrip to a sliding block inside the junction box. Attached to the lower end of the sliding block were the throttle lower cable and oil pump cable, the arrangement allowing both functions to be controlled from the throttle twistgrip. Whilst this method works well enough, it is necessary to check the throttle and oil pump cable adjustment regularly to ensure that the correct proportion of oil is delivered to the engine.

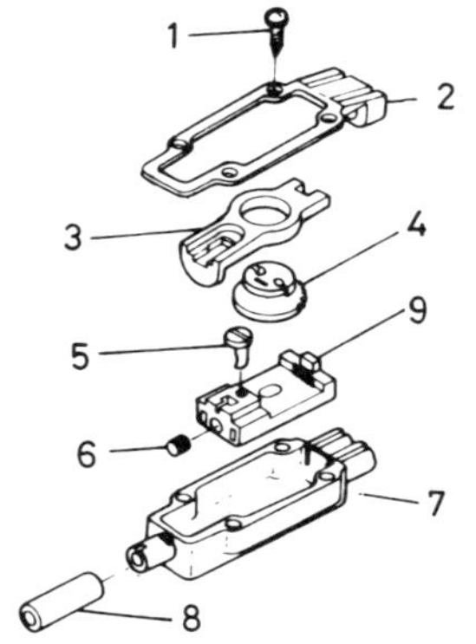

Fig. 8.4 Self-adjusting junction box – component parts

1 Screw – 4 off
2 Cover
3 Rotor guide
4 Rotor
5 Set pin
6 Compression spring
7 Junction box
8 Dust seal
9 Slider

2 The revised junction box described here eliminates the need for regular checking and adjustment and ensures that the oil pump adjustment is maintained at all times. The new junction box comprises an outer casing, or cylinder, in which is carried a slider. The throttle upper cable attaches to the end of the slider, moving it up the cylinder as the throttle twistgrip is opened. Set into the slider is a circular rotor with slots for the throttle lower cable and oil pump cable at opposite sides of its outer edge. The rotor is able to turn in the slider, and it is this movement which provides the self-adjusting capability.
3 The operation of the junction box mechanism is shown in Fig. 8.5. In A the throttle twistgrip is at rest, and it will be noted that there is excessive free play in one of the lower cables (1). As the twistgrip is turned, the initial movement of the upper cable causes the rotor to turn in the slider until the free play has been taken up as shown in B. In stage C, further movement of the throttle twistgrip brings the lock piece (3) into contact with the serrated edge of the rotor, locking it in place and thus ensuring equal movement of both lower cables.
4 In practice, the mechanism should require no attention unless there is reason to suspect that it has jammed or if one of the cables requires attention or renewal. The junction box is attached to the left-hand side of the frame and can be reached after the legshields have been detached. Bend back the clip which secures the upper cable to the frame and turn the junction box round to reveal the cover screws. Remove the four screws and lift the cover away to reveal the slider assembly and cables.
5 The upper cable is easily freed by unhooking it from its locating slot. Slide off the dust seal and disengage the cable from the cylinder. To free the two lower cables, turn and remove the set pin. This is the white slotted-head component immediately above the rotor. The rotor guide can now be lifted away, freeing the rotor. Turn the rotor until the first cable can be slid out of its recess, then remove the second cable in a similar fashion. If the cables are to be renewed, they can be fitted at this stage and the remaining junction box components fitted by reversing the removal sequence.
6 If the operation of the unit has been suspect, check that the slider moves freely along the cylinder and that the rotor is free to turn in its recess. If necessary, apply some silicone grease to the moving parts. Reassemble the junction box and cables, not forgetting the small compression spring which fits between the slider and the lip of the rotor guide. Before refitting the cover, pull down each of the lower cables in turn and open the throttle twistgrip. Check that the rotor turns in the slider, indicating that the automatic adjustment is operating normally. Note that the rotor should be locked by the small lock piece at the lower end of the slider and should engage with the serrated edge of the rotor to retain the adjustment until the twistgrip is released. Refit the cover, securing it with its four screws.

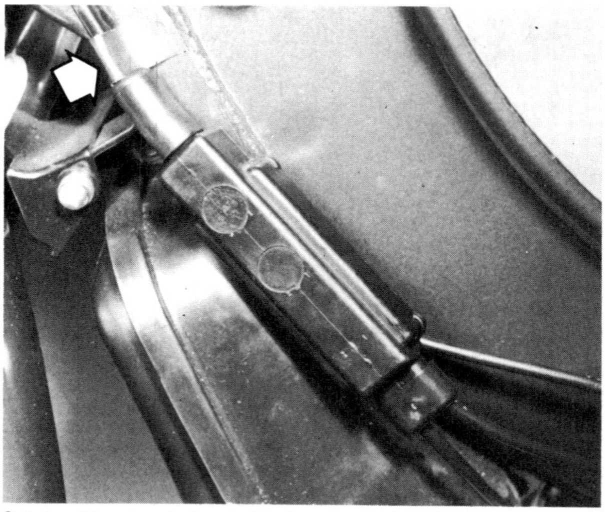

3.4 Junction box is located below legshields. Note cable clip (arrowed)

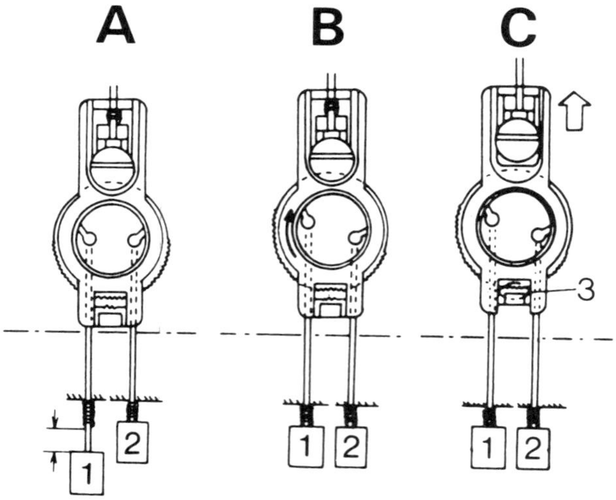

Fig. 8.5 Self-adjusting junction box operation

1 Oil pump cable
2 Throttle cable
3 Lock piece

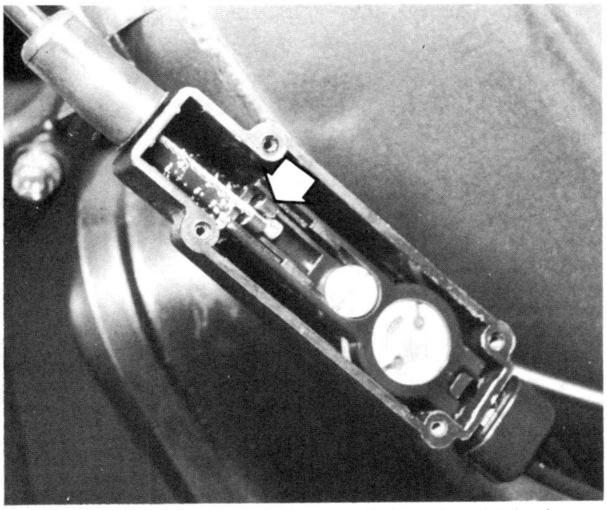

3.5a Unhook the upper cable (arrowed) from the slot in the slider

3.5b Remove the set pin (arrowed) and remove the rotor guide

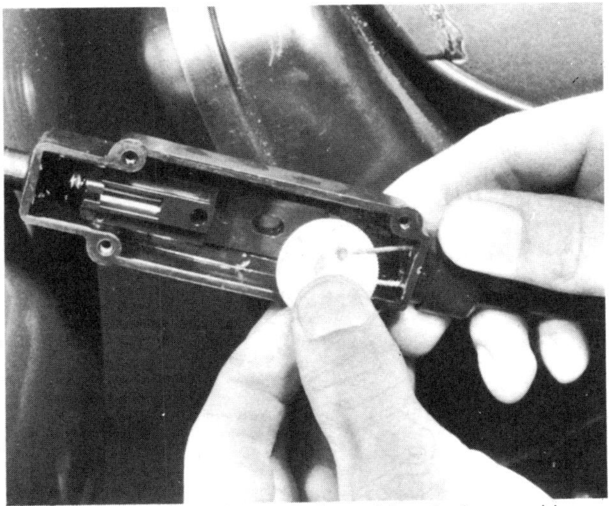

3.5c Lift the rotor out of the cylinder and free the lower cables

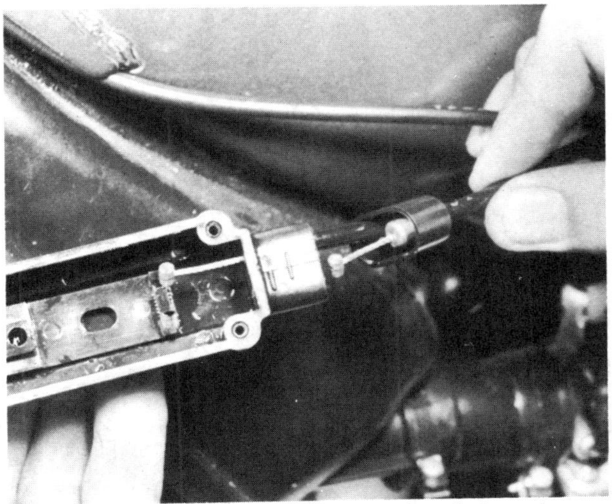

3.5d Disengage cable through centre hole in cylinder end

4 Carburettor modifications: general description

1 With the exception of changes in the jet sizes according to the various models (see Specifications) the carburettor arrangement has remained largely unchanged. The only exception is the omission of the pilot air screw (slow running screw) on the V80 model from 1983 onwards. This means that routine adjustment is confined to regulating the idle speed only.

5 Reed valve assembly and intake system: general description

1 As was the case on the previous models, the V50 and V80 models covered in this supplement employ reed valves to control more precisely the induction timing. In the V80 machines, the reed valve is of the three-petal type, rather than the two-petal version used on the smaller machines. The valves are entirely automatic in operation and require no regular maintenance. If they are to be removed for any reason, take great care not to damage the fragile reed petals. Before refitting the unit, wash it carefully in clean petrol, then check the petals, stopper plate and seating face for signs of damage. Though unlikely on a machine of this type, the petals can occasionally fracture in use, and the valve should be renewed if there is any doubt as to its condition. Refit the valve using a new sealing gasket.

2 Machines produced from 1983 onwards, the V50 MDL (19M) and V80 MDL (19N), have a slightly modified intake arrangement. An extra stub on the intake manifold is connected by a short hose to a small plastic canister. This functions in a similar manner to the "boost bottles" fitted on many competition two-strokes, giving better throttle response during acceleration. Like the reed valve it is automatic in operation and requires no regular attention.

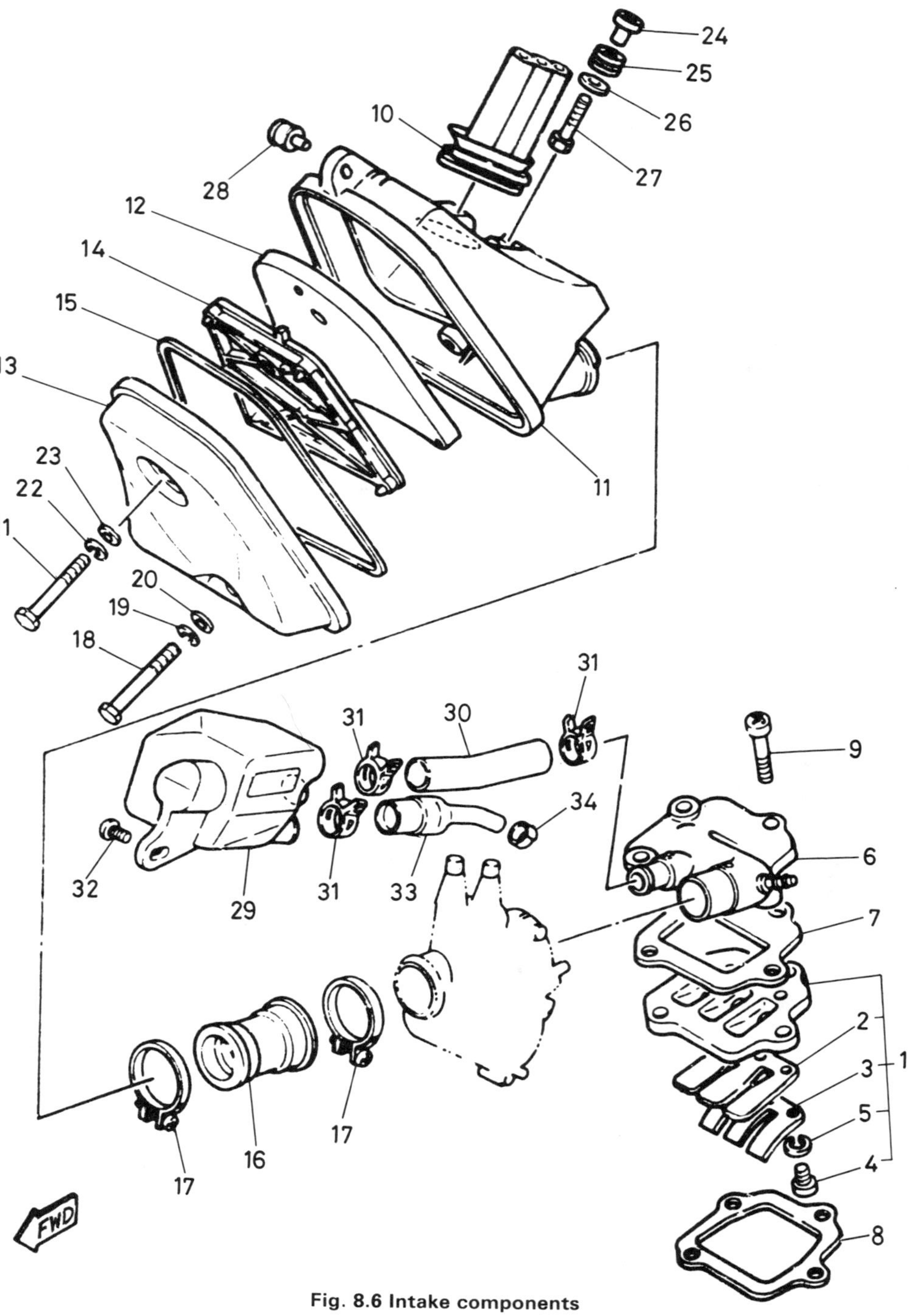

Fig. 8.6 Intake components

1 *Reed valve assembly*
2 *Reed petal*
3 *Stopper plate*
4 *Screw – 3 off*
5 *Spring washer – 3 off*
6 *Reed valve cover*
7 *Gasket*
8 *Gasket*
9 *Screw – 4 off*
10 *Air intake hose*
11 *Air filter casing*
12 *Air filter element*
13 *Cover*
14 *Element frame*
15 *Seal*
16 *Inlet hose*
17 *Clamp – 2 off*
18 *Bolt*
19 *Spring washer*
20 *Washer*
21 *Bolt*
22 *Spring washer*
23 *Washer*
24 *Spacer*
25 *Grommet*
26 *Washer*
27 *Bolt*
28 *Screw and washer*
29 *Air chamber*
30 *Hose*
31 *Clamp – 3 off*
32 *Screw*
33 *Vacuum control valve*
34 *Clamp*

6 Air filter: general description and cleaning – V50 MDL (19M) and V80 MDL (19N)

1 The later models make use of a simplified air filter employing a flat foam element in place of the cylindrical pleated paper element of the earlier models. The filter assembly is mounted at the front of the machine, between the two legshields. To gain access to the element, remove the two cover screws and lift away the cover together with the element.
2 Carefully peel away the element, taking care not to tear it. The element can be cleaned by washing it in petrol to remove any dust and old oil. Allow it to dry, then moisten it with a small amount of two-stroke oil prior to refitting. Note that if it is torn or damaged in any way it should be renewed.

6.1 Air filter cover is retained by two screws

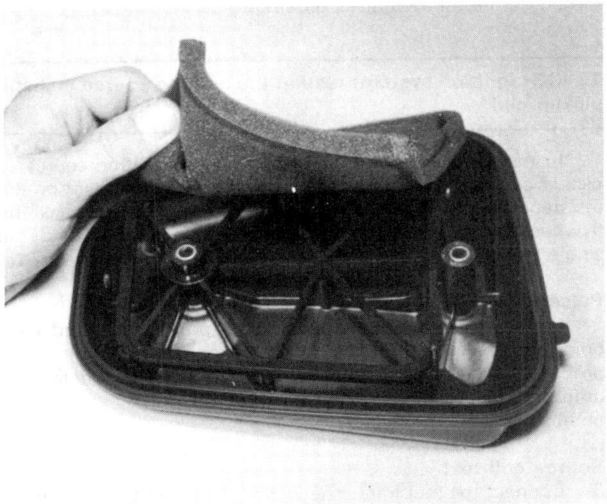
6.2 Element can be lifted away from cover for cleaning

7 Fuel tap: general description – V50 MDL (19M) and V80 MDL (19N)

1 The V50 and V80 models produced from 1983 onwards are fitted with a slightly revised fuel tap in which the vacuum chamber has been moved from the side to the rear of the tap body. In all other respects the tap is similar to the earlier versions. See the accompanying photograph for details.

7.1 Models produced from 1983 onwards are fitted with revised fuel tap

8 Capacitor discharge ignition (CDI) system: general description

1 The coil and contact breaker ignition system of the earlier models has been replaced by a capacitor discharge ignition (CDI) system on all models covered by this Chapter. The system produces a stronger spark than a conventional contact breaker arrangement, and by eliminating the mechanical components, there is no need for periodic adjustment and renewal. The heart of the system is the CDI unit, which is bolted to the frame behind the left-hand side panel.
2 A capacitor inside the unit stores an electrical charge until a trigger pulse is applied to a thyristor (silicon controlled rectifier). The trigger pulse is derived from a pair of pulser coils incorporated in the flywheel generator assembly. The pulser coils are energised by a magnet in the rotor; as the rotor sweeps past the coils a small current is generated. This is passed to the thyristor, which becomes conductive. The capacitor discharges through the ignition coil, producing a spark at the plug electrodes. As the engine speed rises the gap between the two trigger pulses is effectively reduced, and this effect is employed to advance the ignition timing.

9 CDI ignition system: fault diagnosis

1 With the elimination of the mechanical aspects of the ignition system, it is unlikely that frequent attention will be required. In the event of a fault developing, the cause can often be traced to a broken or loose wiring connection, or less commonly, a failed ignition system component. It is important that fault diagnosis is approached in a logical manner, following the sequence described below.
2 Remove the spark plug and check its condition as described in Chapter 4. If in any doubt as to its condition it is advisable to renew it as a precautionary measure. Fit the plug into the plug cap and lodge it against the engine so that the metal body is in contact with the bare metal of the cylinder or cylinder head. Position the plug so that the electrodes can be seen when the kickstart lever is operated.

8.2 View of generator stator showing ignition pickup coil (arrowed)

Important note: the energy levels in electronic ignition systems can be very high. On no account switch on the ignition whilst the plug or plug cap is being held; shocks from the HT circuit can be unpleasant or even dangerous. Secondly, ensure that the plug body is soundly earthed while the system is checked for sparking. The ignition system components can be seriously damaged if the HT circuit becomes isolated.

3 Having observed the above precautions, turn the ignition switch "ON" and operate the kickstart lever. If the system is in good condition, a regular, fat blue spark should be evident at the plug electrodes. If the spark is non-existent, or thin and yellowish in appearance, further investigation will be required. Before proceeding further, switch the ignition off and remove the key as a safety measure.

4 The most likely ignition faults are listed below, starting with the most probable causes. Work through the list systematically, referring to the subsequent sections for full details of the necessary tests and checks.

a) Defective spark plug or plug cap
b) Loose, corroded or damaged wiring connections, broken or shorted wiring between any of the ignition system components
c) Faulty ignition switch
d) Faulty ignition HT coil/CDI unit
e) Faulty pickup coil
f) Faulty ignition source coil

10 CDI ignition system: checking the wiring

1 The wiring should be checked visually, noting any signs of corrosion around the various terminals and connectors. If the fault has developed in wet conditions, it follows that water may have entered any of the connectors or switches, causing a short circuit. A temporary cure can be effected by spraying the relevant area with one of the proprietary de-watering aerosols, such as WD40 or similar. A more permanent solution is to dismantle the switch or connector and coat the exposed parts with silicone grease to prevent the ingress of water. The exposed backs of connectors can be sealed off using a silicone rubber sealant.

2 Light corrosion can normally be cured by scraping or sanding the affected area, though in serious cases it may prove necessary to renew the switch or connector affected. Check the wiring for chafing or breakage, particularly where it passes close to part of the frame or its fittings. As a temporary measure, damaged insulation can be repaired with PVC tape, but the wire concerned should be renewed at the earliest opportunity.

3 Using the wiring diagram at the end of the manual, check each wire for breakage or short circuits using a multimeter set on the resistance scale or a dry battery and bulb wired as shown in the accompanying illustration. In each case, there should be continuity between the ends of each wire.

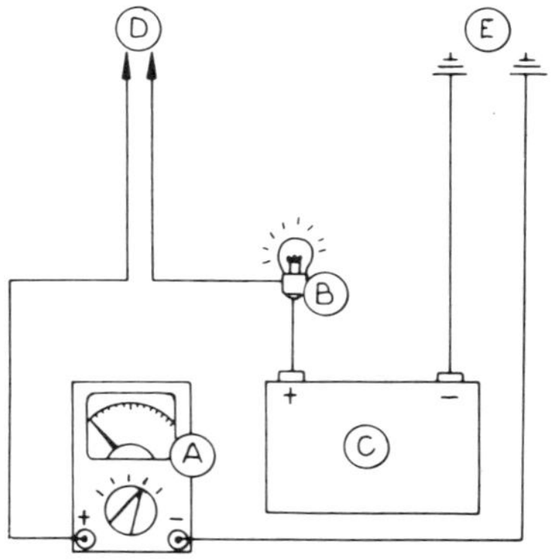

Fig. 8.7 Method of checking wiring and connections

A Multimeter
B Bulb
C Battery
D Positive probe
E Negative probe

11 CDI ignition system: checking the ignition switch

1 Again using the multimeter or battery/bulb arrangement as described above, in conjunction with the wiring diagrams at the end of this Chapter, check that the switch connections are being made or broken as indicated in the switch contact diagram. If the switch proves faulty it should be renewed, though it is worth trying to effect a repair by spraying WD40 or similar into the switch before a new unit is ordered.

12 CDI ignition system: testing the ignition source coil and pickup coil

1 In the event of a suspected fault in the ignition source or pickup coils, these can be tested using a multimeter set on the resistance scale (ohms x 1 or ohms x 10). Trace back the flywheel generator wiring to the six-pin connector and the single bullet connector and separate them.

Pulser coil test

2 Connect the multimeter negative (–) probe to a sound earth point and select the ohms x 1 range. Connect the positive (+) probe to the white/red terminal of the six-pin connector and note the reading. A figure of 20 ohms $\pm$ 10% should be obtained.

Source coil test

3 Connect the multimeter negative (–) probe to a sound earth point and select the ohms x 10 range. Connect the positive (+) probe to the black/red terminal of the separate bullet connector and note the reading. A figure of 295 ohms (2J6 and 3K3) or 330 ohms (19M and 19N), should be obtained.

4 In either of the above tests a small discrepancy from the specified reading can be accepted, which may be caused by the particular meter used. Note however that a reading of zero resistance indicates a short circuit, whilst infinite resistance indicates an open circuit.

13 CDI ignition system: testing the CDI unit

1 In the absence of test data on the CDI unit, the only practical method of checking it is by substitution. Few owners will have a spare unit to hand, but most Yamaha dealers will be able to check the unit quickly and simply by this method. The CDI unit is mounted behind the left-hand side panel, to the rear of the finned alloy casing of the rectifier (see photograph).

14 CDI ignition system: checking the timing

1 The flywheel generator stator is fixed in relation to the crankcase, and this means that the ignition timing setting cannot be adjusted. This is no real disadvantage because there is no reason to have to adjust the preset firing point as is the case with conventional coil and contact breaker systems. In the event of apparent ignition timing problems it is possible to check this using a stroboscopic timing lamp (strobe). If possible, use a zenon tube type in preference to the cheaper and less effective neon tube strobes, connecting it according to the maker's instructions. If using a zenon tube strobe, note that a separate 12 volt car or motorcycle battery will probably be needed to power the unit.

2 Remove the flywheel generator cover and note the position of the timing mark on the rotor and the static index mark on the crankcase. The latter takes the form of one edge of a raised step in the casting (see photograph) and we found it necessary to remove the footrest assembly to be able to look squarely onto the marks. Start the engine and direct the strobe lamp at the static mark. The timing mark on the rotor should appear to be 'frozen' in alignment with the static mark in the position shown in the accompanying photograph.

3 In the unlikely event that the timing is incorrect, the rotor should be removed and the condition of the Woodruff key and slot checked. If the rotor has been fitted incorrectly, the key may have sheared or the slot worn, allowing the error to occur. If this does not locate the problem, the fault must lie in the pulser coil or the CDI unit. The former can be checked as described above, whilst the latter can be checked by substitution of a new unit. It should be stressed that faults of this nature are very unusual.

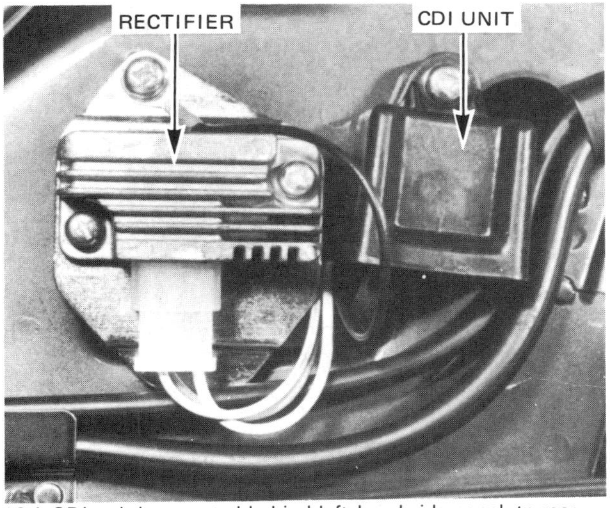

13.1 CDI unit is mounted behind left-hand side panel, to rear of rectifier

14.2 Rotor timing mark (A) should align with edge of shoulder (B) on casing

14.3a Correct extractor tool should be used to draw off the rotor

14.3b Note improvised holding tool used whilst removing or tightening rotor nut

15 Brake adjustment: general information

1 The models covered in this update Chapter are equipped with wear indicators on the front and rear brakes. When adjusting the brakes, note that the front brake lever should have 5-8 mm (0.2-0.3 in) free play between the lever and lever stock, whilst the rear brake pedal should have 20-30 mm (0.8-1.2 in) free play at the pedal end.
2 If there is insufficient adjustment left at the cable or rod, it is permissible to move the brake arm by one spline at a time to restore adjustment. Note that this only applies if the wear indicator is below the maximum limit when the brake is applied; if it is at or near its limit, renew the shoes before attempting adjustment. If the indicator is disturbed, make sure that it is refitted so that the notch aligns with the punch mark on the end of the brake cam.

15.1 Later models feature wear indicators. Note punch mark which should be aligned with slot in indicator

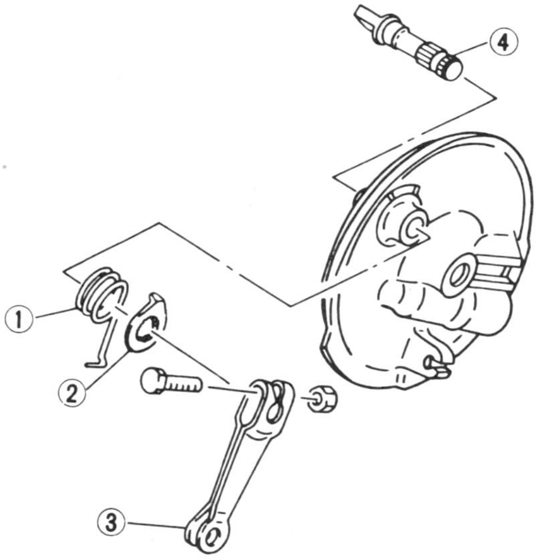

Fig. 8.8 Front brake plate showing wear indicator

1 Spring
2 Wear indicator plate
3 Operating lever
4 Brake cam

16 Instrument panel: V50 MDL (19M) and V80 MDL (19N)

1 The instrument panel on the above models is revised to incorporate the fuel gauge, thus forming an integral part of the speedometer head. Access to the wiring connections and speedometer cable requires the removal of the headlamp unit which is retained by two screws. At the rear of the nacelle is a separate panel housing the warning lamps and the ignition switch. These are reached by removing the panel which is held by two screws. See the accompanying photographs for details.

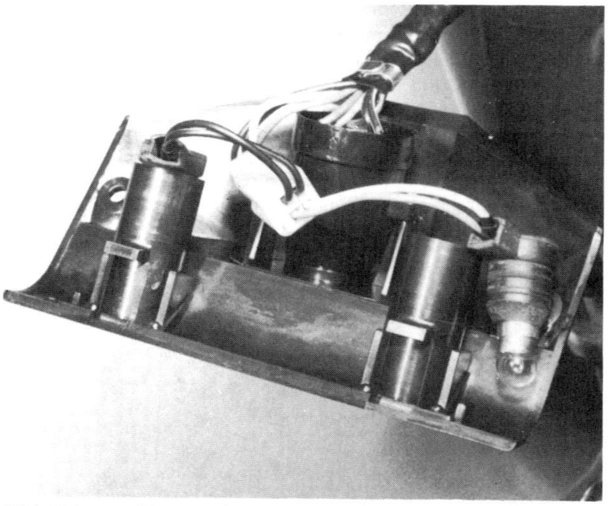

16.1 Sub panel houses ignition switch and warning lamps

17 Fuel gauge: general description and fault diagnosis – V50 MDL (19M) and V80 MDL (19N)

1 The post-1983 models are equipped with a fuel level gauge which is built into the left-hand side of the speedometer head. The gauge is controlled by a float-type sender unit mounted in the top of the fuel tank.
2 In the event of a fault in the fuel gauge system, always check first that the battery is fully charged, that the electrical system is functioning normally and that the fuse has not blown; the system will not operate correctly if this is not the case. If the fault persists, follow the sequence shown below. Note that a multimeter will be required to perform most of the checks.
3 Pull off the oil tank filler cap and lift away the plastic shroud which fits around its neck. Locate the fuel gauge sender wiring connector. Separate the connector and connect the green lead on the gauge side to earth, using a length of wire. Switch on the ignition and note the fuel gauge reading. If it shows 'full' it is safe to assume that the meter movement is intact and that the fault lies in the sender. In this case, refer to Section 5 for details. If on the other hand the meter needle remains at the 'empty' position, proceed as follows.
4 Using a multimeter set on the dc 20V scale, connect the positive (+) probe to the green lead and the negative (–) probe to earth. Switch on the ignition and note the reading. If battery voltage (approximately 6 volts) is shown, the meter can be assumed to have failed and should be renewed together with the speedometer head. If no reading is shown, check for a break in the brown lead between the fuse and the meter connector near the instrument panel. If necessary, repair or bypass the damaged wire.
5 If a sender fault is indicated, remove the sender unit from the tank. It is retained by four screws and care should be exercised when manoeuvring the float out of the tank (see

photograph). The sender can be checked using a multimeter set on the ohms x 1 scale. Connect a probe to each of the two sender leads and note the resistance reading at the empty (float fully down) and full (float fully up) positions, comparing them with the figures shown below:

Fuel gauge sender resistances

Full	2-12 ohms
Empty	87.5-102.5 ohms

6 If the sender resistances are correct, the fault must lie in the black (earth) lead or connections; these should be checked and repaired or bypassed, as necessary. If the sender unit is faulty it will probably be necessary to renew it. Before ordering a new sender, however, it is worth checking the resistance windings and wiper arm for corrosion. These are visible after the pressed steel cover has been removed (see photograph). Light corrosion can be polished off using very fine abrasive paper or an ink eraser. Take great care not to break the fragile resistance wire when doing this. If the windings are broken it may be possible to get the unit repaired by a local auto-electrical specialist.

17.3a Lift away the plastic shroud above the oil tank

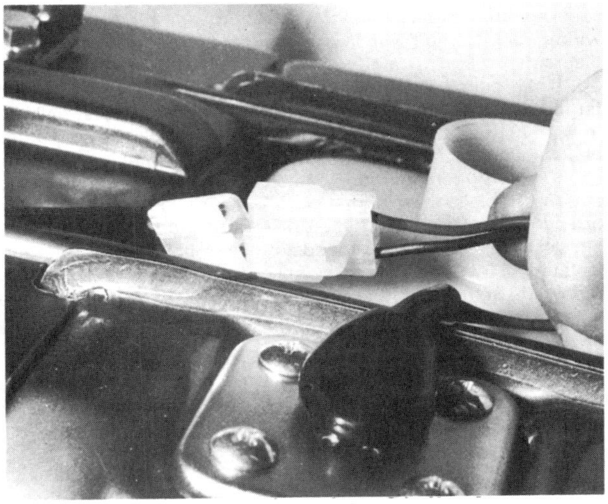

17.3b Separate the sender wiring at the connector

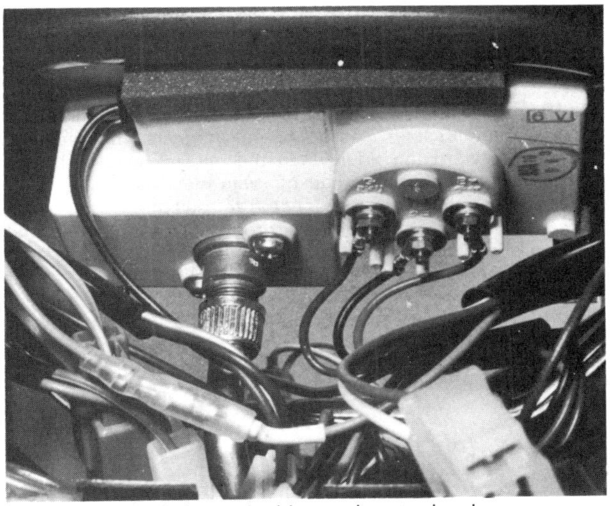

17.4 Fuel gauge is integral with speedometer head

17.5a Sender unit is retained by four screws

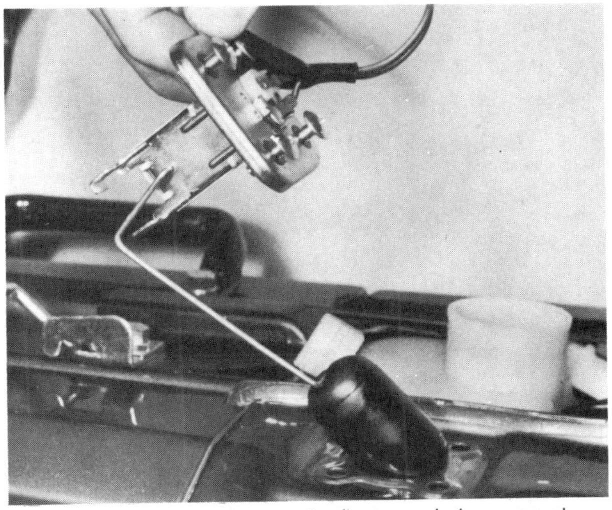

17.5b Take care not to damage the float arm during removal

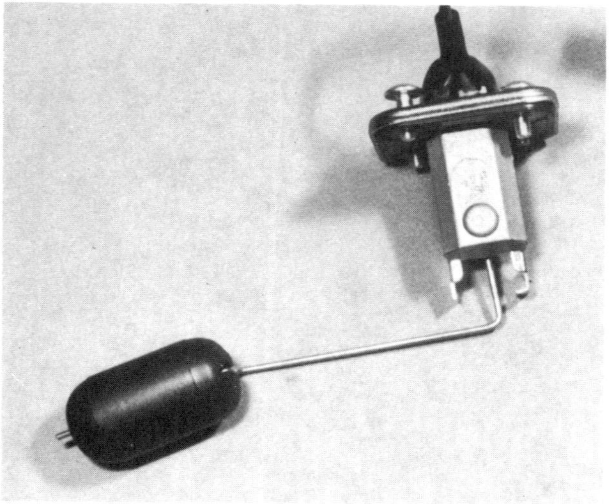

17.6a Pressed steel cover can be removed to reveal windings and moving contact

17.6b Light corrosion can be polished off with fine abrasive paper

18 Oil level warning lamp: description and fault diagnosis – V50 MDL and V80 MDL, 1983 onwards

1 The models produced from 1983 on were equipped with an oil level warning lamp. As its name suggests, this circuit is designed to warn the rider when the oil tank level falls to a seriously low level. The circuit consists of a float-type switch located in the oil tank and connected to a warning lamp on the instrument panel. As the oil level drops, so too does the float, eventually closing two contacts and lighting the warning lamp.

2 This is a very simple circuit and is unlikely to give rise to many problems. In the event of a fault developing it is most likely to be caused by a blown bulb, and this should always be checked first. If this fails to resolve the problem, check the wiring back to the switch unit, using the accompanying wiring diagrams.

3 If the bulb and wiring are intact, the switch unit should be removed for checking. It is a push-fit in the oil tank, just forward of the filler cap, and can be reached after the plastic shield has been lifted away. Pull out the switch unit and unplug the wiring connector. Switch operation can be checked using a multimeter set on the resistance (ohms) scale or a simple battery and bulb arrangement. Connect the test probes to the switch leads and check that the switch conducts when held upright and is isolated if inverted. If the switch proves faulty, it should be renewed. Remember that the safety of the engine is to some extent dependent on the warning lamp operating reliably.

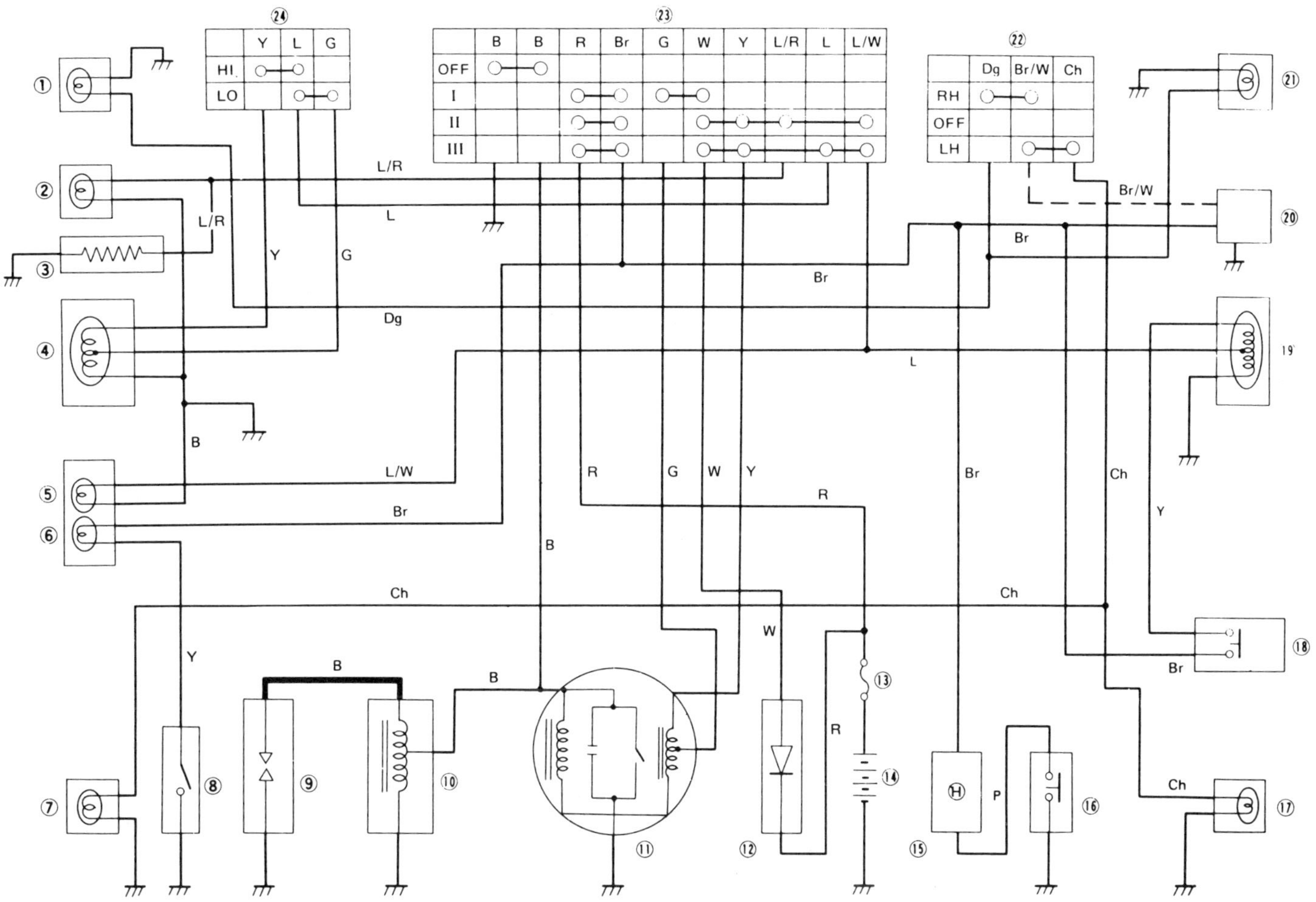

1 Front right-hand indicator
2 Ignition light
3 Resistor
4 Headlamp
5 Instrument light
6 Neutral indicator light
7 Front left-hand indicator
8 Neutral indicator switch
9 Spark plug
10 Ignition coil
11 Generator
12 Rectifier
13 Fuse
14 Battery
15 Horn
16 Horn switch
17 Rear right-hand indicator
18 Brake stop lamp switch
19 Tail/stop lamp
20 Indicator relay
21 Rear right-hand indicator
22 Indicator switch
23 Ignition switch
24 Headlamp dip switch

B Black
Br Brown
L Blue
R Red
G Green
P Pink
Y Yellow
W White
Lg Light green
Dg Dark green
Ch Dark brown
Sb Light blue

Wiring diagram – V50 (544), V50 P (1E9), V75 (545) and V90 (546) 6 volt models

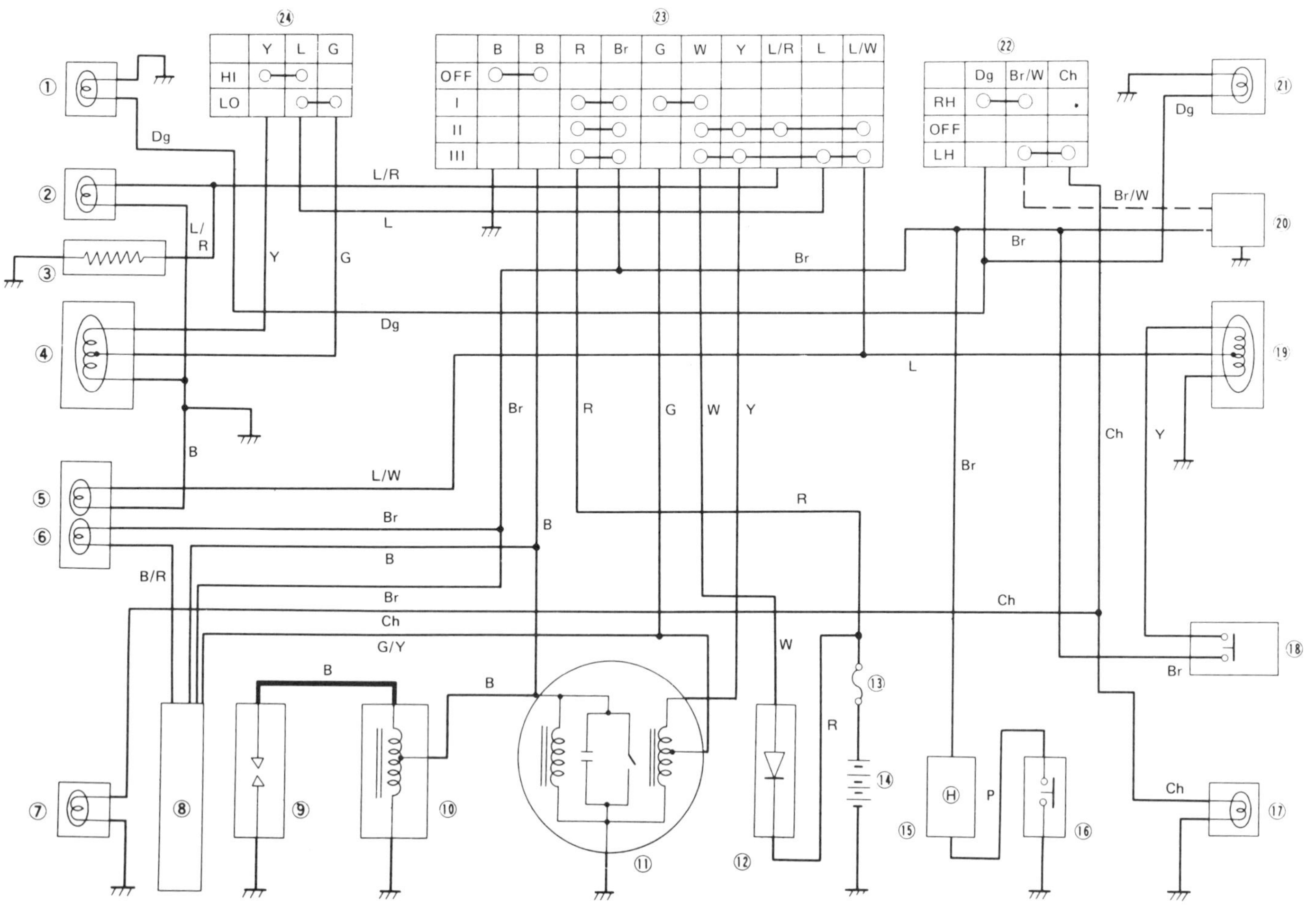

1 Front right-hand indicator
2 Ignition light
3 Resistor
4 Headlamp
5 Instrument light
6 Oil level warning light
7 Front left-hand indicator
8 Oil level warning switch
9 Spark plug
10 Ignition coil
11 Generator
12 Rectifier
13 Fuse
14 Battery
15 Horn
16 Horn switch
17 Rear right-hand indicator
18 Brake stop lamp switch
19 Tail/stop lamp
20 Indicator relay
21 Rear right-hand indicator
22 Indicator switch
23 Ignition switch
24 Headlamp dip switch

B Black
Br Brown
L Blue
R Red
G Green
P Pink
Y Yellow
W White
Lg Light green
Dg Dark green
Ch Dark brown
Sb Light blue

Wiring diagram – V75 A (595) model

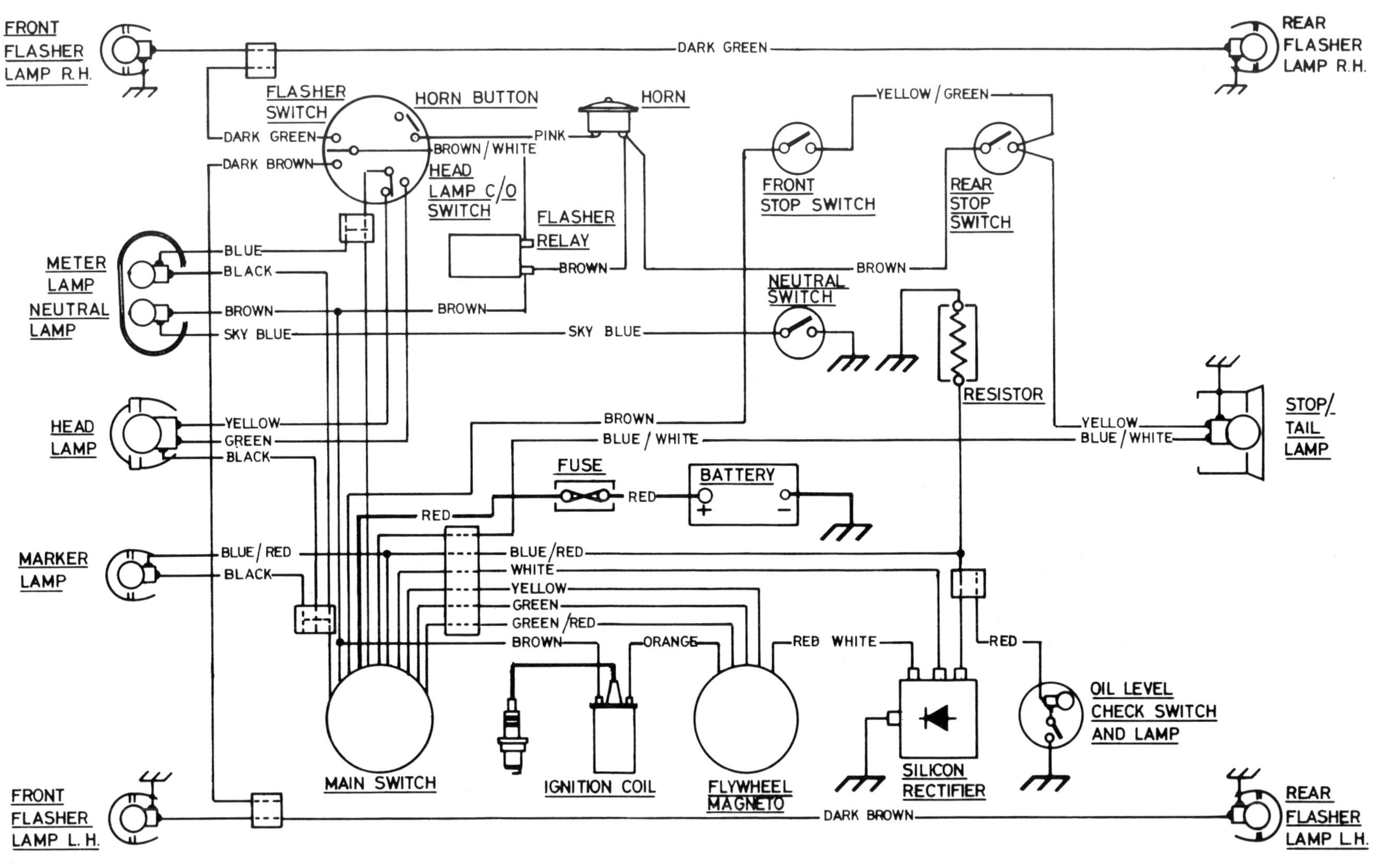

Wiring diagram – V90 (12 volt) early model

Note: No wiring diagram is available specifically for the 12 volt V90 model. This general diagram however, will be of assistance

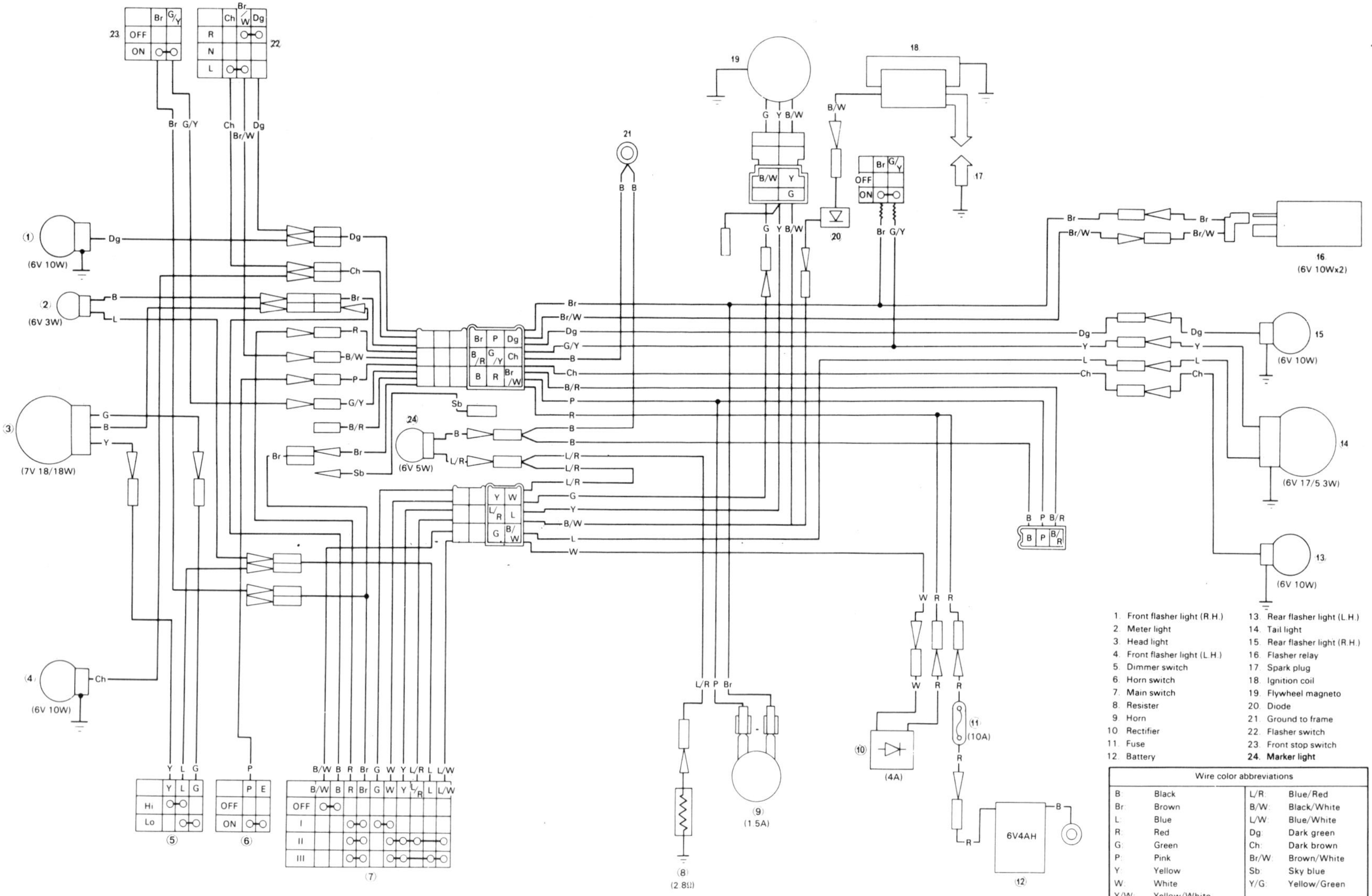

1. Front flasher light (R.H.)
2. Meter light
3. Head light
4. Front flasher light (L.H.)
5. Dimmer switch
6. Horn switch
7. Main switch
8. Resister
9. Horn
10. Rectifier
11. Fuse
12. Battery
13. Rear flasher light (L.H.)
14. Tail light
15. Rear flasher light (R.H.)
16. Flasher relay
17. Spark plug
18. Ignition coil
19. Flywheel magneto
20. Diode
21. Ground to frame
22. Flasher switch
23. Front stop switch
24. **Marker light**

Wire color abbreviations

B	Black	L/R	Blue/Red
Br	Brown	B/W	Black/White
L	Blue	L/W	Blue/White
R	Red	Dg	Dark green
G	Green	Ch	Dark brown
P	Pink	Br/W	Brown/White
Y	Yellow	Sb	Sky blue
W	White	Y/G	Yellow/Green
Y/W	Yellow/White		

Wiring diagram – V50 MA (3K6) model

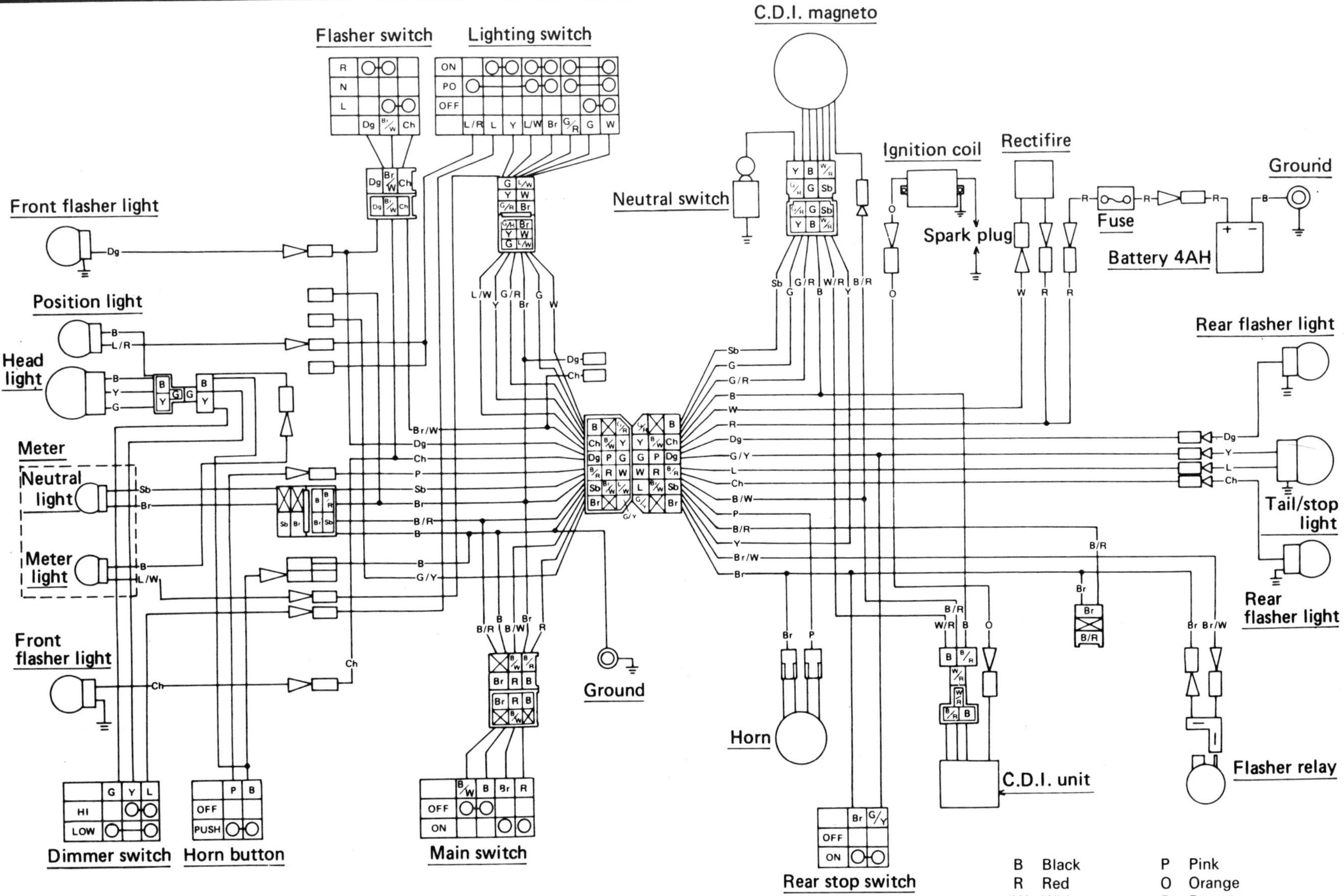

Wiring diagram – V50 MA (2J6) and V80 (3K3) models

Note: *neutral switch and indicator light not fitted to V50 model*

B	Black	P	Pink
R	Red	O	Orange
W	White	Br	Brown
G	Green	Ch	Dark brown
Y	Yellow	Dg	Dark green
L	Blue	Sb	Light blue

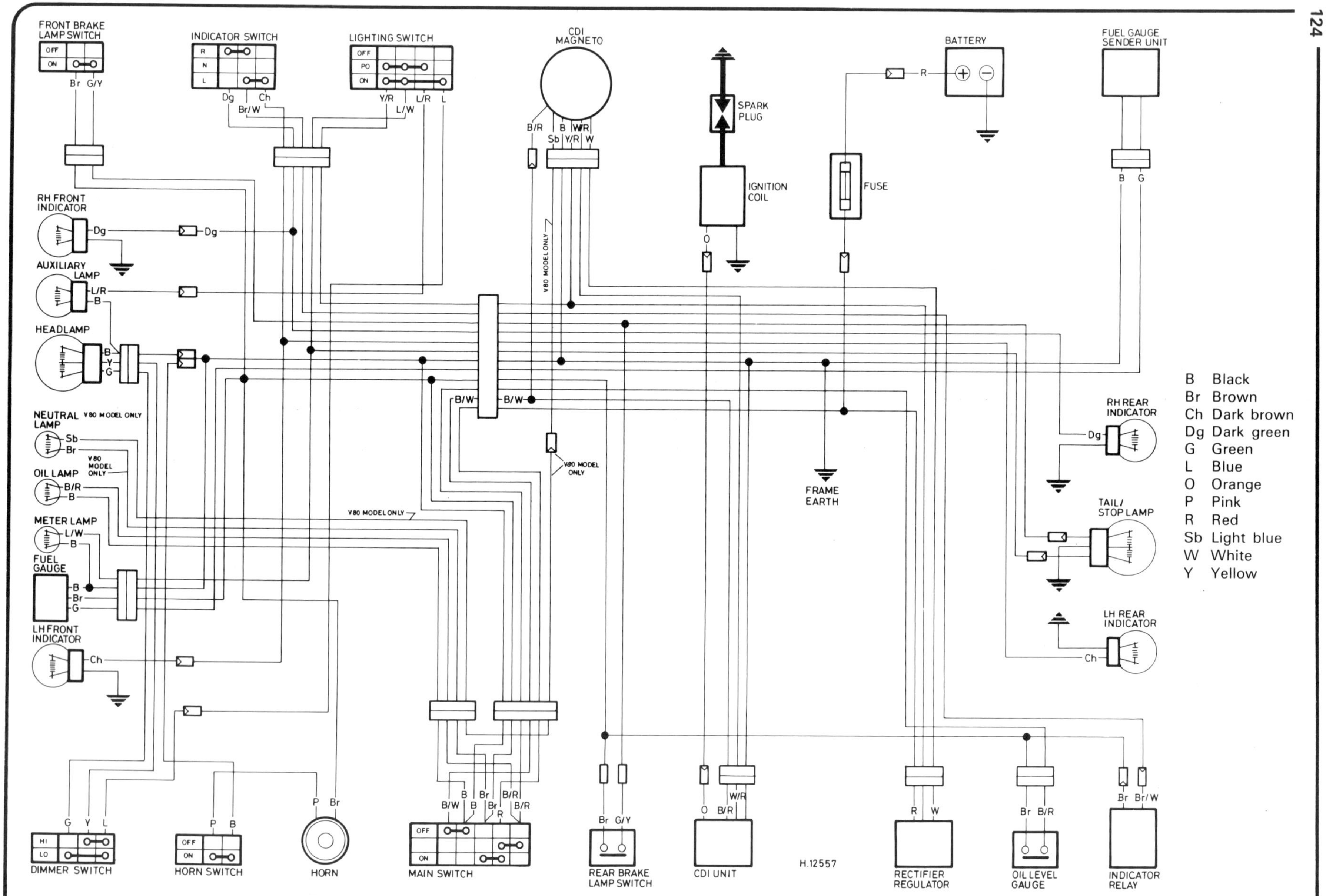

Wiring diagram – V50 MDL (19M) and V80 MDL (19N) models

Conversion factors

Length (distance)					
Inches (in)	X 25.4	= Millimetres (mm)	X 0.0394	= Inches (in)
Feet (ft)	X 0.305	= Metres (m)	X 3.281	= Feet (ft)
Miles	X 1.609	= Kilometres (km)	X 0.621	= Miles
Volume (capacity)				
Cubic inches (cu in; in³)	X 16.387	= Cubic centimetres (cc; cm³)	X 0.061	= Cubic inches (cu in; in³)
Imperial pints (Imp pt)	X 0.568	= Litres (l)	X 1.76	= Imperial pints (Imp pt)
Imperial quarts (Imp qt)	X 1.137	= Litres (l)	X 0.88	= Imperial quarts (Imp qt)
Imperial quarts (Imp qt)	X 1.201	= US quarts (US qt)	X 0.833	= Imperial quarts (Imp qt)
US quarts (US qt)	X 0.946	= Litres (l)	X 1.057	= US quarts (US qt)
Imperial gallons (Imp gal)	X 4.546	= Litres (l)	X 0.22	= Imperial gallons (Imp gal)
Imperial gallons (Imp gal)	X 1.201	= US gallons (US gal)	X 0.833	= Imperial gallons (Imp gal)
US gallons (US gal)	X 3.785	= Litres (l)	X 0.264	= US gallons (US gal)
Mass (weight)				
Ounces (oz)	X 28.35	= Grams (g)	X 0.035	= Ounces (oz)
Pounds (lb)	X 0.454	= Kilograms (kg)	X 2.205	= Pounds (lb)
Force				
Ounces-force (ozf; oz)	X 0.278	= Newtons (N)	X 3.6	= Ounces-force (ozf; oz)
Pounds-force (lbf; lb)	X 4.448	= Newtons (N)	X 0.225	= Pounds-force (lbf; lb)
Newtons (N)	X 0.1	= Kilograms-force (kgf; kg)	X 9.81	= Newtons (N)
Pressure				
Pounds-force per square inch (psi; lbf/in²; lb/in²)	X 0.070	= Kilograms-force per square centimetre (kgf/cm²; kg/cm²)	X 14.223	= Pounds-force per square inch (psi; lbf/in²; lb/in²)
Pounds-force per square inch (psi; lbf/in²; lb/in²)	X 0.068	= Atmospheres (atm)	X 14.696	= Pounds-force per square inch (psi; lbf/in²; lb/in²)
Pounds-force per square inch (psi; lbf/in²; lb/in²)	X 0.069	= Bars	X 14.5	= Pounds-force per square inch (psi; lbf/in²; lb/in²)
Pounds-force per square inch (psi; lbf/in²; lb/in²)	X 6.895	= Kilopascals (kPa)	X 0.145	= Pounds-force per square inch (psi; lbf/in²; lb/in²)
Kilopascals (kPa)	X 0.01	= Kilograms-force per square centimetre (kgf/cm²; kg/cm²)	X 98.1	= Kilopascals (kPa)
Torque (moment of force)				
Pounds-force inches (lbf in; lb in)	X 1.152	= Kilograms-force centimetre (kgf cm; kg cm)	X 0.868	= Pounds-force inches (lbf in; lb in)
Pounds-force inches (lbf in; lb in)	X 0.113	= Newton metres (Nm)	X 8.85	= Pounds-force inches (lbf in; lb in)
Pounds-force inches (lbf in; lb in)	X 0.083	= Pounds-force feet (lbf ft; lb ft)	X 12	= Pounds-force inches (lbf in; lb in)
Pounds-force feet (lbf ft; lb ft)	X 0.138	= Kilograms-force metres (kgf m; kg m)	X 7.233	= Pounds-force feet (lbf ft; lb ft)
Pounds-force feet (lbf ft; lb ft)	X 1.356	= Newton metres (Nm)	X 0.738	= Pounds-force feet (lbf ft; lb ft)
Newton metres (Nm)	X 0.102	= Kilograms-force metres (kgf m; kg m)	X 9.804	= Newton metres (Nm)
Power				
Horsepower (hp)	X 745.7	= Watts (W)	X 0.0013	= Horsepower (hp)
Velocity (speed)				
Miles per hour (miles/hr; mph)	X 1.609	= Kilometres per hour (km/hr; kph)	X 0.621	= Miles per hour (miles/hr; mph)
Fuel consumption*				
Miles per gallon, Imperial (mpg)	X 0.354	= Kilometres per litre (km/l)	X 2.825	= Miles per gallon, Imperial (mpg)
Miles per gallon, US (mpg)	X 0.425	= Kilometres per litre (km/l)	X 2.352	= Miles per gallon, US (mpg)

Temperature

Degrees Fahrenheit = (°C x 1.8) + 32

Degrees Celsius (Degrees Centigrade; °C) = (°F - 32) x 0.56

**It is common practice to convert from miles per gallon (mpg) to litres/100 kilometres (l/100km), where mpg (Imperial) x l/100 km = 282 and mpg (US) x l/100 km = 235*

Index

Printed by
J H Haynes & Co Ltd
Sparkford Nr Yeovil
Somerset BA22 7JJ England